North Carolina Faces the Freedmen

North Carolina Faces the Freedmen

Race Relations During Presidential Reconstruction, 1865–67

Roberta Sue Alexander

Duke University Press   Durham 1985

© 1985 Duke University Press
All rights reserved
Printed in the United States
of America on acid-free paper
Library of Congress Cataloging in Publication Data
Alexander, Roberta Sue, 1943–
North Carolina faces the freedmen.
Bibliography: p.
Includes index.
1. Reconstruction—North Carolina. 2. Freedmen—
North Carolina. 3. North Carolina—Race relations.
I. Title.
F259.A64   1985   975.6'041   84–28758
ISBN 0–8223–0628–X

To My Mother
And in Memory of My Father

Contents

Tables and Illustrations

Tables

Illustrations

Preface

Defeated in battle, white southerners returned home after the Civil War to rebuild their lives and their society. Blacks, rejoicing over emancipation, sought to construct a new life for themselves and their families. Both races, during the tumultuous, confusing period immediately after the Civil War, had their dreams and their visions. They also had their fears and their prejudices. How each attempted to translate its aspirations from dreams to reality is one of the most fascinating stories in American history—and one of the most difficult to recreate.

For almost one hundred years scholars have tried to explain the Reconstruction era. Until the 1930s historians of the Dunning school told a tale of white victims who attempted to build a just society but were thwarted by innumerable obstacles, not the least of which was the presence of ignorant, lazy freedmen who were manipulated by vindictive, greedy white radicals. The white southerner is at center stage in this story; blacks are caricatures and stick figures.[1] More recently, revisionist historians have set forth a different account of this era, in which the white southerner is no longer the victim. Revisionists argue that these southerners, aided by President Andrew Johnson, undermined the implementation of the Republican program. Blacks failed to achieve full equality largely because of difficulties at the national level. The failure of a just Reconstruction program resulted from either a flawed, limited Republican program or the actions of a determined or an incompetent president who stymied Republican legislation and encouraged white southern obstinacy.[2]

This national perspective, while going far to correct the racist assumptions of the older interpretations, left much work to be done. Scholars like Joel Williamson, Peter Kolchin, Herbert Gutman, Edward Magdol, and Leon Litwack have recently enlarged our focus by contributing to our understanding of the black community, especially in its transition from slavery to freedom.[3] Others have examined the economic difficulties the South encountered as it tried to build a free labor economy.[4]

Yet to understand the obstacles that Republican legislators and southern blacks faced throughout Reconstruction and beyond, one must understand the complex interactions between the two races. Neither the black nor the white community can be understood in isolation. Moreover, while blacks were not puppets, neither were whites merely responding to national signals. As Leon Litwack noted: "The two races in the South interacted in ways that dramatized not only a mutual dependency but the frightening tensions and ambiguities that had always characterized the 'peculiar institution.'"[5] To understand this dependency as well as these tensions, one needs to explore the early Reconstruction years in detail. The actions and attitudes of southern whites and blacks during these few crucial years go far in explaining the challenges any Reconstruction policy faced.

Perhaps even more important, an analysis of Presidential Reconstruction is crucial to comprehending how each race dealt with the social revolution brought about by emancipation. During this time the South was relatively free of northern interference. Therefore this era shows most clearly what southerners hoped the future would be and how they intended to implement these plans. Leon Litwack's *Been in the Storm So Long* provides a strong foundation for understanding the period. Yet, in part because of its massive scope, this book has its limitations. Rarely does it reveal the dominant sentiments of either whites or blacks. Moreover, while readers certainly experience the rhetoric of the period, they are often left wondering what the reality was.

As Otto Olsen and Michael Les Benedict have both argued, what is needed are more detailed state studies. Olsen wrote: "Although a radical revision of Reconstruction history has been underway for two generations, the standard studies of southern states have remained white supremacist products of the Dunning school" with some notable exceptions. "This fact has constituted a serious flaw in Reconstruction historiography because evaluations and interpretations of that period are so vitally dependent upon the southern state record."[6]

This study attempts to help fill the gap in our knowledge of race relations at the state level during the crucial transition era of Presidential Reconstruction. North Carolina is an important state whose history is still in need of revision. J. G. de Roulhac Hamilton's *Reconstruction in North Carolina*, written in 1914, is the only comprehensive study of the

Tarheel state's, Reconstruction history. Trained by Dunning, Hamilton viewed Reconstruction as a crime—a crime that the South, and especially North Carolina, did not deserve. In arriving at this conclusion, however, Hamilton practically ignored the period of Presidential Reconstruction, which he incorrectly believed was an era when "the government was practically military in that the state government performed its function only through the acquiescence of military commanders." Moreover, he failed to examine the black community in any systematic or scholarly fashion.[7]

Several historians have since published important correctives to Hamilton's thesis, offering new perspectives. Horace Raper's 1951 study of Governor William Holden points out the economic and political reforms launched during the era of Republican rule. Raper also contributes to an understanding of why Holden failed to maintain control of the state's political machinery during Presidential Reconstruction.[8] Otto Olsen, in his study of carpetbagger Albion Tourgee, suports Raper's thesis that the white Confederate-Conservative coalition, fearful of Holden's appeal to the common man, organized to control Presidential Reconstruction. This coalition continued its resistance during Congressional Reconstruction. And throughout the entire Reconstruction era, Olsen argues, racism based on economic rivalry and deep-seated prejudice motivated the conservative leadership in North Carolina to resist reform and to struggle to maintain white supremacy and home rule.[9] Dwight Billings, in his sociological analysis, sees economic developments in much the same light; economic changes, he argues, were shaped by the old planter elite's desire to maintain its hegemony.[10]

While all these studies point to the entrenched racist ideology of North Carolina's white conservative leadership, none analyzes comprehensively the interrelationship between the white and black communities. W. McKee Evans does this in his excellent 1966 monograph on Reconstruction in the Cape Fear region in the eastern part of the state. He details the reestablishment of the old leadership, the struggle by blacks to gain their full complement of rights, and finally the violent means employed by white conservatives to regain control. Social disorder and violence characterized the region, he argues, because while political control was temporarily wrenched from the hands of the old elite, economic power remained "in the hands of a relatively few prominent families."[11]

From these works, historians have gained a much more accurate picture of Reconstruction in North Carolina than the version Hamilton originally presented. One begins to appreciate the determination with which the antebellum white leadership fought the challenges to the old order. One also begins to see how blacks attempted to change this old order so they could achieve a measure of equality. But none of these studies provides a statewide perspective on the social, economic, political, and cultural developments of the era. And, as Otto Olsen maintained, we cannot fully understand why Radical Reconstruction failed until we have detailed state studies containing comprehensive analyses of the white and black communities.[12]

Focusing on the struggles of North Carolina blacks and whites as they dealt with the trials of adjusting to a free society, this study hopes to add to our understanding of the complex interactions that characterized this era. Both races were confronted by a series of new and difficult situations. By analyzing political events, social institutions, economic developments, criminal activities and court proceedings, and education in North Carolina during Presidential Reconstruction, one sees how the hopes and aspirations of blacks and whites ran in opposite directions, making it impossible to create a Reconstruction policy that everyone could accept. One can see, in detail, how correct Michael Perman was when he asserted that southern leaders would not change unless coerced.[13] And since North Carolina for many reasons should have been one of the more flexible of the former Confederate states, these findings would certainly hold true in other parts of the South.

North Carolina, then, is an important state in which to study Reconstruction. While the state's political history, economic variety, and topographical features parallel those of many other southern states, on racial issues it was considered one of the most liberal states in the South. Statistics show that North Carolina was predominantly rural, dominated by moderate sized farms and a relatively modest slave population. In 1860, 69 percent of all its farms were under one hundred acres and the average per capita wealth was only $836. Moreover only 27.7 percent of North Carolina families owned slaves, and of these about 71 percent owned fewer than ten. The state's slave population was only one-third of the total, ranking North Carolina sixth among the slaveholding states. Only sixteen of the state's eighty-nine counties had more slaves than

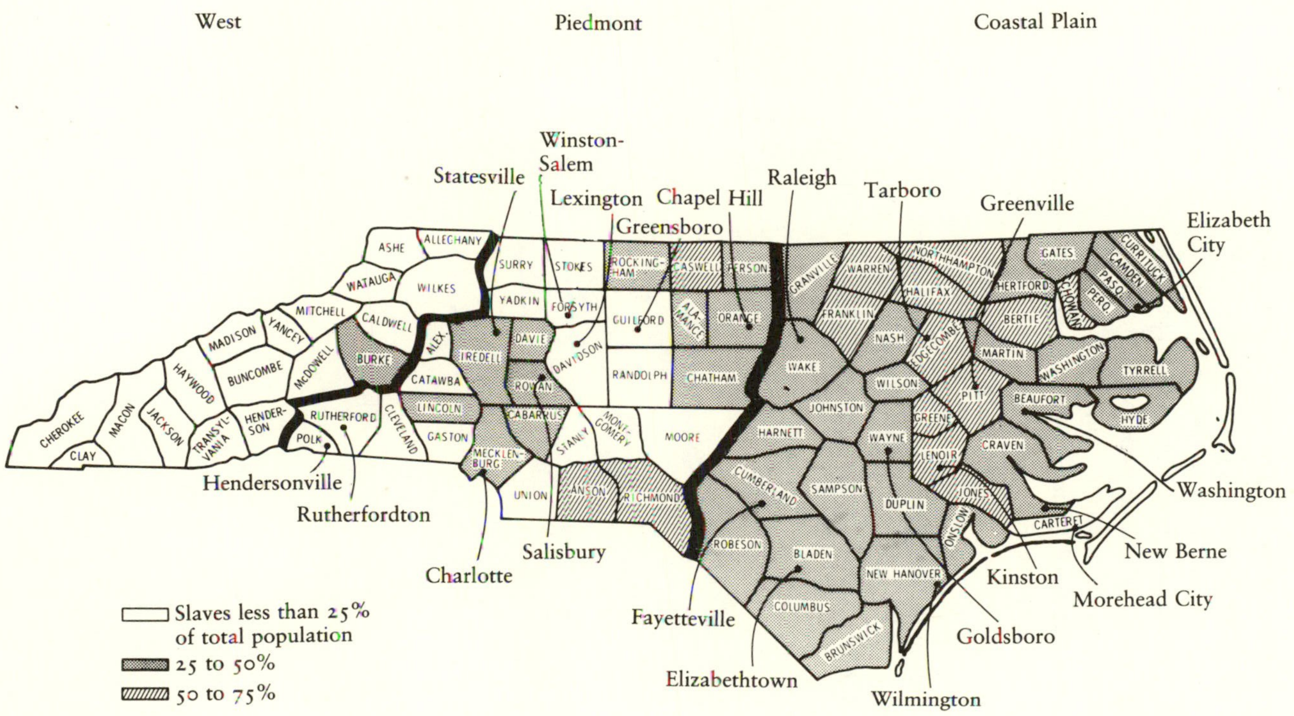

Map 1. Distribution of Slaves

whites, and all but three of these were located in the coastal region. On the other hand, the free black population—30,463 in 1860—was comparatively large, second only to that of Virginia among the Confederate states. Still, free blacks represented only 3.3 percent of the total population and 8.4 percent of the black population.[14]

The state's moderate temperament is well illustrated by the reluctance with which it left the Union and the strong unionist sentiment evident there throughout the war. But despite its unionist tradition, its relatively small black population, and its few great planters, turmoil and conflict characterized its Reconstruction period. A detailed examination of North Carolina during this era shows how the state's white leadership, initially unhampered by Republican legislation, planned to form its postbellum society and how North Carolina blacks struggled against these plans.

Acknowledgments

A great number of people over a great many years contributed to this work by generously offering their time, their advice, and their knowledge. This book began in the memorable seminar Dr. John Hope Franklin took to North Carolina in the winter of 1966. Before and since, as a teacher, my dissertation adviser, and a friend, Dr. Franklin has been a continual source of inspiration as I strove to meet his high standards. His careful and thorough criticisms and comments along with his words of encouragement kept my research focused and the analysis clear. My debt of gratitude to him is immeasurable. I am also grateful to my classmates in the seminar who generously shared their research and theses as I expanded the seminar paper into a dissertation.

I also wish to thank others who spent long hours reading the manuscript in its different stages and who offered wise counsel and insightful criticisms: Henry D. Shapiro of the University of Cincinnati, John Dittmer of the Massachusetts Institute of Technology, and Don Critchlow of Notre Dame University. And I am especially indebted to my colleague, Patrick Palermo, whose superb critical abilities helped correct many stylistic and analytical errors. His constant encouragement inspired me to continue to rethink, to clarify, and to rewrite.

Archivists and librarians, too numerous to mention by name, at the North Carolina State Archives, the University of North Carolina at Chapel Hill, Duke University, the National Archives, and the Library of Congress were most helpful. I owe a special debt to Ellen McGrew and Beth Crabtree at the North Carolina Archives, Dr. Caroline Wallace of the Southern Historical Collection, and Sarah Jackson at the National Archives, all of whom went out of their way to help me uncover many important documents. The University of Dayton and the National Endowment for the Humanities provided several grants that gave me the time to complete this work. Dewey Grantham and my colleagues in the

1976–77 NEH seminar at Vanderbilt all offered many helpful suggestions. Mrs. Linda McKinley typed and retyped the manuscript many times with speed, accuracy, and a critical eye. The final responsibility is, of course, entirely my own.

Chapter VII appeared originally, although in somewhat different form, as an article in the *North Carolina Historical Review* 53 (April 1976): 113–32. I wish to thank the North Carolina Division of Archives and History for permission to use material from the article in this work.

Finally, I would like to thank my husband, Ronald B. Fost, who continually inspires and calms me, and my parents, Mr. and Mrs. Bernard M. Cohn, who made my education possible and to whom this book is dedicated.

1 The "Great Social Revolution" Begins

I shall be broken without my servants.—Mrs. Catherine Roulhac, May 21, 1865, Ruffin–Roulhac–Hamilton Papers

When I first saw the Yankees I was afraid of 'em. . . . [Then] they come down and talked with us and told us we were free and then I was not so scared of 'em.—Ransom Sidney Taylor, *North Carolina Narratives*, 15: 340

A "GREAT SOCIAL REVOLUTION" began in the southern United States in 1865.[1] Bertcha Lane and her daughter Hannah belonged to former Governor Charles Manly until the end of the war. Bertcha's husband, Allen Lane, a stonecutter who hired his time and lived with his wife and child, was owned by Susan and Emma White. When the war ended, Bertcha told her former master she was going to leave. Despite the fact that Manly offered Bertcha and her husband a free house, free wood, and help in feeding their children, Bertcha insisted on leaving. She explained: "I have never been free and I am goin' to try it. I am goin' away and by my work and the help of the Lord I will live somehow."[2]

Clara Jones decided to stay with her former owners, Rufus and Sally Jones, after Sally Jones tearfully told her that "she can't do without her niggers." Clara's husband, William, who had lived on the neighboring McGee plantation, moved to the Jones's farm to be with Clara and took the name of Jones. Then, in Clara's words, they went into farming "wid a purpose an' believe me we makes our livin'."[3]

These accounts illustrate just a few of the many decisions blacks had to make upon emancipation. They had to choose vocations and employers, select names, and reunite families. While faced with many difficulties they were optimistic. Bertcha and Clara's reminiscences clearly show this attitude of hopefulness and determination. They could now work to achieve the American Dream: independence, happiness, and success.

Whites, on the other hand, were anxious and fearful about the future. Their dreams had been shattered. As the Confederate governor of North Carolina, Zebulon B. Vance, observed: "The immediate emancipation of . . . slaves, without one moment's preparation, of either themselves or their masters, brings us with breathless haste, face to face, with some of the most startling and dangerous questions of the age."[4]

For North Carolinians the Civil War officially ended on April 18, 1865, when General Joseph E. Johnston surrendered to General William T. Sherman at Bennett House near Durham. Nine days later General John M. Schofield, commander of the Department of North Carolina, issued General Order 31 declaring that "hostilities . . . have definitely ceased."[5] But conditions were chaotic. While Federal troops had marched through only a small portion of the state, all of North Carolina shared the economic and emotional problems of recovery. During the war military maneuvers, pillaging troops on both sides, and simple neglect had caused devastation to the state's agriculture and manufacturing. Land had lain untended for long periods of time, farm animals were in short supply, and currency had disappeared or was valueless. Widespread lawlessness created additional hardships, as bands of civilians and former Confederates plundered the countryside.[6]

But such hardships were merely physical. The land could be reclaimed; crime could be suppressed. Materially and psychologically, the sudden emancipation of more than 330,000 slaves was more difficult to deal with. The *Philadelphia Inquirer*'s Raleigh correspondent astutely observed, "Aside from this complication [of the presence of the freedmen] the problem of reconstruction would be simple and easy."[7]

On April 28, 1865, General Schofield made the situation clear in General Order 32: "To remove a doubt which seems to exist in the minds of some of the people of North Carolina, it is hereby declared that by virtue of the [Emancipation] Proclamation . . . , all persons in this State heretofore held as slaves are now free."[8] But despite the clarity of this order, North Carolina whites, as the *Daily Union Banner* of Salisbury observed, exhibited considerable "perplexity . . . on the subject of the freedom of the slaves, and most of the people seem at a loss precisely what to do in the matter."[9]

Some solved their "perplexity" by simply ignoring the issue. In May and June there were reports that in some areas blacks "had not heard that they were free."[10] Even where slaves had heard the news, some were afraid to do anything about it. In September one former slave who operated a ferry across the Yadkin River told John R. Dennett, on special assignment in the South for *The Nation*, that he was in the same condition as before the war. His mistress had neither begun to pay him wages nor told him that he was free. And he said that he was afraid to ask her lest she claim that he was "insultin' to her and presumin'."[11]

A few whites wishfully believed that slavery had not yet been legally abolished. Mrs. Catherine Roulhac claimed that her slaves were not free, either "lawfully" or "constitutionally."[12] As late as September two white North Carolinians in different areas of the state reported that some citizens still maintained that blacks were not "legally free."[13] The freedmen themselves complained that many "wholly denied" their freedom.[14]

For the most part North Carolina planters worked to minimize the effects of emancipation. In June Federal officer Colonel Boynton noted that he found many who hoped "in some undefined way, [that] they will yet control the slaves, amounting with some to a conviction." In October Sidney Andrews, a northern journalist touring the South, reported that "slavery still exists as a fact even if abolished as a name." He maintained that "many of the people hope some system of peonage or apprenticeship will be established as soon as the State gets full control of her affairs."[15]

Many whites did not wait that long. They refused to give their former slaves more than room, board, and clothing,[16] unable to see that this was no different from the old slave situation. Often they whipped blacks who refused to work under these conditions.[17] Some angry whites even killed the freedmen. The *New Berne Times* reported that near Warsaw a former slaveholder, returning to his plantation after the war, found that his former slaves had "made a crop." When they refused his orders to leave, he murdered six of them.[18] In Salisbury, "two prominent men . . . and one of the wealthiest, most refined and respectable young ladies" were on trial before military courts for shooting blacks.[19] From August 1, 1865, to the end of 1866, the Freedmen's Bureau listed fifteen freedmen murdered by whites.[20]

North Carolina blacks, on the other hand, jubilantly greeted emancipation. But they too were unsure about what to expect. Most realized, however, that first they had to prove to themselves and to their former owners that they were truly free. Thus, as William A. Graham, writing from Hillsboro, noted, they deserted their former masters "in search of freedom."[21] Thousands had fled to Union lines during the war. After Federal troops seized New Berne in March of 1862, large numbers of eastern North Carolina blacks flocked to that city. As northern troops expanded their control of eastern North Carolina, thousands of others congregated in New Berne, Washington, Beaufort, and on Roanoke Island.[22]

After the war countless more former slaves temporarily left their homes. In June a Freedmen's Bureau agent in Charlotte reported that "the whole population of Blacks [was] . . . completely wild. The sudden transition from Slavery to Freedom had caused them to become a restless and wandering People Stragling [sic] over the country in Search of Freedom."[23] Disgustedly, David Schenck of Lincoln County contended that "every fool negro thinks freedom consists in leaving his master and being idle."[24]

While most blacks left voluntarily to test their freedom, many were driven off by their former masters. This was especially true of women, children, and the aged who could not pay their way by their work.[25] Other former owners forced the freedmen to leave their homes because they felt they were "impertinent."[26] Most of those who drove their former slaves away, however, did so in the summer after the crop had been "laid by" in order to avoid paying them any wages. In June and July the Freedmen's Bureau received more than a hundred complaints of such cases for the central area of the state alone.[27]

Many blacks who left or were driven away from their former homes eventually congregated in the towns. In fact they became so numerous that the Raleigh *Daily Standard* contended that overcrowding was causing them to contract diseases and incur "fearful risks in their morals and habits of industry."[28]

When blacks arrived in the towns, many were already in poor health. One Beaufort man wrote that the freedmen there were "nearly naked and look as if they were half starved."[29] The thirty thousand freedmen in Wilmington were said to be "in a state of great destitution."[30] The *New Berne Times*, describing a congregation of about one hundred fifty to three hundred freedmen living in tents recently vacated by Union troops on a farm outside New Berne, claimed that the ex-slaves were "dying at the rate . . . of about a half a dozen a day."[31] Two northern teachers working in New Berne confirmed that the condition of the hundreds of freed-men coming there daily was "wretched in the extreme." Significantly, however, they added that "they seem well satisfied with their escape from slavery and present prospects."[32]

The Freedmen's Bureau worked to alleviate the suffering. The Bureau undertook a variety of tasks ranging from care for the destitute, to super-vising labor contracts, trying cases involving blacks and whites, and coor-dinating educational activities.[33] In all these endeavors, however, it was understaffed. The assistant commissioner supervised all Bureau activities in the state. Below him were four superintendents, one each for the eastern, southern, central, and western districts. Each district was then subdivided into subdistricts, composed of two to four counties each and supervised by an assistant superintendent.[34] Given the fact that each subdistrict was so large, one superintendent noted that "of course it is utterly impracticable under the circumstances to render that complete protection to the Freedmen that doubtless the Administration con-templated in the institution of this Bureau."[35] A Kinston citizen wrote that because there was no Bureau officer in his county whites "have more opportunity to encroach upon the rights" of blacks.[36]

Besides the problems of understaffing, the Bureau in North Carolina also suffered from a high turnover in personnel. There were, for example, five different assistant commissioners between 1865 and 1867 plus two more acting assistant commissioners. The same pattern held true for the superintendents and assistant superintendents. [37] This high turnover rate was probably caused, in part, by the fact that most Bureau supervisors were Union officers, many of whom were being mustered out of the army and returning home.

As a result, a third problem arose. On occasion the Bureau appointed North Carolina citizens as agents when not enough army officers were available. Approximately a dozen North Carolina whites served in these positions. Some performed well. Others, however, "proved unfit . . . , not being able to comprehend that a negro can be a free man, or can have any rights which a white man is bound to respect." Moreover, when Bureau officers remained in North Carolina as citizen agents, as they sometimes did after being mustered out of the army, they often found that they lost the respect of the native whites and the confidence of the blacks that they had commanded as members of the United States Army.[38]

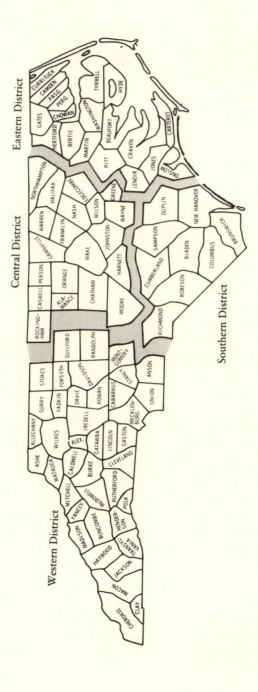

Map 2. Freedmen's Bureau Districts

Despite these difficulties the Freedmen's Bureau did adequate work in North Carolina. Its first task was to set up camps for destitute freedmen. No monthly records are available giving the exact number of freedmen in these camps immediately after the war. At the end of September 1865, however, Dr. M. K. Hogan, surgeon-in-chief of the Bureau in North Carolina, reported the following figures: in the two settlements near New Berne, there were about seventy-five hundred freedmen—five thousand at the Trent River Settlement and twenty-five hundred at the Johnsonville Camp. Three thousand five hundred were living at the Roanoke Island Settlement. In two smaller camps near Beaufort—Near Town and Hammocks—there were between three hundred and five hundred people.[39] Other small and less permanent camps also existed. One, for example, in Plymouth, was disbanded by the end of October or sooner.[40] Camps were also operating in Salisbury, Morehead City, Wilmington, and Greensboro. Charlotte and Raleigh each had a camp and a hospital.[41]

Camp conditions varied considerably, depending in part on the resources available at individual sites and in part on the competence of the Bureau officer in charge. The freedmen in the camp near Salisbury were reported to be healthy and "quartered in comfortable shanties."[42] By September 1865 the Trent River Settlement near New Berne, established in 1863 as a temporary refuge for the freedmen, had become a bustling village. Less than three hundred of the approximately five thousand black residents were receiving government assistance. In fact the income received from the freedmen's labor in August was $935 while expenses were "several hundred dollars less." Many freedmen had selected plots of land, acquired horses, mules, and carts, and were farming. Others had opened shops or were engaged in "mechanical" work. Captain Horace James, the Bureau superintendent for the camp, noted that the land had been worth about $10 per acre before the war. But since the freedmen had come, he estimated that it could be sold to them in lots at $200 per acre "and be cheap at that." To support this claim, James cited an example of "one little building erected for a shop [that] sold . . . for $55."

Yet despite all this prosperity and hard work, the freedmen did not own the land. Captain James had proposed, in September 1865, that the land be sold to them either by the federal government, "setting it apart . . . as being abandoned land; or that we should purchase the whole, of the old owners . . . , and immediately dispose of it to the people who have placed improvements on these lots." In December Colonel Eliphalet Whittlesey, commissioner of the Bureau in North Carolina, wrote that he was trying to obtain those lands "where the freedmen had built houses." These efforts failed, however, and the land was eventually returned to its white owners.[43]

Elsewhere in North Carolina freedmen were often destitute. Writing in September 1865, Major Charles J. Wickersham, superintendent for the Southern District, reported that in his area there was "much sickness in the freedmen camps," creating a great need for doctors and medicine.[44] One former slaveholder claimed that the freedmen in and around Wilmington were "crowded together [and] scantily fed." She also argued that those camped close to the rice fields were "dying by the thousands."[45] Roanoke Island was in a similar deplorable condition. Unlike the Trent River camp this area was barren and impossible to farm. Because of this condition the freedmen were unable to support themselves and had to rely almost entirely upon the government for support. But that support was inadequate, causing a great many hardships.[46]

Despite evidence of suffering among some freedmen and hard work by many, numerous white North Carolinians complained about the army and the Freedmen's Bureau, arguing that they encouraged idleness among the ex-slaves in these camps. The Raleigh *Sentinel* labeled the Bureau settlements "camps for the encouragement of vagrancy," causing former slaves "to depend on the government for support."[47] Some whites worried that their farms would go untended, adding to the financial loss engendered by the war. Further, they claimed that white women would face numerous hardships if they could not employ servants to do the household chores. T. P. Devereux, who had owned a large number of slaves before the war, summarized these attitudes when he contended that "the Negro is a necessity to the prosperity of the Southern States; . . . it will take millions of money and years of privation to obtain another race as equal to their performance."[48]

While the first and major concern of the planter class was to ensure themselves a reliable labor force, many more North Carolina whites worried about such social and psychological issues as law and order, the maintenance of white pride and respect, and the freedmen's place in southern society. They saw the army as the major institution which prevented them from reshaping their society in a way which would solve all these problems. Besides resenting the army's presence simply because it served as a daily reminder of southern defeat and humiliation, many whites felt that legally the military had "unlimited control over the civil and military laws of the State . . . , only limited by the authority invested in the Governor by the President's proclamation."[49] They claimed that they could not act with complete freedom and could not control their own destinies until the troops left.

But in reality even if the army had the authority it did not have the manpower to control the state. The figures for North Carolina bear out John Hope Franklin's contention that the small number of soldiers left in the South after the Civil War did not justify southern white complaints. By August 1865 more than two-thirds of the Union troops in North Carolina had been discharged. In September only about nine thousand remained. By October 1866 fewer than two thousand troops were stationed in the state. Moreover, by the end of 1865 most of the remaining soldiers had been withdrawn from the towns and cities.[50] Thus the number of troops was always too small to interfere very much.

James E. Sefton, in his generally reliable overall history of the Federal army in the South, maintains that one of the main reasons for southern white discontent was that a disproportionately large number of the troops which did remain were black.[51] But in North Carolina, at least, this was not the case. The greatest difference between the number of white and black troops was reached in September 1865, when the ratio was approximately four to five (3,972 white soldiers and 5,296 blacks). Even this small disproportion so distressed General Ruger that he ordered "no further reduction of white troops" along with the mustering out of blacks. He also suggested that black soldiers be used only "for garrison duty at the Forts & Depots on the Sea Coast, and the white troops for duty in the interior of the State." By March 1866 only one black regiment remained in both North and South Carolina.[52] Still, the army was generally hated.

A few white North Carolinians admitted that the troops were well behaved and that military rule was not as bad as they had feared.[53] Many more, however, complained that the troops were undisciplined. Some alleged that soldiers were drunk, disorderly, and riotous.[54] More important, many native whites did not like the effect that the troops had on the freedmen. They claimed that the presence of Federal troops made the freedmen "insolent and idle," for these northern soldiers treated blacks with as much respect as they did whites, socialized with the former slaves, and believed the testimony of blacks when they charged their white employers with such "crimes" as nonpayment or abuse. A Freedmen's Bureau agent summarized these feelings well when he explained that while whites were "not maliciously opposed to constituted authority," trouble often occurred between them and northerners because the native whites were "universally prejudiced against the 'nigger'" and resented the northern presence that forced them to treat freedmen fairly.[55]

Whites most resented the presence of black troops. Provisional Governor William H. Holden received numerous complaints from the citizens of Wilmington, New Berne, Beaufort, Morehead City, and Windsor. These complaints ranged from charges of "misbehavior" and "insolence" to "shocking outrages," thievery, and arresting whites for "no offences."[56] White Wilmington citizens also feared a black insurrection. On June 18,1865, for example, one Wilmingtonian claimed that "daily outrages" by black troops "or by other negroes instigated by them, have excited serious and well-grounded fears for the safety of our unarmed and defenseless people." In July the mayor and commissioners of the town wrote Holden about their fears of an insurrection. The next month they again wrote about the "spirit of rebellion" among the black troops. This time they asked Holden "to aid them in procuring 100 'Spencer' Rifles or Navy Revolvers with which to arm the police & other citizens, so that we may not be entirely defenceless in the case of an emergency."[57]

The vast majority of these complaints were exaggerated and white fears were unfounded. What these whites viewed as "insolence" and "shocking outrages" were generally acts done by blacks merely carrying out their duties as soldiers. Some whites viewed as an "outrage" any action by any black, soldier or freedman, that did not comply with their views of the black man's place in society. Some even openly admitted to these prejudices. The Raleigh *Progress*, for example, reporting on black troops in Goldsboro in May 1865, noted that they "drill well, their discipline is good . . . , and when off duty we have seen nothing like insubordination or plundering among or by them."[58] In August, however, the *Progress* editorially asked that black troops be removed "from our towns and villages." While still conceding that "the colored troops conduct themselves well and that the discipline is good," it explained that "our prejudices can't be overcome in a moment." Black troops, it claimed, had "demoralizing influences . . . on the negro population," which caused "whites to feel that they are constantly subject to the bursting forth of an eruption that may engulf all before it." The *New Berne Times* agreed.[59] In other words, many whites feared that if blacks did not "keep their place" an insurrection would inevitably result.

Reports from Wilmington also show that prejudice was the reason for the charges against the troops. The mayor's and commissioners' main complaint was that black troops had arrested the chief of police because he was carrying a gun. They failed to note that it was illegal at the time for Wilmingtonians to be armed. Such an arrest, they said, was "an indignity, not only to said Chief of Police, but to the civil government of this town." But what they feared most was that if this "indignity" was not "publicly rebuked," it would "greatly work to lessen the influence of the Commissioners & their officers over the colored population of this town, and be productive of much trouble."[60] The other "outrage" the mayor and commissioners reported was really a mass meeting of blacks where they probably called for equal rights. The city officials claimed that this gathering caused "great excitement . . . in the community" and therefore, they concluded, blacks were exhibiting "a spirit of rebellion."[61]

The *Wilmington Herald*'s view is probably a truer picture of reality:

> All of this talk about the negro troops is mere prejudice. . . . Those now in this city are among the best that have been put into the field. They are splendidly disciplined. . . . They are modest and respectful in their bearing; civil and gentlemanly, yet firm in the discharge of their duties, especially when brought in contact with whites; . . . and quiet and peaceable when off duty. Since their advent here the city has been remarkably quiet, the street fights and disturbances so common a week ago have entirely ceased.[62]

The Raleigh *Standard*'s Wilmington correspondent confirmed that the "colored troops . . . keep perfect order and surprise all in their drill and discipline." A week later, however, while still admitting that "the colored troops keep perfect order, and behave, while off duty," he explained that whites wished these troops removed because their presence was "galling" and caused Wilmingtonians to make "magnified representations . . . , as the imagination of a good many is stretched, in regard to them."[63]

General Samuel A. Duncan, a Union officer stationed in Wilmington, investigated white fears of a black conspiracy and reported that such anxieties were "utterly groundless, and absurd in the extreme."[64] General Thomas H. Ruger, commander of the Department of North Carolina, after his investigation of all the complaints forwarded to him, came to the same conclusion. The few instances of misconduct, he contended, were no more numerous than one would expect of white troops. The problem as he saw it was that "the people are sensitive on the subject of colored troops, whose presence is distasteful to them, and regarded as having a tendency to demoralize the colored people in general."[65] The Raleigh *Sentinel* also noted the orderly nature of black troops and made the significant observation that the complaints from Wilmington and New Berne coincided with "the organization of police of those places."[66] Obviously the complainants were anxious to regain control over the black population in these areas and the troops were standing in their way.

Nevertheless, Governor Holden asked President Andrew Johnson to remove black troops from the towns, explaining that their presence "has greatly increased the jealousy and unkind feeling between the white and colored citizens." On September 20 General George C. Meade, commander of the Military Division of the Atlantic, ordered all remaining black troops transferred to forts and depots on the coasts. Only white troops would be used in populated areas.[67] The Wilmington *Daily Journal* expressed its "relief" when the blacks left, "as the colored regiments in a great measure are composed of men who were formerly slaves, and very naturally their presence was obnoxious to those who formerly owned slaves, and were used to commanding them."[68] Thus the white elite, fearful of the consequences of emancipation, endeavored to maintain the status quo antebellum. Their former slaves, on the other hand, worked to acquire what they considered true freedom.

2　The Freedmen Begin Their Struggle for Freedom

We trust that in this country and in this State we may live, and . . . in this State we may die; not as rogues, not as convicts, not as vagabonds, but as men of intelligence, men of industry and men worthy of protection and rights, and men capable of exercising judgment to the interests of the State and the United States.—"A Colored Man of Raleigh," *Journal of Freedom*, October 21, 1865

WHILE WHITE LEADERS struggled to reassert their control over the black population, their former slaves—individually, in mass meetings, and in a statewide freedmen's convention—began their quest for "true freedom." What freedom meant to each ex-slave differed. Some merely wanted economic opportunities; others demanded full equality. But despite these differences most agreed that they wanted independence, opportunities, and respect.

While struggling to achieve this freedom, blacks showed surprisingly little vindictiveness. Many spoke kindly of whites. John Nixon, a delegate-elect to the state freedmen's convention, told Wilmington blacks that they were "in a land of friends."[1] Even the more radical Abraham H. Galloway, a black Union soldier, admitted that "we have many warm friends among the whites."[2] The statewide freedmen's convention, which met in the fall of 1865, noted that "born upon the same soil, and brought up in an intimacy of relationship unknown to any other society, we have formed attachments for the white race which must be as enduring as life, and we can conceive of no reason . . . [why anyone] should now sever the kindly ties which have so long united us."[3]

Others called upon their fellow blacks to remain peaceful and tried to assure whites that they had no "intention of stirring up strife."[4] The North Carolina A.M.E. Zion Church, in December 1865, asked its members "to avoid all irritative expressions both in . . . private and public discourse."[5] John Nixon went further when he urged black Wilmingtonians attending a mass meeting to ignore ill treatment by whites and to "go on and bow to them, and treat them all right, and be loyal to them."[6]

Directing his attention to the white community, a Fayetteville delegate to the state freedmen's convention declared that "there never would be a black rebellion. The Negroes wanted nothing so much as to live in peace with the white people of the States."[7] J. W. Hood, pastor of North Carolina's largest black church, the A.M.E. Zion Church of New Berne, argued that "the rumor concerning the colored people raising an insurrection has no foundation." He believed that such rumors were started by whites who wanted "some pretext for depriving them [blacks] of the rights they now enjoy," especially the right to own side arms for self-defense. He contended that whites wanted blacks disarmed so that they could mistreat the former slaves freely. "The time has been when they [whites] could cane a colored man off the sidewalk with impunity; but they fear that it would not be quite safe to amuse themselves in that way while the colored man is permitted to have the means of self-defense."[8]

The actions of blacks clearly confirmed their assurances. Although North Carolina blacks took part in numerous mass meetings and parades, not one incident of violence was instigated by the freedmen. Many North Carolina newspapers commented on how orderly these demonstrations were. This was true even when whites threatened blacks in attempts to dissuade them from holding such gatherings.[9]

While they remained peaceful blacks generally refused to remain docile slaves. Their desertion of their old homes was only an initial response to freedom. Official reports indicate that by December the freedmen had returned to work. O. O. Howard, commissioner of the Freedmen's Bureau, noted a steady decline in the number of rations issued by the Bureau in North Carolina. Moreover, many of the rations were issued to white women and children who were "families of soldiers who had died in the [Confederate] service." By September 1865 only five thousand freedmen out of a population of over 330,000 were receiving aid from the government, and most of these were women and children. By December most blacks had made contracts and were back on the farms.[10]

But the freedmen continued to demonstrate their newly acquired independence in many other ways. Reports from many sections of North Carolina recorded white complaints about blacks putting "on airs" and acting "impertinent" or "saucy and insolent." Black women wore veils and carried parasols like white women. Freedmen refused to yield the sidewalk to whites. Thus a white Concord man argued that "freedom's made 'em so sassy there's no livin' with 'em. I heerd that some of 'em's been sayin' the niggers'll rule the day here within two months time. I just want one to *say* that to me. The niggers that talk like that'll git killed certain."[11]

Most commonly blacks yearned for economic independence. Whites were disturbed when they realized that a freedman would prefer "buying a poor old mule and a poor old cart and going into business for himself" rather than work on a white man's farm.[12] Many blacks believed that the government would grant them forty acres and a mule, and it took much convincing by the Freedmen's Bureau to persuade them that this would not occur.[13] In other words, as Captain Horace James of the Freedmen's Bureau noted, what blacks wanted were "the common rights of citizens. . . . They want liberty to buy and sell and get gain; to select and favor their own church, school and party; to defend themselves; to litigate with, and implead, one another; to hold written documents, instead of verbal promises; and to manage their own affairs."[14]

Blacks worked to achieve these rights in many different ways. Some, individually or in small groups, asked for "the full rights of citizenship, inclusive, of course, of the right to vote."[15] Others, like some Colored Men of Raleigh," requested limited suffrage. In a letter to the editor of the *Sentinel* they emphasized their desire to improve themselves and others of their race through "industry, economy, frugality, [and] temperance." But they argued that the right to vote was essential in achieving this goal. However, they conceded that not all blacks were as yet capable of voting. Therefore, they wanted the vote given to those who "can read and write, those that have been in respectable standing in the various Churches for five years and those that have and do own 500 dollars worth of property." They asked: "How do you or can it be expected of us to improve our condition unless you as the leading people, allow us." The *Sentinel* praised this letter as being written in "a different spirit from that evinced by the speeches and declarations of the colored people generally. They have most frequently demanded *suffrage as a right*, and *for all*. The above asks it as a manifestation of clemency, as an unmerited favor to that part of the colored race who have proven themselves worthy, as a means of elevation." But continuing in this paternalistic tone the *Sentinel* argued that suffrage as a right does not elevate anyone: "In desiring suffrage, the blacks would reverse nature and reason." Moreover, limited suffrage would not, the *Sentinel* feared, "satisfy the clamors of the rest."[16]

Faced with this kind of sentiment many North Carolina blacks realized that they had to organize. Within months of emancipation they began to form "Societies, leagues, combinations, [hold] meetings, with little routine or record, but much of speechmaking and sage counsel" to demonstrate their awareness of their freedom and to express their views. They started Equal Rights Leagues in at least two North Carolina towns—Wilmington and Beaufort—and Union Leagues in Raleigh, New Berne, and Kinston. These organizations were devoted to the struggle for equal rights for all.[17]

Blacks also held numerous demonstrations and meetings. Their first recorded mass demonstrations occurred on the Fourth of July 1865. They saw these parades as a way of asserting their freedom, for such celebrations had been prohibited in antebellum times. At least two thousand blacks from Raleigh and the surrounding countryside marched down the main streets and in front of the governor's home. The parade "was orderly, the people well dressed." Members of the African Methodist church, the Baptist church, and the Union League marched as groups with the African Methodist church band leading the way. The banners the marchers carried showed clearly that these blacks understood what their freedom meant. One banner proclaimed: "No Slave lives beneath this flag!" Another demanded "Equal Rights before the law: the only equality we ask." Realizing the necessity for self-improvement a third proclaimed: "'You may now learn to read yourselves, and also instruct others'—Governor Holden."[18]

More than two thousand freedmen in Beaufort also celebrated the Fourth of July under the auspices of the Salmon P. Chase Equal Rights League. Here too the procession was orderly and the banners "appropriate, and their mottoes significant." A. H. Galloway, a black Union soldier, delivered a speech to the group demanding "*all* equal rights *before the law*, and nothing more."[19] In New Berne "a colored Burying Society" and another unidentified group ("whether they belong to the schools or the leagues, we do not know") marched, the latter "with a colored band and banners flying."[20] Blacks in Kinston "also had a procession and an oration."[21] The white press was unanimous in its praise of these Fourth of July parades, all commenting on the orderliness of the freedmen and many applauding the moderation of their banners.[22]

The largest and most formal assemblage that blacks organized during this period was a statewide freedmen's convention, which met in Raleigh from September 29 through October 3, 1865. During September many blacks attended meetings throughout the state to choose delegates. These mass meetings were launched in response to a call made by a gathering of blacks in New Berne on August 22. Published in at least three North Carolina newspapers, this statement called upon freedmen to "rise up in the dignity of men." It continued: "The time has arrived when we can strike one blow to secure those rights of Freedmen that have been so long withheld from us." It went on to announce plans for the convention, and urged: "from all sections let delegates be sent to represent you. Let the entire colored population of North Carolina, assemble in their respective town-ships, and speak their views."[23] The president of the New Berne meeting—Jonathan R. Good, a native North Carolinian and a free barber with a good income before the war—explained that the convention was "to take such measures as will advance the welfare of the colored people of this State. . . . The white people . . . are about to hold conventions for the purpose of reconstruction, and it is necessary that the colored people should take such steps as may influence these conventions and promote our good."[24]

North Carolina newspapers reported only eight countywide mass meetings held to select convention delegates, while two other sources noted two more such meetings. But since at least thirty-four counties sent delegates to the convention, it is likely that more mass meetings were held than reported. Those that were reported were all held in the heavily black areas of southeastern and northcentral North Carolina. Most met in cities; a few were held in predominantly rural areas. Generally the meetings were well attended. A Freedmen's Bureau agent reported that fifteen hundred people attended the meeting in Tarboro. A "respectable" number of blacks gathered in Elizabeth City, and the Chapel Hill meeting was large enough to be called a "crowd." The *Wilmington Herald* reported that in that city on September 13 "the African population, in full force, assembled." The next week another Wilmington meeting was reported as "one of the largest gatherings of the kind ever."[25]

All the meetings reported were described as efficiently run and conforming to conventional organizational rules. After the acting chairman called the meeting to order each gathering elected a president or chairman, one or more secretaries, and sometimes one or more vice-presidents. Then the chairman appointed a committee to prepare resolutions. While this committee was working, one or more people usually addressed the group. Then the resolutions were presented and approved. Finally, delegates to the freedmen's convention were either elected or appointed.

At most of these county meetings, blacks called for legal and political rights. The Wake County meeting, held in Raleigh on September 9, was the one exception. While choosing delegates to the convention, this group passed resolutions questioning the wisdom of holding such a meeting before the state's constitutional convention met. They feared that the convention "would be injudicious" to the black population, since whites might construe it "as an attempt on the part of our people to forestall or to dictate its [North Carolina's state constitutional convention] actions or legislation concerning us." The Raleigh group thus suggested that the freedmen postpone their statewide gathering until after the state's constitutional convention, "inasmuch as we should first know what the disposition of the State authorities are toward us, in order to act intelligently."[26]

Ignoring this advice, at all the other meetings organized throughout the state blacks resolved to gain their rights. But even at these other gatherings the tone was generally moderate. Many specifically denied any desire for social equality. They recognized that they had to educate themselves and their children, work hard, and maintain peaceful relations with whites. They also, however, enunciated their beliefs that the rights to testify in the courts and to vote were essential if their freedom was to be preserved. Some were willing to accept qualified suffrage, based on education or wealth, if such restrictions were applied equally to both races. But this limited suffrage, they argued, was a mandatory minimum. As those attending the Edgecombe County meeting held in Tarboro on September 16 succinctly put it, "Representation and taxation should go hand in hand; and it is diametrically opposed to Republican institutions to tax us . . . , and at the same time deny us the right of representation."[27]

John P. Sampson, a native North Carolinian who had recently returned to his home state after attending college in Ohio and serving as the editor of the *Colored Citizen* of Cincinnati for some time, spoke at a Wilmington meeting on September 21 and elaborated on the point raised at the Tarboro gathering. He claimed that without the right to vote the black man's "liberty is a mockery." Voting, he contended, is a right, not a privilege, and that "no class of men can, without insulting their own nature, be content with any deprivation of their rights." Further, argued Sampson, "by depriving us of suffrage you affirm our incapacity to form an intelligent judgment . . . ; you declare before the world that we are unfit to exercise the elective franchise, and by this means lead us to undervalue ourselves . . . and to feel that we have no possibilities like other men." Thus, he said, to deprive blacks of the right to vote in a democracy was "to brand us with the stigma of inferiority," and he labeled the charge of inferiority "an old dodge." Using time-honored American logic, he argued: "If we know enough to pay taxes . . . , we know enough to vote. *Taxation and representation* should go together. If we know enough to shoulder a musket or fight for the flag . . . , we know enough to vote." Finally he displayed his own prejudices by concluding, "If we know as much when sober as an Irishman knows when drunk, we know enough to vote."[28]

Abraham H. Galloway was the most radical speaker to address any of these preconvention meetings. At the August 28 New Berne meeting he argued that "the only way you can close the negro man's mouth is to throw the ballot down his throat." Sarcastically he claimed that New Berne whites feared that if blacks were allowed to vote they would have the majority and elect him, Galloway, as mayor. And while maintaining that he did not want social equality, he attacked whites by asserting that while they opposed social equality they slipped "around at night, trying to get into negro women's houses." He continued that despite this white hypocrisy he did not wish "to be considered as the white man's enemy" for he thought "the white man [was] . . . as good as a negro—if he will only behave himself." But even Galloway was willing to accept limited suffrage, based on "the test of education," if such a test were applied equally to both blacks and whites.[29]

The few North Carolina newspapers that commented upon these meetings and on the call for the convention generally disapproved of the proceedings. The *New Berne Times* set the editorial pattern early when on August 31 it reacted to the original call for the convention by noting that it had published the circular calling for the convention "only to satisfy curiosity, and to show that negroes are wide awake to the importance at least of agitation." The *Times* labeled demands for full citizenship "foolish and unreasonable." It also argued that "if the object of the . . . proposed convention is to consult about and ask assistance in educating, refining and christianizing their race . . . , then their object is a good one. . . . But if the object . . . is to set up a claim for immediate political equality with the whites, their labor will be in vain." The *Wilmington Herald* contended that the mass meeting there merely showed "that these people have 'mass meetings on the brain.'" It accused "fanatical agitators" from the North of filling the minds of the freedmen "with wild notions of their right to the ballot," and urged blacks to work rather than to take part in "useless political tom-foolery."[30]

The Reverend George Rue—minister at New Berne's A.M.E. Bethel Church, chaplain of the 32nd United States Colored Troops, and delegate-elect from Craven County to the freedmen's convention—indignantly responded to the *Herald*'s attacks: "We are neither crazy, nor all so ignorant as he [the editor of the *Herald*] may think, and furthermore, . . . we do not seek his counsel nor ask his advice. . . . In our meetings we are asking for our rights, earnestly and respectfully, and shall continue asking until our demands are granted."[31]

In some cases whites went further than simple verbal condemnation. Some in Chapel Hill threw stones at the building where a mass meeting was being held, forcing blacks to leave. In Tarboro several meetings were reportedly called but many blacks "were prevented from attending by threats of personal violence from their badly reconstructed white neighbors." Sidney Andrews, a northern journalist touring the South, claimed that many delegates to the freedmen's convention "were obliged to leave their homes in the night, are asking [for] safe-conduct papers from the military authorities, and will even then quietly return home in the night." And the delegates did appoint a committee of three to ask General Thomas H. Ruger, commander of the Department of North Carolina, to protect "certain delegates returning home where bitter feelings exist against the colored Convention." There is also evidence that one delegate, Isham Sweat of Fayetteville, experienced economic retaliation. Sweat claimed that his white customers stopped patronizing his barbershop after he was elected a convention delegate.[32]

Despite this white opposition the freedmen's convention met on September 29, 1865, in the African Methodist Church of Raleigh. A small white wooden building on a back street, it was "neatly but cheaply furnished" with a carpeted floor and cushioned seats and could hold about four hundred people. Its only ornament was a large plaster-of-paris bust of Abraham Lincoln, over which were the words: "With malice toward none, with charity for all, with firmness in the right, as God gives us to see the right, let us strive on toward the work we are in, to bind up the nation's wounds."[33]

According to the offical roll of delegates 106 men from thirty-four of the state's eighty-nine counties attended the convention. The delegates decided, however, that because some who came did not have credentials "on account of the interference of the whites in some counties," and because some counties had sent too many delegates and others too few, all would be admitted and the meeting would be made a mass convention. Therefore, according to several observers, approximately 120 men from forty counties participated.[34]

Most of the representatives came from the coastal region, the eastern cities, and the heavily black central areas. Only two western counties sent delegates. There are several possible reasons for this. John R. Dennett, a northern correspondent for *The Nation*, argued that "at this present time the Negroes in central and western North Carolina have given but little thought to political subjects, and take no great interest in them. In Wilmington, Newbern, and Beaufort, judging by their representations at the convention, the case is different."[35]

There are, however, other possible reasons. Poor communications and the high cost of travel were doubtless important considerations.[36] For example, the Charlotte *Western Democrat* (the leading newspaper in the west) never mentioned the convention before, during, or after it met.[37] Another possible explanation is simply that the majority of blacks lived in the eastern half of the state. Western blacks, especially where they were vastly outnumbered by whites, may also have been afraid to hold mass meetings and to send delegates.

Besides their regional backgrounds, other differences existed among the representatives. While a few were born in the North or in other

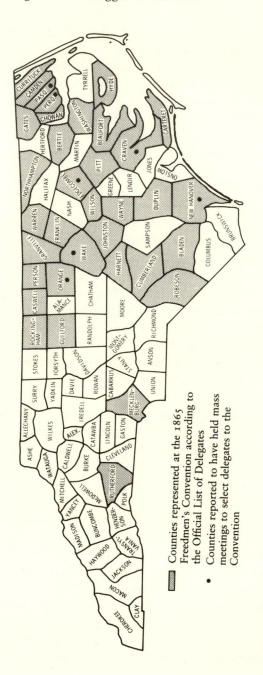

Counties represented at the 1865
Freedmen's Convention according to
the Official List of Delegates

• Counties reported to have held mass
meetings to select delegates to the
Convention

Map 3. 1865 Freedmen's Convention

southern states, most were native North Carolinians. Of the sixty-seven delegates whose birthplaces can be determined, sixty-two were from North Carolina, although two of these had been educated in the North. Two were born in Virginia, one in Alabama, one in Pennsylvania, and one in Massachusetts. Moreover, northern journalist Sidney Andrews asserted that "with few exceptions, those who took part in the debate or were in any way responsible for the action of the convention, were not only North Carolinians by birth, but . . . men who have always lived and expect to continue living in the state."[38]

Most of the delegates were probably former slaves. Only eleven can be identified as having been free before the war. Four were definitely ex-slaves, and forty-nine others can be assumed to have been slaves as they appear in the 1870 census as being native North Carolinians but cannot be located in the population schedule of the 1860 census, which listed only free persons.[39] Despite the fact that most delegates were freedmen, half of those on whom such information can be found were literate. According to the 1870 census,[40] thirty-nine could read and write and five others could read but not write. Only twenty-four were listed as not being able to read or write.

The delegates were unusual in other important ways. While most North Carolinians engaged in agricultural pursuits, only thirteen delegates were farmers and another eleven farm laborers. Twenty-two were artisans—carpenters, barbers, blacksmiths, and the like.[41] Another two were grocers and six were laborers. There was also one caulker, one boatman, and one turpentine dealer. Ten were ministers and three were teachers. About half of these artisans and professionals lived in rural areas while the remaining thirty-eight of the seventy-one so identified lived in cities and towns.

Moreover, many of the delegates owned some land and had acquired some wealth. Twenty-nine, according to the 1870 census, had no personal or real property, but seventeen owned both. An additional nine had some personal but no real property, and nine others had no personal but some real property. In sum, of the sixty-four delegates who appeared in the census (approximately 60 percent of those on the official delegate roll), almost 55 percent (thirty-five delegates) owned property. And some of these holdings were fairly large. Of those who owned property, three owned assets of $100 or less, ten had property valued at between $100 and $500, twelve between $500 and $1,000, and ten owned property worth over $1,000.

Their literacy, their occupations, and their wealth all imply that the delegates were generally the rural and urban black elite. Not surprisingly, many remained black leaders. Nine were elected to state offices after 1868 when blacks won the vote, and others continued to be active on the local level although they did not hold elective office.

Despite the fact that these delegates were wealthier, were better educated, came from more skilled occupations, and had more experience with freedom than the typical black North Carolinian in 1865, they certainly did not have the kind of background or experience found among typical white legislators. But they came to the convention with, as Andrews noted, "a new sense of responsibilities of manhood, and a new sense of the manner in which they must meet these responsibilities."[42] Dennett maintained that even those who were uneducated displayed great native intelligence. One, for example, acknowledged: "Yes, we are ignorant. . . . I am ignorant for one." But he continued: "They say we don't know enough to know what the word constitution means. But if we don't know enough to know what the Constitution is, we know enough to know what justice is. I can see for myself down at my own court-house. If they makes a white man pay five dollars for doing something today, and makes a nigger pay ten dollars for doing that thing tomorrow, don't I know that ain't justice."[43] Thus Andrews concluded that "the great body of delegates . . . had a pretty clear conception of what they wanted to do."[44]

While "crowds of colored citizens" watched as "interested spectators," the convention proceeded smoothly and efficiently. On the first day New Berne delegate J. W. Hood was elected president. Originally from Pennsylvania, he had lived in New Berne since 1863 when the Union army occupied that city. The minister of New Berne's A.M.E. Zion Church, he remained in North Carolina as an active leader until his death in 1918. He was a leading member of the meeting which had called for this convention. In his presidential address to the convention Hood labeled the meeting the most important assembly ever to meet, for blacks had "come together as one man," with their watchword "equal rights before the law." In pursuing these rights, however, he maintained that both races had to live together "and the best way is to harmonize our feelings as much as possible, and treat all men respectfully." He also asserted that while some whites were "ruffians" most were "gentlemen and ladies." After these cautious, conciliatory comments Hood became more radical as he listed three rights he believed blacks must have: the right to testify in court, the right to serve on juries, and the right to vote. He acknowledged that some blacks might not be fully prepared to use all these rights wisely but argued: "Give the colored men rights at once, and then they will practice them and the sooner know how to use them."[45]

Isham Sweat, A. H. Galloway, and James H. Harris also delivered speeches on the first day of the convention. Sweat, a native North Carolinian from Fayetteville, was an ex-slave, self-educated, and a barber by trade. He told the convention that the freedmen must be granted equal rights before the law, including the right to vote. Galloway, a delegate from New Berne, had been one of the first to call for a convention. A former North Carolina slave who escaped to Ohio in 1857, he had returned to his native state as a Union soldier. In his address he reiterated the main theme from his earlier speeches: the need for universal manhood suffrage. James H. Harris of Raleigh was also a native North Carolinian. Born free and self-educated, he had been an upholsterer before the war. Later he became a teacher and one of the state's most prominent black political leaders. He was one of the most moderate delegates at the convention, and his address advised blacks "to be cautious and proceed slowly in their work."[46]

On the second day of the convention the resolutions drawn up by the business committee were read and adopted.[47] Many of these resolves demonstrated a great awareness of current events and a loyalty to the federal government, especially to the Radical Republicans. Evidence of this awareness is particularly important since some historians have claimed that blacks were unaware of what freedom meant and that they were "duped" by white northerners into supporting the Radicals.[48] After proclaiming their loyalty to the United States the delegates resolved "that we hail the event of emancipation, with the Freedmen's Bureau governing the interests of the colored men in the South; . . . the amendment to the Federal Constitution [the Thirteenth Amendment, forever prohibiting slavery] and its endorsement by various State Legislatures and Conventions; the progress of enlightened sentiment . . . as turning a bright page in the history of progressive civilization, a triumph of just principles, a practical assertion of the fundamental truths laid down in the . . . Declaration of Independence."

Further, they praised "the efforts of that portion of the Republican party, of which Messrs. Chase, Sumner, Stevens and Greeley are the head, to secure to the colored citizen his rights through the action of Congress." Exhibiting pride in the achievements of blacks in the United States and abroad, the delegates also hailed "the recognition of independence of Hayti and the Republic of Liberia by our govt; [and] the admission of Mr. Rock, a colored lawyer, to the bar of the Supreme Court." They also lauded "the rapid progress being made on the part of our young men in the glorious cause of education, [and] in pursuing useful and honorable avocations," applauded the establishment of more than seventy-five hundred schools for blacks in the South, and recommended that all North Carolina freedmen "educate themselves and their children."

The final resolution established a committee "to prepare an address to the constitutional convention of the State of North Carolina . . . representing the wishes of this convention on the subject of Equal Rights."[49] The committee was composed of four native North Carolinians and one northerner. James H. Harris, who spoke with moderation on the first day of the convention, was chairman of the committee. Like Harris the other members of the committee were leading black citizens. Jonathan R. Good, the presiding officer of the New Berne mass meeting which had called for the freedmen's convention, served in the 1874 North Carolina House of Representatives. Isham Sweat of Fayetteville, one of those who addressed the convention at its opening session, was a member of the 1868 North Carolina House. John Randolph of New Berne, a former slave like Sweat, was a carpenter and teacher by trade. The Reverend George A. Rue was the only northern-born member of the committee. He had come from Massachusetts to New Berne as a chaplain in the army and took up the post of minister at the A.M.E. Church in New Berne.

This committee brought in its report on October 2, the third day of the convention. Despite Hood's call for complete political and legal equality and despite the resolutions passed the previous day praising the work of the Radical Republicans, the address "to the Constitutional Convention of North-Carolina and the Legislature to assemble thereafter" was written in a humble, respectful tone. More important, it did not ask for any specific legal or political rights. It opened by "earnestly disclaiming all wish to . . . dictate in the solemn and important duties which have been intrusted in you," and expressed confidence in "your justice, wisdom and patriotism, to guard the interests of all classes." Almost apologetically it explained that while "it was impossible for us to remain indifferent spectators" during the Civil War, "you will do us the justice to admit that we have remained throughout obedient and passive. . . . Our brethren have fought upon the side of the Union, while we have been obliged to serve in camp . . . and raise subsistence for the Confederate army. Do you blame us that we have, meantime, prayed for the freedom of our race?" The petition also prayed for continued harmonious relations between whites and blacks in North Carolina. Slavery had led blacks to form close attachments with whites "and we can conceive of no reason that Our God [who] bestowed freedom should now sever the kindly ties which have so long united us."

The address then focused on economic matters. It pointed out that government agents and Union troops would not remain in the South much longer to protect blacks from "unreasonable prejudice, and unjust men." Therefore, it continued, blacks had to find, "at home" the necessary protection and sympathy they merit by their "industry, sobriety and respectful demeanor." The presentation also acknowledged that many former masters had promptly freed their slaves "and have manifested a just and humane disposition towards" them. But other planters, it said, "have either kept the freedmen in doubt; have wholly denied his freedom, or have grudgingly conceded it." Some had forced ex-slaves to leave the plantations. Others had refused to pay freedmen at all or had not paid them a living wage. Therefore the petition urged the state convention and the legislature to pass "some suitable measures . . . to prevent unscrupulous and avaricious employers from the practice of . . . acts of injustice towards our people." This legislation must also guarantee "adequate compensation for our labor" because "our first and engrossing concern . . . is, how we may provide shelter and an honorable subsistence for ourselves and families." The address also requested "such encouragement to our industry as the proper regulation of the hours of labor and the providing of the means of protection against rapacious and cruel employers and for the collection of just claims." Futher, it urged the legislature to make "some provision . . . for the care of the great number of orphan children and the helpless and infirm."

In addition to these economic considerations, the petition explained that black children needed education so that they "may be made useful in all the relations of life." It also asked for the removal of "the disabilities under which we formerly labored, and to have all the oppressive laws which make unjust discriminations on account of race or color wiped from the statutes of the State." It did not elaborate on this request, however, nor did it list any specific "disabilities," but relied solely on the white man's goodness and sense of justice. While this petition made an implicit request for fair treatment in the courts, it did not call directly for legal equality, nor for the right to vote. Economic concerns were paramount.[50]

It is difficult to explain why this address was so moderate in both tone and substance, after the more radical speeches delivered on the first day of the convention, demanding immediate political equality, and the resolutions passed on the second day praising the Radical Republicans. The two northern journalists who observed the proceedings, John R. Dennett and Sidney Andrews, argued that after the first day a more moderate group of native North Carolinians, headed by Harris, wrested control from the Wilmington–New Berne faction that was comprised largely of northern-born or northern-educated blacks. However, there appears to be little evidence supporting this view. In fact the Harris committee was dominated by the supposedly more radical faction. While Harris, as chairman, might have been a moderating influence, another theory seems more plausible. During the first two days of the convention blacks were talking among themselves. But the moderate resolutions proposed by the Harris committee and approved by the delegates were directed to white North Carolinians, specifically to the elected representatives of the state's constitutional convention and legislature. The black delegates seem to have adopted a political strategy of caution. Hoping to persuade whites that compromise and reconciliation were the best policies, they decided for political reasons on a moderate course—at least temporarily. Even Harris, the most moderate of the convention's leadership, hoped for eventual political and legal equality. The convention seemed to believe that it was better strategy to ask merely for economic opportunities; political equality could come later. But earlier and subsequent proceedings make it clear that the delegates did not want to wait too long.

On the last day of the convention several more radical resolutions were discussed and passed. Most of the afternoon the delegates debated a proposed recommendation from the business committee that "colored teachers and preachers be employed" to teach black children and to serve black congregations whenever possible. Those favoring the proposal argued that it would "stimulate education among the young men and women." The opposition feared "it would serve to set up another wall between blacks and whites." The reasons for the proposal and the strong feelings on both sides are impossible to determine. There seemed to be no clear-cut division between moderate and radical or native versus northern delegates. A compromise was finally proposed by several delegates who "favored the general policy enunciated in the resolution, but opposed its passage, on the ground that some of the more ignorant of their people would look upon it as a recommendation not to send their children to the schools established by the Freedmen's Bureau and the Aid Societies of the North." The convention tabled the committee's resolution and passed a substitute motion proposed by the compromise group. This resolution merely thanked the northern benevolent societies "who have so liberally provided for the education of our children" and also the Freedmen's Bureau "for their effort in our behalf."[51]

John P. Sampson of Wilmington then moved that after the convention adjourned it should "resolve itself into a North Carolina State Equal Rights League." The delegates adopted this motion and elected James Harris president, John R. Good vice president, and Isham Sweat corresponding secretary. They also elected an eleven-man executive committee and adopted another resolution "encouraging sub-Leagues in every County." Next a previously appointed committee presented a proposed constitution for the League, which was also adopted. The preamble explained that "feeling the stern necessity of encouraging a well ordered and dignified life, . . . we are met in concert with the determination to organize more permanently, consolidating all efforts looking to our general elevation." Article II of the constitution noted that the purpose of the League was "to secure, by political and moral means . . . the repeal of all laws and parts of laws, State and National, that make distinctions on account of color." The constitution established Raleigh as the League's headquarters and stipulated that membership was open to all who subscribed to the League's principles and who contributed "to its funds as he or she may be able." In order to facilitate the unified efforts spoken of in the preamble, church organizations, societies, and schools could become auxiliaries of the League.[52]

By establishing this League with a stated purpose of securing, "by political and moral means" the repeal of all discriminatory legislation, the convention met the demands of its more radical members. Most delegates clearly wanted full equality. Some, however, were willing to be humble and respectful, waiting to see what the state's constitutional convention and legislature would do. Therefore while sending a modest address to the state convention the delegates also organized themselves so they could press their demands further if neither the constitutional convention nor the legislature enacted the laws they wanted.[53]

Sidney Andrews, evaluating the work of the convention, maintained that it "was a body of which the negroes of this or any other Southern State might well be proud, and which no Northern man could see without feelings of hearty respect." He believed the address to the constitutional convention was "one of the most remarkable documents that the time has brought forth. . . . This is their first political act; and I do not see how they could have presented their claims with more dignity, with a more just appreciation of the state of affairs, or in a manner which should appeal more forcibly either to the reason or the sentiment of those whom they address."[54]

North Carolina's white press, however, generally attacked the convention and its work. The Salisbury *Union Banner* labeled it "a high festival of ebony." The Raleigh *Sentinel* praised the moderate tone of the freedmen's address to white North Carolinians but opposed the extension of equal rights to blacks and blamed the agitation over rights for the freedmen on "New England fanaticism." The state might eventually grant blacks citizenship, it continued, but only if the freedmen stopped "holding colored Conventions" and making "threatening speeches." The Raleigh *Progress* also applauded the petition to the state constitutional convention and the legislature and urged these bodies to "maturely consider their duties and obligations to this unfortunate race, and then act with wisdom, discretion and justice." But it too opposed "the extension of the right of suffrage or other political privileges" to blacks and said it had hoped that the convention would have been more moderate and have made "no insolent or unreasonable demands." The only way blacks can improve their condition, it argued, was by not making enemies of whites.[55] The attitudes expressed by these newspapers were also the attitudes of most white North Carolina leaders as they faced the freedmen and the issues of their status in the South.

3 The "White Man's Government"

This is the white man's country and the white man's Government, and the white man intends to govern in them.—*New Berne Times*, June 24, 1865

We have no prejudices against the negro . . . and if everybody, North and South, will quit talking about "negro equality" and "negro suffrage," and strive to inaugurate some fair measure to compel him to work, they will do more good for the negro in that way than in any other.—*The Western Democrat* (Charlotte), July 25, 1865

AS BLACK NORTH CAROLINIANS struggled to assert their freedom, North Carolina whites worked to establish what they believed to be the proper postbellum race relations. Intellectually they knew slavery was dead. On July 1, 1865, Colonel Whittlesey, assistant commissioner of the Freedmen's Bureau in North Carolina, clearly told them:

> The negro has become free. . . . He cannot with safety be treated with neglect, or scorn, or cruelty. Withhold from the freedmen fair wages for their labor, deny them a right to a fair hearing before courts of justice, discourage their efforts to accumulate property and to acquire learning, and you will drive from the South its real wealth—its productive labor. On the other hand, give to the freedmen that which is just and equal, give them all the facilities possible for improvement and education, and you will secure in the state its best supporters and its truest friends.[1]

Yet old convictions died hard. For thirty years or more white southerners had been developing an elaborate rationale for slavery based on constitutional rights, historical precedents, social considerations, economic principles, biblical sanctions, and ethnological arguments. They had come to believe that blacks were inferior, lazy, and indolent, and that if set free they would merely become shiftless vagabonds, thieves, and gamblers.[2] The war and Lincoln's Emancipation Proclamation could not kill these beliefs which many North Carolinians reiterated either directly or implicitly throughout Presidential Reconstruction. They argued that God "never intended" blacks to "be [the] equal, politically or socially, of the white man," and that they had been better off as slaves.[3]

These attitudes caused many to maintain that blacks still had to be guided and controlled. They argued that unless whites forced them to do otherwise blacks would refuse to work and would live lives of crime. An observer, writing to Thaddeus Stevens, noted that the North Carolina freedman was "sneered at by all and informed daily yes hourly that he is incompetent to care for himself—that his race is now doomed to perish from off the face of the Earth—that he *will not* work—that he is a thief by nature[,] that he lies more Easily and naturally than an honest man breathes."[4]

Because they believed blacks to be a lazy, thieving, potentially dangerous, depraved race, many whites feared that continued northern occupation would be a further "corrupting" influence on the freedmen. By returning to the Union quickly they hoped to regain control over the black population. But before restoration could be accomplished North Carolina would, at a minimum, have to carry out President Johnson's reconstruction program. On May 29, 1865, Johnson issued two proclamations that established his framework for reunion. The first granted amnesty and pardon to those who would take an oath of allegiance to the United States and promise to support emancipation. Fourteen excepted classes had to apply for special pardon. Among these groups were civil and diplomatic officials of the Confederacy, colonels and generals of the Confederate army, Confederate governors, those who left seats in Congress or the judiciary to aid the rebellion, and those former rebels whose taxable property was estimated at over $20,000.

The second proclamation appointed William W. Holden provisional governor of North Carolina and outlined the procedure the state would have to follow. Holden was to reorganize the state government by appointing "loyal persons" to state and federal positions and then to convene a constitutional convention which would emancipate the slaves, declare the ordinance of secession null and void, and repudiate the Confederate debt.[5]

For one small group of white North Carolinians, predominantly from the western counties, compliance with federal law was easy. They had always been unionists. Many had either fought in the United States army or had been engaged in fifth column activities in the South during the war. They elected a man to Congress who could take the required congressional ironclad test oath, swearing that he had *always* been loyal to the United States. This group often clashed with former Confederates and sometimes faced persecution and discrimination in the state courts.[6]

Most other North Carolina whites were what Whitelaw Reid aptly called "reluctant unionists." They were Union men, he said, "if they can have the Union their way—if the negroes can be kept under, and themselves put foremost." While there were a minority of "malignant rebels" who were openly hostile to the North and the federal government and another minority faction who wanted to submit to all the federal government's demands, the reluctant unionists quickly emerged as the dominant group in the state. After Johnson's proclamation of amnesty and pardon, most "began to talk of their rights." While claiming that they would obey all laws and apply for special pardons when necessary, these whites viewed such action as "eat[ing] dirt" and wanted to eat it "in the easiest way" they could.[7] Many politically aware whites, therefore, had ulterior motives in professing loyalty. The Raleigh *Standard* stated the alternatives clearly: "Shall we accept the plan proposed by the President, and live under civil law, or shall we reject it and continue to be ruled by the military." More important, it noted that once civil government was restored, "white men shall be enabled to rule the black."[8]

But even though North Carolina whites wanted to return quickly to the Union, they either could not or would not do what northerners felt was necessary. Their pride had been wounded by the war but it had not been killed, and the pre-war communication gap was still there. The factors that had contributed to starting the Civil War—two different cultures with two different attitudes on slavery and states' rights—had not been destroyed by that war.

While whites immediately attempted to gain reentry into the Union, the question of the status of the black population continually plagued them and their efforts and prevented them from complying fully with northern demands. To North Carolina whites the freedmen's position within their society was the pivotal question. All reconstruction activities were affected by this concern. Whites, for example, held union meetings between April and June of 1865 to proclaim their renewed loyalty to the

United States. But even at these gatherings reluctant unionist sentiment dominated. Of the thirty-six meetings reported by various North Carolina newspapers, all but fourteen added requests, demands, or conditions to their loyalty resolutions, such as that blacks be colonized, that slavery be gradually rather than immediately abolished, and that blacks be denied the vote.[9]

During the campaign to elect delegates to the state constitutional convention, candidates hotly debated the issues that faced the convention: the abolition of slavery, the repudiation of the Confederate debt, and the declaration of the ordinance of secession null and void. Although these were President Johnson's minimum demands, whites still fought over whether or not they should comply. And the election results were mixed; North Carolinians elected men of all political opinions. Moreover, many voters stayed away from the polls, too bitter even to participate in an election for a convention that would carry out the president's requirements.

Because of this informal boycott the convention that convened on October 2 was the most unionist of the elected bodies to meet in North Carolina during Presidential Reconstruction. One hundred twenty-six men served as delegates in the 1865 and 1866 sessions of the convention. Most were former Whigs who had only reluctantly supported secession. While the majority had supported the Confederate war effort once secession occurred, three served in the Union army and at least seven more could take the ironclad oath, swearing that they had always been loyal to the Union. And of the fifty-eight delegates whose political activities after the war can be traced, thirty-eight became Republicans while only twenty-eight became Democrats.

In other ways the convention delegates seemed typical of any southern elective body of the period. The majority were middle-aged, the average age being forty-seven and a half. Lawyers dominated, followed by farmers. The delegates were also better educated, wealthier, and had owned more slaves than the average North Carolinian.[10] This profile might explain why Dennett called the convention an "imposing body." In fact, he was surprised that so many of the delegates had come from "the better class of people" because he had been led to believe that Union men had "little property and . . . no social standing."[11] In North Carolina at least this was not true.[12]

In spite of the delegates' unionist leanings the convention's actions showed that reluctant unionism was still present. One overriding theme dominated the debates on the floor of the convention and in the press: if the convention did not fulfill all of the president's demands, North Carolina would not get back into the Union. Thus political necessity was the overriding force motivating the delegates.

The ordinance forever abolishing slavery passed unanimously. Even here, however, many delegates probably voted for the ordinance more out of expediency than from any conviction that slavery was wrong or destructive to the state's economy. Many probably agreed with the *Sentinel* which argued that "our people are not convinced that its [slavery's] abolition is right or just—that it is best for the negro, or best for the South or best for the future prosperity of the whole country, yet as the North demands it, the South will make the sacrifice in good faith for the sake of peace and Union."[13]

The ordinance declaring secession null and void encountered more resistance because, as Mecklenburg County delegate Alexander McIver explained, he did not want North Carolinians "to stulify" themselves "by denying its [the secession ordinance's] validity." However, only twenty voted for a substitute proposal and when the original ordinance declaring secession "null and void" came to a vote it passed 105 to 9.[14]

The longest debate centered on the ordinance "prohibiting the payment of all debts created or incurred in aid of the late rebellion." Many feared that repudiation would financially destroy the state and many of its citizens. Only after a firm telegram from President Johnson, in response to Holden's inquiries, did the delegates vote to prohibit "the payment of all debts created or incurred in the aid of the late rebellion." Many still opposed repudiation in principle, however, and blamed Holden for forcing the vote. This bitterness contributed to Holden's defeat in the November gubernatorial election.[15] During this fall campaign—when candidates were running for Congress, the General Assembly, and for governor—the primary issues were pride and reunion. The position of the black man was not generally discussed because all candidates agreed that blacks should not be granted legal or political equality.

In a fairly close gubernatorial race Jonathan Worth—a prominent Whig politician who had only reluctantly followed his state out of the Union—defeated Holden, the Johnson-appointed provisional governor, by 31,643 votes to 25,704. Worth generally won in the more secessionist-oriented eastern areas while Holden carried the more unionist west; the two split the central part of the state. Because Worth received most of his support from the ultra-secessionist counties, many northerners regarded his election as a victory for the die-hard Confederates. But the political views of both men were actually similar at the time. Both supported President Johnson and his Reconstruction policy, both had good unionist records, and both opposed black suffrage and court testimony. The election results were more an indication of Worth's personal popularity and the animosity that many felt toward Holden than of any substantive differences between them. Holden had alienated the unionist Whigs when he refused to recommend special pardons for leading Whig politicians in order to further his own career. He also was no friend to the secessionist Democrats, for after initially declaring as a secessionist Democrat he had become a supporter of the Whig Zebulon Vance during his term as governor, and then had broken with Vance to run against him in 1864 as a "peace" candidate.[16]

The results of the campaign for North Carolina's seven congressional seats are more indicative of the reluctance of North Carolina's unionism. All of the candidates stated that blacks should not be given the right to vote. Given this agreement the campaign centered on two issues: did a candidate support Holden or Worth for governor, and, more important, could he take the required ironclad or test oath that said he had never supported or aided the Confederacy? North Carolina's response to this second question is a good indication of the extent to which whites were willing to obey national law in order to gain readmission to the Union.

The election results indicate that the majority of North Carolina's electorate believed that honor was more important than acquiescing to the federal government's requirements. W.N.H. Smith, a member of the 1865–66 General Assembly, predicted before the election that those who were originally secessionist "will find recovery of their political fortunes hopeless" but that "our people will *reject*, with scorn, the candidate who can say . . . that *he can take the test oath*." And he was correct. In five of the seven congressional districts at least one of the candidates could take the required test oath. But in only one of these districts, the seventh—in the western, ultra-unionist part of the state—was such a candidate elected.[17]

Hundreds of North Carolinians also refused to ratify the ordinance abolishing slavery, passed by the constitutional convention. Although most recognized the counterproductive results of voting against this measure, many could not bring themselves to vote for it, so they simply did not vote. Only about 38 percent of those who voted for governor also voted on this ordinance. Thus the measure passed by large majorities— 18,527 to 3,696. It was defeated in only seven counties, all in the heavily black eastern part of the state. But in other counties located throughout the state, including the far-western areas where slaves were few and where citizens strongly opposed secession, the vote was very low or very close.[18] Reluctant unionism and antiblack sentiment was present throughout the state. As the Raleigh *Standard* cogently noted: "We cannot understand how any one who had taken the amnesty oath binding him to the abolition of slavery, could vote against the anti-slavery ordinance of the Convention. But hundreds did so."[19] Obviously these North Carolinians had taken the amnesty oath only to regain their political privileges and their property. They were indeed reluctant unionists—and political realists.

The same can be said for the members of the state legislature who convened in Raleigh on November 27, 1865. Their backgrounds differed in many ways from those delegates who served in the constitutional convention. Only twelve of the 124 members of the House of Commons and fourteen of the fifty-five members of the Senate had been delegates at the convention. Whigs still predominated but the number of antebellum Democrats increased significantly. The number of Civil War secessionists also increased while the number of those who had supported Holden's "peace" candidacy in 1864 declined. There was also a significant decline in the number of those who became Republicans after Presidential Reconstruction. These political affiliations indicate that this General Assembly was composed of men more likely to be reluctant rather than unconditional unionists.

The members of the legislature were slightly younger[20] and more of them had served in the Confederate army than the convention delegates. In addition, only one member of the state legislature can be identifed as being able to take the test oath. Apparently by November whites were turning to their young war heroes as political leaders.

Issues directly or indirectly involving the position of the freedmen dominated the legislators' time. One of their first actions was to ratify the Thirteenth Amendment, abolishing slavery. As early as May 1865, the Raleigh *Standard* told North Carolina whites that such action would be necessary before the state could be readmitted.[21] Ratification did not occur, however, without some opposition. Several delegates feared that the enabling clause granting Congress the power to enforce the amendment by appropriate legislation would be interpreted as authorizing it to enact statutes dealing with the political and civil rights of blacks in the states. Despite these fears both houses of the assembly ratified the amendment by overwhelming majorities. But a week later the legislators adopted a resolution "touching" upon the Thirteenth Amendment which pointed out that they had ratified the amendment only because they understood that it did not enlarge congressional power "to legislate on the subject of freed men within the States."[22]

During the legislature's second session its major task was to decide the exact legal status of the freedmen. North Carolinians knew that any laws they passed governing blacks would be carefully scrutinized by northern congressmen and would be weighed heavily when they considered North Carolina's reentry into the Union.[23] But as the Raleigh *Sentinel* explained, since slavery had been abolished the state had to adopt "a code for the regulation of the freedmen."[24] George Howard, a member of the state senate from Edgecombe County, felt that a system of laws was necessary in order to maintain "social order" and to avert "the evils resulting from a sudden change in the status of society."[25]

North Carolina's elected representatives had already been pondering the complex question of the status of the freedmen for many months. The 1865 convention had appointed a committee chaired by John Pool, a prominent former Whig and Civil War unionist, to receive and study the address to that convention by the freedmen's convention. Pool's committee felt that since slavery had been abolished, "new and mutual rights and duties have supervened, which require corresponding legislation." The committee argued that since emancipation had freed blacks from their masters' supervision, "the State" must "assume control" because "the freedman is ignorant of the operations of civil government, improvident of the future, careless of the restraints of public opinion, and without any real appreciation of the duties and obligations imposed by the change in his relations to society." In the interests of both whites and blacks, it contended, laws had to be enacted to educate the freedmen, to

aid their material welfare, and to promote the "general peace and prosperity of the State." Legislation that would lead to social or political
equality, the committee argued, would be counterproductive.[26]

Because of the complexity of the subject the convention, at the committee's suggestion, created a commission of three to propose to the
legislature "a system of laws upon the subject of the freedmen and to
designate such laws or parts of laws . . . as should be repealed in order
to conform" with the abolition of slavery. In addition the General Assembly appointed an eight-man joint committee to confer with the commission. Because the assembly and the committees recognized that such a
complex issue required much thought, any consideration of legislation
concerning the freedmen was postponed until the assembly reconvened
in the winter of 1866.[27]

On January 23, 1866, the commissioners submitted their report to
the legislature. First they explained the rationale for their proposed code.
They argued that while few freedmen were honest, this vice was not
inherent in the race. Slavery had encouraged this trait, they said, but fair
laws would correct these bad habits.[28] The commissioners then proposed
nine bills for the General Assembly to consider. Only one—"A bill concerning Negroes, Indians, and persons of color and mixed blood"—dealt
with blacks specifically. The other eight were to be "equally applicable"
to blacks and whites.[29] Nonetheless, these eight bills actually were directed
at the freedmen and were referred to the House and Senate committees
"having charge of the subject of the Freedmen."[30] Although these bills
contained no mention of race, the legislature clearly viewed them as part
of the so-called "Black Code." The commission argued that because "the
industry of the negro race has become greatly relaxed and demoralized,"
the proposed bills, all of which dealt with the encouragement of labor
or the prevention of crime, were necessary.[31]

The commissioners' report immediately became the main topic of
"hotel and barroom discussions," occupying "the thoughts of all."[32]
While some newspapers and prominent North Carolinians quickly pronounced their support of the report,[33] a few legislators immediately
attacked it as too liberal. W.N.H. Smith of Hertford did not want to
include Indians with "persons of color," for "there was no good reason
for degrading them to a level with the Negro." This argument carried
the day and Indians were deleted from the bill. William Jenkins of Warren

characterized as erroneous the intimation in the commission's report "that free negroes are citizens." Atlas Dargan of Anson contended that blacks were, *by nature*, "thriftless, improvident, depraved and illiterate" and "creature[s] swayed by impulse and passion." Indeed, he said, it would be better to stay out of the Union rather than to give blacks the right to testify in North Carolina courts, as the commission had recommended.[34]

The legislature spent two months debating the nine proposed bills. The sections of the Code dealing with judicial liberties for blacks were clearly designed for northern consumption, as these rights were the minimum the North would accept. In this proposed legislation blacks were given the same legal privileges that whites held and were granted "the same mode of trial by jury." All punishments for criminal violations were to be the same for whites and blacks, except for the crime of "assault with an *intent* to commit rape upon the body of a white woman." For this offense a black man was to suffer death.[35]

Governor Worth argued that besides appeasing the North by making all but one punishment the same for whites as for blacks, such a provision guaranteeing equal punishments would benefit white North Carolinians as well. He believed that this section, combined with the proposal to allow blacks to testify in court, would enable "the jurisdiction of our courts" to be "fully restored"; there would be no more interference by the military or by the Freedmen's Bureau—a most popular goal among white North Carolinians.[36]

The longest debate in the General Assembly centered on the proposal to allow black testimony in all cases "where the rights of persons or property of persons of color, shall be put in issue . . . ; and also in pleas of the State, where the violence, fraud or injury alleged shall be charged to have been done by or to persons of color." In all other civil and criminal cases testimony by blacks was not permitted "unless by consent of the parties of record."[37]

While the commission's report recommending the passage of the "act concerning Negroes . . ." gave, at most, one-paragraph explanations for other sections of this bill, the commissioners felt called upon to write several pages to justify this provision on testimony, because they knew that most whites were adamantly opposed to it. The report attempted to defend allowing black testimony both morally and practically. First, it argued that the "present helpless and unprotected condition of the race demands it." The abolition of slavery had removed the master as the slave's source of security; the courts were the only acceptable substitute. Without the right to testify, blacks would have to resort to violence to defend themselves. Further, the commission argued, "the admission of such evidence is necessary to secure the colored people in their property." If this newly acquired property was not protected by the courts, the commission maintained, blacks would lose the desire to work for and preserve it, and might become vagrants. On the other hand, said the commission, the right to give testimony would encourage blacks to be industrious and honest and would protect them from "depraved white men" who tried to lead them astray.

In addition to these practical considerations, the report argued that the state had a moral duty: "It is not . . . our policy to degrade them [blacks]. On the contrary, our true policy is to elevate them. . . . They must be educated out of their ignorance, and reformed out of their vicious habits." Appealing to historical precedent, the commission pointed out that all of the civilized countries of Europe granted the right to testify to everyone, including heathens and pagans. At least, it argued, the majority of the freedmen were Christians.[38]

Many legislators, newspaper editors, and ordinary citizens rallied to the commission's defense, repeating its arguments and adding new ones of their own. Many stressed that granting blacks the right to testify would not lead to political or social equality, a widespread fear throughout the state. They also contended that the right to testify would encourage blacks to be industrious, for they would know that their property would be protected. Moreover, they argued, allowing blacks to testify would have little impact anyway. With all-white juries and white judges, black citizens' testimony would "be taken for just its value."[39]

But, more important, these supporters maintained that political expediency demanded black testimony. Rufus Y. McAden, in a speech before the House, argued that "the action of the Legislature upon this bill, decides whether or not North Carolina accepts fully the reconstruction policy of President Johnson; whether or not she desires the removal of the military government and the restoration of civil government with its manifold benefits."[40] S.F. Philips contended that while he had originally opposed Negro testimony he now felt that political necessity demanded that the legislature grant it. He believed that positive action on Negro testimony would help the president in his fight with northern radicals, who would impose restrictions even more "repressive" than black testimony. He argued "that the Proceedings [of the Legislature] would be viligantly [sic] scrutinized by those who are hostile to what we conceive to be our rights and happiness." How, he asked, "can we say, leave the freedmen to us, we will do him justice, refusing in the same breath to allow him to tell his tale before a jury of white men and white judges?"[41]

Many also maintained that by granting blacks the right to testify, the state could rid itself of the Freedmen's Bureau. North Carolinians knew that Holden and General Ruger had agreed that because Negro testimony was not admitted in the state courts all cases involving blacks would be heard either by the Freedmen's Bureau or by military courts. Thus the most telling argument was that blacks already had the right to testify in the Freedmen's Bureau courts. Therefore, as Rufus Y. McAden asserted, "the object of the bill is merely to change the manner of trial; to try our people before our own judges and juries, before courts that are familiar with the character of the negro; know his ignorance and his universal disposition to lie, and consequently are able to adjudge cases correctly according to the law and evidence."[42]

Some North Carolinians, in and out of the legislature, were not persuaded by any of these arguments. William A. Jenkins of Warren argued that "this was a white man's government." He feared that if blacks were granted the right to testify they would soon gain the right to vote. He also "was unwilling to sanction the inauguration of any new system of legislation which would appease the radical majority of the North."[43] Atlas Dargan of Anson also believed that North Carolinians were "too prone . . . to yield to outside pressures." He maintained that "no one had kindlier feelings towards that unfortunate race. . . . He had owned many, had never punished one." But he would never grant the right "to swear against the lives and property of white men" to "a creature swayed by impulse and passion—who was influenced more by stomach than intellect—to whom the proffer of a hogjowl was an irresistible argument." Further, he asserted, there was "no reason to believe that the concession" of this right "would lead to the removal of the Freedmen's Bureau, and [he] argued at length, to show that the passage of the bill would lead to a demand for negro suffrage." Many others echoed these sentiments.[44]

After all the debating was over, the bill allowing blacks to testify finally did pass, but only after two stipulations were added. The first stated that blacks would be allowed to bear witness only after the Freedmen's Bureau moved out of the legal and judicial arena. The legislature passed this proviso despite the fact that they were informed that President Johnson opposed it; it was needed to win the support of those who had promised their constituents that they would oppose Negro testimony. The second stipulation instructed the courts "that whenever a person of color shall be examined as a witness," he should be warned to tell the truth.[45] This section leaves considerable doubt as to whether or not a black man's testimony would be considered at all by a white jury. There were clearly limits as to how far North Carolina would go even in the name of political expediency.

While the legislature spent more time debating the testimony issue, it seemed most deeply concerned with the problem of developing a new labor system to replace slavery. Most of the Black Code was dedicated to ensuring the community that blacks would work. As early as June 1865, the Raleigh *Standard* claimed that until the status of the freedman was determined by the state legislature "there can be no system [of labor]—no stability, and consequently but little comfort." Legislation was necessary to suppress vagrancy and to encourage and reward labor.[46] The Raleigh *Sentinel* agreed, claiming that "blacks are proverbially averse to labor. None ever yet attained a ready aptitude and disposition to labor who were not previously trained under compulsion." Thus while laws had to be passed to force the employer to pay fair wages, most legislators felt it was more important to enact provisions to force "the blacks to perform their contracts fully. . . . They must be taught that liberty is not licentiousness." Several other newspapers concurred.[47]

Many individuals outside the legislature also stressed the economic need for a Black Code. A Mecklenburg County planter felt that there ought to be laws apprenticing all black children under the age of twenty-one to their former masters and forcing adult blacks to work. One of Beaufort's "town dignitaries" believed that the freedmen should be placed "under the control of the Legislater [sic]," so it could "fix their wages, and prevent vagrancy." The grand juries of Buncombe and Transylvania counties, complaining that most freedmen were "lazy and indolent," asked for "stringent laws . . . [to] compel them to become useful to themselves and *the white race in their proper sphere as laborers*."[48] B. F. Moore, a delegate to the constitutional convention and a member of the commission that prepared the proposed code, went even further when he called for legislation that would authorize the sale of blacks for a term of years if they violated their contracts.[49]

The legislators, agreeing with their constituents, enacted several provisions to ensure North Carolina employers a black labor force. Blacks were allowed to make contracts, but for articles worth over ten dollars contracts had to be witnessed by a white person who could read and write.[50]

Next, the apprenticeship section of the "Act Concerning Negroes . . . , " while providing that all masters were "bound to discharge duties to them [black apprentices] as to white apprentices" and stipulating that black children were to be bound out in the same manner as whites, contained three discriminatory provisions. First, black girls could be bound out to the age of twenty-one while white girls could be apprenticed only until their eighteenth birthday. A more oppressive section stipulated that the county courts could bind out black children "when the parents with whom such children may live do not habitually employ their time in some honest, industrious occupation." No such provision existed for white children. Last and most disturbing, in binding out black apprentices former masters, when judged suitable persons by the court, were entitled to preference over all others.[51] The Raleigh *Standard* correctly surmised that this provision would "*look* to the Northern mind like a disposition to cling to slavery . . . and besides it deprived the freed colored child of the right of locomotion, and places it [*sic*] in a condition in the eye of the law below that of the white child." Others issued similar warnings, but to no avail.[52] The discriminatory provisos were enacted, and many white North Carolinians took full advantage of them in what certainly looked like an attempt to reestablish slavery under a new name.[53]

The legislature also passed a vagrancy act. While most states had vagrancy laws, many Republicans had criticized the Mississippi and South Carolina vagrancy statutes as attempts to suppress black liberty. As a result, North Carolina legislators cautiously omitted any mention of race in the law. And several North Carolina newspapers did complain about the large number of white as well as black vagrants in the state.[54] But white North Carolinians were most concerned about the large numbers of blacks who congregated in cities and towns in mid-1865.[55]

The law itself was so vague that it allowed as much discrimination as any court cared to exercise. While vagrancy was a misdemeanor, the court had almost complete discretion as to the penalty. The offender could be discharged, if he paid the court costs and "enter[ed] into a recognizance, *in such sum as the court shall prescribe*, conditioned for his good behavior and industrious, peaceable deportment for one year." If no such bond were posted, the court could fine or imprison the vagrant, "or both or *sentence him* to the workhouse *for such time as the court may think fit.*"[56] Again, no limits were set on how much the fine would be or how long a sentence the vagrant had to serve.

Federal officials and northerners were very sensitive about southern vagrancy laws because if carefully written they could, for all practical purposes, reenslave the freedmen. The Joint Committee on Reconstruction, therefore, thoroughly questioned two United States Army officers stationed in North Carolina. Colonel Whittlesey testified that he feared that slavery would be reestablished "if there was no fear of any evil consequences from the government or from the people of other States." Lieutenant Sanderson agreed, claiming that the legislature intended to seize black vagrants and sell them. In fact, he pointed out, this had already occurred in Gates County.[57]

The bill "to secure to Agricultural Laborers their Payment in Kind," like the vagrancy law, applied equally to blacks and whites. Ostensibly it was passed to stimulate industry and "to encourage the field laborer, by securing to him the fruits of his toil."[58] While many North Carolinians were willing to pay blacks, the scarcity of money after the war made payment in kind preferable. Many blacks, however, disliked this method of payment, which seemed to them too much like slavery.[59] Employers could—and sometimes did—pay blacks only in food and clothing, thereby keeping them perpetually poor and dependent on their providers. One former slaveholder contended that this practice was "a means of reducing the wages of the negro below their value."[60] The bill "to prevent enticing servants from fulfilling their contracts, or harboring them" was also supposed to apply equally to both races. But it too was designed primarily to control the black laborer.[61]

The General Assembly also provided for the establishment of workhouses or houses of correction. Although the cost of construction was more than the depleted North Carolina treasury could afford, the legislature felt that this disadvantage would be compensated for by forcing blacks to work. Again, the Assembly carefully applied the law to both races,[62] and the commissioners merely explained that "the dread of involuntary labor is much more effectual to suppress misdemeanors and idleness than a few days of imprisonment."[63] However, the Wilmington *Dispatch*, urging the quick construction of a workhouse, argued that "there are now from twenty to thirty negroes imprisoned in our county jail who have been spending several months there at public expense"; they had "served out their time" but could not be released because they could not pay the court fees. "In a workhouse, however, they would be enabled to earn by their labor the fees demanded."[64] Thus if blacks would not work voluntarily, the state could still make use of them by forcing them to labor in workhouses.

This set of work laws, then, helped to solve one of the major problems facing North Carolina after the war: the problem of replacing slavery with a new labor system. They did so, however, by restricting the freed people's choices and opportunities. They also served to keep blacks "in their place" as common laborers. Several other statutes enacted as part of North Carolina's Black Code also had the same result. Social distance was maintained by laws forbidding marriage between blacks and whites and allowing counties to appoint separate wardens of the poor for each race.[65] The one "social privilege" granted blacks was the right—or more accurately, the obligation—to marry. Because marriage was prohibited during slavery, many newly freed black couples were living together illegally. To correct this situation, all emancipated slaves "were deemed to have been lawfully married . . . .at the time of commencement of . . . cohabitation." Freed blacks were required to record these marriages at a fee of twenty-five cents. Failure to so file was a misdemeanor punishable "*at the discretion of the court.*" For each month after September 1, 1866, continued failure to comply with the law would constitute a separate offense.[66] The commission asserted that such penalties were necessary to help blacks, because living together unmarried demoralized them and made it impossible for whites to elevate them.[67] But this seemingly noble explanation hardly seemed to justify such potentially severe penalties. If it chose the court was left free to fine or imprison freed blacks and reduce them to virtual slavery.

The General Assembly also wanted to legitimize marriages in order to reduce the number of illegitimate children. While the "act more effectually to secure the maintenance of bastard children . . . , " again did not mention race, it was proposed, as were all the other acts previously discussed, by the commission on freedmen and was obviously directed toward former slaves. The commissioners specifically mentioned the freedmen when explaining why such a bill was necessary. The legislators claimed that the statute was designed to "elevate the race" by forcing blacks to perform their parental duties. But the penalties imposed on the father who did not support his child indicates an economic motive. If the father could not or refused to pay the court costs and the money necessary for child support, he would be sent to the workhouse for not more than twelve months. Alternatively he could "bind himself as an apprentice . . . for such time and at such price as the court may direct." Again, the court had great discretionary powers—and in a few cases, it did abuse them.[68]

North Carolina whites also felt a strong need to curtail the increase in crime, most of which they blamed on the freedmen. Part of the reason why many whites felt labor laws were necessary was that they firmly believed that blacks would steal if they were idle. William A. Graham's complaint was typical: he argued that "thefts are of daily and nightly occurrence . . . and negroes with arms are traversing the country under pretense of hunting but really for stealing." He urged the legislature to pass a bill that would make the *intent* to steal a crime.[69]

The General Assembly gladly complied. The *intent* to steal horses or other livestock was deemed a misdemeanor; but the guilty were to be punished "as if convicted of larceny," even though "such animal may not have come into the actual possession of the person so offending." Any person "commanding, counselling, advising, aiding or abetting any such unlawful acts" was to be "punished in like manner." Anyone trespassing would be guilty of a misdemeanor and anyone stealing would be guilty of larceny.[70] Again, while none of these laws mentioned race, all were proposed by the commission on freedmen and reported out by the committees on freedmen in the General Assembly. And given many white North Carolinians' attitudes toward blacks and their supposed disposition to a criminal way of life, it is probable that these laws were, in the main, directed at the freedmen.

As in antebellum days, whites feared black revolts.[71] In the Black Code the General Assembly specifically retained two antebellum provisions, amended to apply to all "free persons of color" rather than the former antebellum words, "free negroes." Reflecting white views that out-of-state blacks might threaten North Carolina's peace and agitate native freedmen, one section fined any black person entering North Carolina from another state $500 "from time to time" until he left the state. Moreover, if a native black left the state for over ninety days he was to be treated as an out-of-state black and assessed the same penalties if he returned home. If these blacks could not pay their fines, they were to be hired out. The second antebellum statute retained in the Black Code prohibited blacks from owning guns, swords, or knives unless they obtained a license one year in advance of purchase.[72]

The General Assembly also enacted new legislation to deal severely with troublemakers or insurrectionaries. The "act to punish seditious language, insurrections and rebellions in the State" imposed the death penalty on anyone joining into or aiding any conspiracy or insurrection. Moreover, any person, who "by words spoken, written or printed," tried to "excite in any person whatever a spirit of insurrection, conspiracy, sedition or rebellion," would be sentenced to the pillory for one hour, "receive one or more public whippings, not less than thirty-nine lashes each, and imprisoned twelve months."[73]

The North Carolina Black Code, then, had six provisions that were frankly discriminatory: the provision making the intent to rape a white woman punishable by death for a black man; the apprenticeship section; the limitations on a black person's movements; the law prohibiting blacks from owning or carrying firearms or other weapons; the provision making intermarriages illegal; and the limitations on blacks testifying in the courts. The remainder of the code in theory applied equally to both blacks and whites. There was enough discretion given to the courts, however, that blacks could in fact be discriminated against.

Colonel Whittlesey, head of the Freedmen's Bureau in North Carolina, after witnessing the actions of the North Carolina General Assembly, concluded that if northern troops or the Freedmen's Bureau were removed from the state, white North Carolinians would "re-establish slavery just as it was before . . . [or] they would enact laws which would make the blacks virtually slaves."[74] Clinton A. Cilley, superintendent for the Western District, believed the code showed that North Carolina whites "wish to impress it thoroughly on the Blacks that they are inferior, and must be so kept by law."[75]

North Carolina's Black Code succeeded in this latter goal, although it was fairer than codes in some other southern states. For example, blacks in Mississippi were deemed vagrants for "unlawfully assembling themselves together either in the day or night time." They were also unable "to rent or lease any lands or tenements except in incorporated cities or towns." Louisiana blacks were not allowed to enter St. Landry parish "without special permit in writing" from their employers, nor was any black in the parish allowed to be out after 10 P.M. without written permission from his employer. Louisiana blacks had to work for whites and could not rent or own a home there.[76] Still, the North Carolina black man or woman was clearly inferior in the eyes of the law, placed somewhere between slave and citizen.

Yet the North Carolina Black Code was apparently too liberal for many North Carolina legislators. The "Act Concerning Negroes . . ." passed in the House by a vote of fifty-one to fifty. In the Senate, it was first defeated, then reconsidered and passed twenty-two to nineteen.[77] The *Wilmington Herald* argued that many voted against the bill in the Senate because "it was so mangled by amendments . . . that its best friends hardly know it."[78] The *Herald*'s argument was partially correct. Some men did vote against the act because they opposed its discriminatory features, especially those dealing with black testimony and apprenticeship. But in the House not more than eleven of the fifty votes cast against this law fall into this category. In the Senate, only three of the nineteen negative votes were based clearly on opposition to discriminatory passages. The majority of those opposed to the code were conservatives who felt that the laws did not go far enough in restricting blacks.[79]

The more liberal constitutional convention that reconvened in May of 1866 did eliminate, at Governor Worth's suggestion, most of the code's discriminatory sections. It repealed the two provisos added to the section dealing with black testimony, the provision for more severe punishment for blacks than for whites for the crime of assault with intent to commit rape, and the sections limiting the movements of blacks in and out of the state and prohibiting them from carrying or owning weapons. Worth urged these actions mainly to rid the state of Bureau interference with the judicial process. The Bureau had assured Worth that it would turn over all cases in which blacks were involved to the state courts once these discriminatory sections were removed.[80]

The 1865–66 General Assembly also passed other laws that, while applying to both races equally in theory, also helped to control the freedmen and to separate the races without subjecting the state to charges of discrimination. The most important of these was the Militia Law, by which the Assembly attempted to ensure law and order. The all-white militia was to be called out to quell any "insurrection among free persons of color" or "when there may be outlaws or negroes, committing depredations or *in any way* alarming the citizens of any county."[81] Like many other North Carolina laws of this period, this act was so vaguely worded that it could be interpreted to mean almost anything; in this case, the militia could be used against blacks for the flimsiest reasons. The tendency of some white citizens to believe unsubstantiated rumors of insurrection and to feel that any attempt by blacks to assert their freedom was a "depredation" meant that this law posed a real threat for blacks.

Although blacks benefited little from the state and were allowed no voice in its government, they were still taxed. In "An Act Entitled Revenue," every laborer, with a few exceptions, was assessed one dollar a year. If the laborer was employed by another, his employer was to pay the tax for him and "retain the same out of any moneys due him."[82] Besides this state tax, counties added an additional tax of between one and two dollars.[83] A Freedmen's Bureau agent pointed out that the total tax was often three dollars and that this sum represented 2.5 to 3 percent of a laborer's yearly wage. On the other hand, real estate was taxed at less than one-fifth of 1 percent. This agent argued therefore that while the tax claimed to put "black & white on the same footing," it was "actually a heavy discrimination in effect against the freedman" because "the great preponderance of colored men" were laborers. Thus blacks were "compelled to pay an unjust & extortionate share of the public expenses."[84] In addition—as George Hawley, another Bureau agent, complained—while blacks were severely taxed, "the destitute and helpless freed people receive[d] no aid" from the state as whites did.[85] The Bureau was unable to overturn the tax law, for technically it applied equally to both races.[86] The 1866–67 General Assembly did alter the law, decreasing the state tax from one dollar to fifty cents, but the inequities cited by the Bureau agents remained.[87]

Various city and county legislative bodies also passed discriminatory laws during this same period. In Forsyth County, and probably in all other North Carolina counties, cemeteries were segregated. In Roxboro, a town in Person County, city officials repealed all the slave laws but retained all the old discriminatory laws against free blacks. Fayetteville citizens reinstated the old slave code as soon as Sherman's troops left, decreeing that blacks could not meet unless a white man was present, nor could they carry canes. Moreover, the city council passed an ordinance prohibiting them from parading "for the express purpose of preventing a celebration of the 4th of July." And three blacks, arrested for minor offenses, were publicly whipped, although only one had been convicted. New Berne whites also enforced the old slave code, including the prohibition against the founding of schools for blacks. The commissioners of the town of Washington denied anyone from New Berne or Plymouth the right to enter their city under a threat of a fifty-dollar fine. Although no distinction was made between whites and blacks in the wording of this regulation, the Freedmen's Bureau agent stationed in Washington maintained that he had "good reasons for believing, that it was intended to prevent any colored person from coming here" from New Berne or Plymouth. He pointed out that while "a large number of Whites have been permitted to come here without hinderance," a black man was arrested "on the ground that he had visited" one of the forbidden cities. In Elizabeth City an ordinance instructed the "town Constable . . . to prevent the assembling of crowds of persons on the side walks of the streets . . . , obstructing the same to the inconvenience and annoyance of Ladies passing along the Streets." Again there was no written distinction as to race but the city council, when citing some examples of people who so assembled, listed only blacks.[88]

The trend toward conservatism can be seen even more clearly in the actions taken by the 1866–67 General Assembly. The central issue in the October 1866 elections for members of the Assembly and for governor was whether North Carolina would support the proposed Fourteenth Amendment as a means to reenter the Union, or would elect candidates opposed to any more concessions to the North. The Fayetteville *News*, supporting the latter position, expressed the view of the majority when it explained that the choice was between men who supported the Fourteenth Amendment and those "who will not be willing, merely for the sake of the State's being restored to the 'Union,' to sacrifice every principle of right and justice."[89] The *Rutherford Star* argued the unionist position: "The choice [is] between the Howard [Fourteenth] Amendment and go into the Union; or the radical plan of *reorganization, confiscation, negro suffrage and stay out*." The *Star* felt that the Fourteenth Amendment was the better alternative.[90]

Governor Worth, representing the Conservative Party, was half-heartedly opposed by Alfred Dockery for governor. Dockery, a wealthy Richmond County farmer who had owned numerous slaves, supported the Fourteenth Amendment but declined to run for governor. The Raleigh *Standard* and other radical papers, however, urged their subscribers to vote for him anyway.[91]

North Carolina voters overwhelmingly supported Governor Worth's reelection. The *Goldsboro Daily News*, in urging its readers to vote for Worth, argued that "if this vote is to keep us out of the Union 60 years longer, let us give it, and prove by acts, that though defeated in the field, we have not forgotten our rights, as freemen; and willing, though we be, to get back into the Union upon the plans suggested by the President, we are equally willing to undergo the privation of territorial government, before we will be driven by radicals, as a flock of sheep to be murdered at their will and pleasure."[92] Worth supporters also won a large majority in both houses of the General Assembly. In at least nine counties men who had served in either the convention or the previous assembly were defeated for reelection by more conservative, sometimes politically unknown candidates. Interestingly, these counties were not in the black belt but were for the most part areas located in the center of the state where relatively few slaves had been held.[93] In several other counties there were no candidates who opposed Worth or who supported ratification of the Fourteenth Amendment.[94] Many ran on their Confederate war records as well as on their stands on the issues of the day, with newspapers often printing military titles along with the names of the candidates.[95]

This conservative General Assembly convened on November 19, 1866. As in the previous elected bodies serving during Presidential Reconstruction, former Whigs predominated. But there was an increase in former secessionists and a decrease in the number of those who became Republicans during Congressional Reconstruction. At least thirty-five members had served in the Confederate army.

The legislature's conservative bent was immediately apparent. The men elected speakers in both houses firmly opposed ratification of the Fourteenth Amendment. In neither body was an advocate of the amendment even a contender for the speakership.[96] During debates on several issues many representatives hissed the more radical representatives and applauded the conservatives.[97]

The General Assembly's most decisive act was its rejection of the Fourteenth Amendment. This proposed amendment proclaimed blacks to be citizens and declared that a state could not deprive a citizen of life, liberty, or property without due process of law. It also proportionately reduced the congressional representation of any state that denied blacks the vote. Another provision repudiated the Confederate debt. But the part despised most by the North Carolina legislators was the third section that excluded from office all those who, after having sworn to uphold the United States Constitution, had aided the rebellion.

In his message to the legislature Worth urged rejection, contending that since the southern states had been "denied representation in the body which proposed" the amendment, the state could not ratify it without losing its dignity. He attacked the third section most vehemently, claiming it would bar "the great body of the intelligence of the State" from holding office.[98] Most North Carolina newspapers also advocated rejection. They too objected primarily to the third section. Many also argued that if North Carolina did demean itself by ratifying the amendment no guarantee existed that it would be readmitted into the Union. But the *Sentinel* conceded what most felt when it stated that even if the state were certain of restoration, the ratification of the Fourteenth Amendment would destroy the South; it was therefore too high a price to pay.[99]

Of course, most members of the General Assembly had been elected on platforms that opposed the amendment. Thus it was not surprising that the Joint Committee on the Constitutional Amendment recommended its rejection. Only one member of the thirteen-man committee dissented from the report. Two other members of the assembly spoke for the amendment on the floor of the legislature. Only six North Carolina newspapers supported it. Those who urged acceptance of the amendment argued that its terms were better than those that would be imposed upon the South if the amendment were rejected. But the representatives refused to listen to these warnings. The Senate rejected the amendment 46 to 1 and the House turned it down 102 to 10.[100]

The legislature next enacted several laws directed at North Carolina blacks. Governor Worth had devoted a great deal of his message to the General Assembly to "the African race," arguing that additional legislation was needed to protect and control the freedmen: "The most prominent subjects demanding new legislation are crime and pauperism." The increased crime, especially that committed by blacks, he contended, placed a great tax burden on the state, and the erection of workhouses, provided for by the previous legislative session, was also costly. Worth suggested, therefore, that convicts and vagrants be forced "to work with ball and chain on the highways or other public works of the counties, allowing them . . . to raise the [court] fine and costs by apprenticing themselves."

In another section of his message, entitled "Apprenticeship," the governor urged the assembly to revise the state's apprenticeship laws to eliminate the discriminatory sections.[101] This the assembly did. It also extended the deadline for blacks to record their marriages or be fined.[102]

The legislature went on to amend the act establishing workhouses to allow two or more counties to build such institutions together for their joint use. Another act gave "county and superior courts authority to sentence criminals to work the public roads." The courts would decide whether or not the criminal was to be made to wear a ball and chain. In addition to serving out their time for the crimes they committed, those convicted could be "required to work out the fine and costs by the county, together with any prison fees that may have been incurred for their confinement previous to their trial and conviction." Another law permitted "the mayor or chief magistrate of any incorporated city or town" to order those unable to pay their fines or penalties "to work on the streets or other public works, until, at fair rates of wages, such . . . persons shall have worked out the full amount of the judgment and costs of the prosecution."[103] While these laws made no mention of race, Worth urged their passage in the section of his message to the assembly entitled "The African Race."

Worth also requested that the assembly provide for the erection of a state penitentiary for convicts who had committed "higher grades of crimes."[104] The creation of penitentiaries had been one of the many reforms begun in the North during the antebellum years, and North Carolina may well have been interested in undertaking what was then considered to be a humane measure. But racial biases were also involved. The Joint Select Committee on a Penitentiary, for example, explained that for other than capital offenses the normal punishment in North Carolina was whipping and imprisonment. But it maintained that whipping was not effective "as a punishment for a large part of our population, now amounting to one-third of the whole; that part, too, the most prone to crime." Blacks, it argued, were used to whippings, but putting them to work in a penitentiary would teach them "habits of industry and a trade by which . . . [they] are able to make an honest living."[105]

The legislature also attempted to impose more control over black laborers by increasing the fine for not fulfilling a labor contract to $200. This act passed after the legislature received a petition from fifteen men from Anson County, explaining that they and the agricultural interests of the state were suffering because of the "persistent efforts of persons, mostly from beyond the limits of our state, to entice, by promises of more liberal wages than we can pay, the Freedmen in our employ to emigrate or change their homes." These farmers argued that they were "wholly dependent . . . upon hired colored labor," and that it was "a source of great annoyance and loss to us for stranger or citizen to come in and cause the Freedman to violate his contract."[106] The legislature also allowed anyone advancing money or supplies to his agricultural employees to place "a lien on the crops which may be made during the year."[107] Thus the foundation of the crop-lien system, which would keep blacks in perpetual poverty for many decades, was laid early after the war.

It is clear from this review of the legislative record of the state and of some local official bodies meeting during Presidential Reconstruction that reluctant unionists had gained control after the first session of the constitutional convention. The lawmakers insisted on all their rights and privileges, but were willing to grant blacks only limited legal rights and economic opportunities. Perhaps even more important, it is obvious from the laws passed that the majority of North Carolina legislators operated on the assumption that blacks were inferior, lazy, and potentially dangerous, and that they had to be controlled. Thus blacks were denied, through legislation, complete rights to life, liberty, property, and the pursuit of happiness.

4   The Black Community Organizes

Will you . . . treat us as human beings with all our rights? It is all we ask.—Minutes of the Freedmen's Convention, Raleigh, 1866

DURING THIS PERIOD blacks had not been sitting idly by, watching their white neighbors decide their fate. After they adjourned their freedmen's convention in October 1865, they continued their struggle for freedom and independence in a variety of ways. They organized their own community to give their lives stability and to have a base from which to launch protests against white abuse.

One of the first tasks that faced the freedmen was to formalize their marriages and reunite families divided by slavery. Southern states had forbidden slaves to marry legally, but now blacks had the opportunity to give their "cohabitations" the sanction of law. Extant records are not complete enough to provide reliable figures on how many blacks married during this early post-emancipation period. But it is clear that significant numbers did. In Wilmington, for example, from March through November 1866, eighty black couples took out regular marriage licenses.[1] During the same year in Edgecombe County, 137 black couples married. In Duplin County the clerk recorded 105 black marriages and 171 white marriages from 1866 to 1868.[2]

More illuminating than the county marriage records, however, are the cohabitation records. Under the Black Code enacted by the state legislature in March 1866, freedmen were to legalize slave marriages if the husband and wife were still living together. Because of the system used in North Carolina, the records varied from county to county. Either justices of the peace or the county clerks recorded the freedmen's marriages. However, most of these officials listed the freedmen's names along with the length of time they had been "cohabiting together as husband

and wife" under slavery. What these records indicate is that most freedmen searched for loved ones and formalized slave marriages soon after the Civil War. These documents also confirm Herbert Gutman's thesis that slaves had stable, long-lasting marriages in which the bonds of affection were obviously quite strong. Given the option of dissolving their slave marriages or reconfirming them, thousands of freedmen chose the latter course.[3]

Fairly complete records exist for marriages recorded during this period in twenty-eight North Carolina counties. These records represent a good sampling, for they include counties located in every geographical region—ranging from a county that had in 1860 a 14 percent slave population to one with a 66 percent slave population; from counties that had sizable numbers of free blacks to those that had very few; and from those where small farms predominated to those where many slaveholders owned hundreds of slaves. By computing the *maximum* possible slave marriages for each county, and then comparing that figure with the number of freedmen who registered their marriages in 1866 and early 1867, one finds that in every county but four, over 30 percent of the *possible* slave marriages were reconfirmed. In twelve of the counties, over 50 percent registered their marriages. The average for the twenty-eight counties was 47.5 percent.[4]

A significant percentage of the slaves who registered their marriages had cohabited together for long periods of time.[5] Many knew the exact day and month as well as the year in which they had become husband and wife. Another indication that the freedmen were continuing a long, meaningful tradition of family life is the fact that sixteen men were listed as either "Senior" or "Junior." Obviously, as Gutman has argued, slaves had developed a sense of family that was important to them. They often named children after the father, and the freed blacks retained these names.[6]

A further analysis of the cohabitation records reveals another interesting point: the majority of those freed couples who recorded their marriages had last names different from each other at the time they officially acknowledged their marriages. As table 2 illustrates, for the twenty-five counties where last names were listed 39 percent of those freed couples registering their marriages had the same last names, while 61 percent had different names.[7] The discussion on the selection of names later in this

Table 1. Minimum percentage of freedmen marriages registered in North Carolina[a]

| County | Slave population, 1860 | | | | | | Number of marriages recorded | Percentage recorded | |
| | 15–20 yrs old | | 20+ yrs old | | Total over 15 | | | | |
	Male	Female	Male	Female	Male	Female		MP, 20+	MP, 15+
Bertie	396	452	1,847	1,833	2,243	2,285	667	36	30
Beaufort	358	318	1,408	1,248	1,766	1,566	338	27	22
Catawba	89	87	320	339	409	177	177	55	43
Chowan	225	169	813	820	1,038	989	327	40	33
Currituck	138	124	618	482	756	606	72	15	12
Duplin	363	390	1,364	1,354	1,727	1,744	686	51	40
Edgecombe[b]	658	582	2,305	2,026	2,963	2,887	983	49	34
Forsyth[c]	115	99	384	339	499	438	154	45	35
Franklin[d]	372	402	1,412	1,374	1,784	1,776	799	58	45
Granville	591	684	2,170	2,137	2,761	2,821	1,316	62	48
Halifax[e]	567	600	2,400	2,341	2,967	2,941	165	7	6
Hyde	177	126	628	517	805	643	199	38	31
Iredell	228	234	786	830	1,014	1,064	362	46	36
Johnston	286	265	959	950	1,245	1,215	548	58	45
Lincoln	108	104	460	431	568	535	226	52	42
Nash	262	269	883	969	1,145	1,238	530	49	38
New Hanover	557	586	2,264	2,266	2,821	2,852	1,804	80	64
Orange	283	287	1,042	1,074	1,325	1,361	912	88	69
Pasquotank	181	163	790	637	971	800	300	47	38
Perquimans	208	144	875	739	1,083	883	229	31	26
Person	299	282	1,014	980	1,313	1,262	592	60	47
Pitt	537	474	1,735	1,692	2,272	2,166	923	55	43
Richmond	302	279	1,077	1,055	1,379	1,334	289	27	22
Robeson	303	289	981	991	1,284	1,280	588	60	46
Stokes	125	140	440	501	565	641	217	49	38
Wake	606	625	2,087	1,991	2,693	2,616	676	34	26
Warren	620	590	2,302	2,075	2,922	2,665	1,428	69	54
Washington	132	135	548	553	680	688	222	41	33

[a]The minimum percentage of ex-slave marriages registered was derived by taking the smaller number of adult male or female slaves twenty years and older (for column 8), and fifteen years and older (for column 9) in each county in 1860 and dividing this figure into the actual number of freed marriages registered. Of course, as Gutman points out, this formula "greatly exaggerates the possible number of slave marriages." (Gutman, *Black Family*, table 35, p. 416.)

Number giving length of marriage	Years married by percentage					Number of years Listed	Percentage slave, 1860	Percentage free black, 1860
	<5	6–10	11–20	21–30	Over 30			
666	29	23	28	13	7	.1	57	2.0
319	30	23	25	12	5	6.0	40	5.0
176	35	23	27	10	5	.6	16	.3
327	31	15	23	17	13	—	54	2.0
70	21	14	36	22	4	3.0	34	3.0
642	30	21	27	9	6	6.0	45	2.0
958	30	26	25	10	7	3.0	58	2.0
148	38	20	25	8	5	1.0	14	2.0
782	30	25	26	11	6	2.0	50	4.0
1,222	27	26	25	11	5	7.0	47	5.0
165	20	25	29	16	10	—	53	13.0
198	26	25	26	16	7	.5	36	3.0
339	26	25	27	10	6	6.0	27	.2
547	34	22	30	13	5	.2	31	1.0
192	31	22	16	12	4	15.0	26	1.0
421	30	26	26	9	8	2.0	40	6.0
1,795	34	25	23	11	6	.5	46	4.0
909	28	24	26	14	7	.3	30	3.0
—	—	—	—	—	—	—	33	17.0
228	27	20	27	14	12	.4	49	5.0
588	30	21	28	13	7	.7	46	3.0
917	29	23	25	15	7	.7	52	.8
192	19	15	19	8	4	34.0	50	3.0
546	32	22	25	8	5	7.0	35	9.0
217	31	23	32	7	7	—	24	.8
663	37	25	19	11	7	2.0	38	5.0
1,417	32	23	25	12	6	.8	66	3.0
203	29	23	21	13	6	9.0	39	5.0

bProbably incomplete, for records cover only May through August, 1866.

cProbably incomplete, for records cover only 1866.

dProbably incomplete, for records cover only April through August, 1866.

eIncomplete, for only three justices of the peace signed records, and they did not cover the entire county.

chapter shows that during slavery slaves most often used the last name of their current master. Thus it appears that the majority of those freedmen who recorded their marriages had been owned by different masters and had lived on different plantations before emancipation.

It is true, as antebellum sources indicate, that married slaves often lived on different plantations and were owned by different men.[8] The two volumes of North Carolina slave narratives compiled by the Works Progress Administration during the 1930s reinforce this fact. Forty former slaves indicated in these narratives that their mothers and fathers, when

Table 2. Numbers of freedmen who recorded their marriages by length of marriage and by last names

	Years married											
	5 or less		6–10		11–20		21–30		Over 30		Total	
County	Same	Different	Same	Different	Same	Different	Same	Different	Same	Different	Same	Different
Beaufort	37	63	31	46	30	54	21	21	12	5	131	188
Bertie	82	111	84	67	108	77	60	29	32	16	366	300
Catawba[a]	14	12	5	9	8	12	4	3	1	4	32	40
Currituck[a]	1	4	—	—	1	4	—	—	—	1	2	9
Duplin[a]	77	126	65	74	84	94	32	35	27	13	285	342
Edgecombe	110	189	118	138	100	141	47	49	36	30	411	547
Forsyth	16	43	15	16	19	19	3	9	4	4	57	91
Franklin[b]	63	176	75	123	72	136	38	51	24	24	272	510
Granville	86	270	100	237	116	207	67	79	23	37	392	830
Halifax[a]	4	10	10	12	17	6	4	2	3	1	38	31
Hyde	6	45	13	37	15	36	13	19	6	8	53	145
Iredell	30	64	32	57	47	49	20	17	14	9	143	196
Johnston	46	139	39	82	51	91	38	31	20	10	194	353
Lincoln	53	17	32	18	27	10	20	6	7	2	139	53
Nash	36	93	65	45	47	63	18	21	14	19	180	241
New Hanover	73	542	80	368	74	345	35	161	29	88	291	1,504
Perquimans[a]	10	50	13	27	16	36	7	21	9	15	55	149
Person[a,b,c]	122	58	90	32	134	26	64	10	32	8	442	134
Pitt	41	225	36	172	45	188	31	112	17	50	170	747
Richmond[a]	9	27	4	21	13	21	1	11	1	7	28	87
Robeson	70	119	60	72	65	80	18	31	15	16	228	318
Stokes	22	45	22	27	36	33	11	5	10	6	101	116
Wake[c]	233	17	164	5	121	5	66	7	43	2	627	36
Warren	103	358	107	226	100	261	54	118	26	63	390	1,026
Washington[a]	1	29	5	13	6	10	3	8	2	2	17	62
Total	1,345	2,832	1,265	1,924	1,352	2,004	675	855	407	440	5,044	8,055

[a]Some records give no last name for either party. These were omitted from this tabulation.

[b]Some records give no last name for the wife. These were counted in this tabulation as the wife having the same surname as her husband.

[c]It is obvious from these records that most of the clerks and justices recording these marriages simply assigned the same last names to both parties. They were counted as having the same last names for the purpose of this tabulation, but it is likely that many had different surnames before their marriages were formalized.

Table 3. Length of marriages of freedmen who had been owned
by different masters while slaves

Number of years	Number of couples
2	6
3	3
4	2
5	4
6	3
9	3
10	1
11	1
12	2
15	4
16	3
17	4
18	1
20	1
30	1
32	1
36	1
40	1
46	1
No length listed	1
Total	44

slaves, lived on different plantations. Thomas Hall, a former Orange
County slave, contended that this was "often the case."[9]

Cohabitation records for six North Carolina counties also indicate
the prevalence of the pattern of married slaves being owned by different
masters.[10] Clerks in these counties listed the name of the former master
along with the name of the freed person recording his or her marriage.
An analysis of these couples and those who had owned them shows that
this pattern affected men and women living in a wide variety of slave
conditions. Fifty couples in these six counties had been owned by separate
masters while they were slaves. For most of these couples, the owners
lived in the same counties, many close together. But in other ways the
experiences of these slaves were very different. Table 3 shows that the
length of the slave marriages of this group ranged from two to forty-six

64 The Black Community Organizes

Table 4. Wealth and slave ownership of former slaveholders who owned slaves married to other slaves owned by another master

Wealth		Number of slaves owned	
$1,000–$5,000	7	1	1
$5,000–$10,000	5	2–5	5
$10,000–$20,000	14	6–10	8
$20,000–$50,000	12	11–20	15
$50,000–$100,000	7	20–50	17
Over $100,000	6	51–100	3
Not found	2	Over 100	2
		Not found	2

years, with the average being about twelve and one-half years. The owners, too, were quite different; according to the 1860 census their wealth ranged from $1,000 to $315,000, and their slave ownership from one to 110. But as table 4 details most were middle-range planters worth about $20,000 and owning an average of slightly over twenty slaves.

But even if it were common for a slave to "marry" someone owned by a different master, one should not assume that this was a more prevalent practice than a slave marrying one of his owner's slaves. If most married slaves were owned by separate masters, historians of the antebellum South most assuredly would have already pointed this out. The obvious question, then, is why was it that in North Carolina the majority of freed couples who recorded their marriages in 1866 and 1867 had been owned by separate masters? One possible explanation is that married couples who had been separated as slaves had a greater psychological need to record their marriages than did those who had been living together on the same plantations.

Despite the ambiguities apparent in the cohabitation records, one conclusion is certain: thousands of former slaves, who came from a variety of experiences during the antebellum years and who had cohabited as man and wife for anywhere from a few months to over fifty years, chose to legalize their marriages and to work to make their families the cornerstone of their new free community. But because of their slave experiences, some had difficulty achieving this goal. It is impossible to determine how many freed people faced the same tragic situation as Owen Smaw, Celia Smaw, and John Bryan. On August 6, 1866, after living as husband and wife for four years, Owen and Celia registered their marriage before the clerk of the Beaufort County Court. Several months later, however, John Bryan—Celia's first husband—appeared to claim his wife. John had been sold several years earlier and was presumed to be dead. Thus Owen and Celia's marriage was cancelled "at the request of all parties." Presumably, John and Celia were then wed.[11]

As might be expected, not all freed people recognized their slave marriages as binding. The Freedmen's Bureau papers contain dozens of cases of husbands or wives deserting their spouses. One Bureau officer summarized the problem when he noted that "there are . . . many cases of trouble and suffering among the Freedmen arising out of the desertion of their families by the husband or wife, thus leaving their little children to the tender mercies of the remaining parent or their former masters. Many deserted their families during the rebellion to obtain their freedom . . . and in many instances the parent has got another husband or wife, not regarding their former marriage while slaves as legal." He also noted that there were "many cases of plurality of wives, or adultery."[12]

Some black women also complained to Bureau officials that their husbands would not support them and their children. Maria Coump, for example, who had been living with her husband for seven years, maintained that she had worked with her spouse raising a crop and that he now wanted to "turn her off" the farm "without allowing her anything for her work."[13] But these examples are exceptions; only about two dozen such complaints exist in Bureau records.[14] On the other hand, thousands of freedmen chose to register their slave marriages and to establish a traditional family life.

Another problem faced by many freedmen attempting to establish a full family life was trying to find their children. Freedmen's Bureau records indicate that hundreds left their former owners in search of loved ones. These efforts were often futile, as was the case in Mattie Curtis's family. After the war Curtis's parents were married by a northern minister and then left to find their fourteen oldest children, who had been sold away during slavery. After a long search they found only three, and, like many others, had to start their new lives with all the family they could find.[15]

Former slaves also faced the task of choosing names. Herbert Gutman has argued that slaves often adopted the name of their ancestors or the first master who owned them as a means of giving stability to their family lives.[16] This may have been true for some North Carolina slaves; if so, one would assume that they would have retained these names after emancipation. But only one former slave can be found to have done this.[17] According to the slave narratives and cohabitation records, most North Carolina slaves had the name, as one former Cumberland County slave maintained, "of the family who [presently] owned" them.[18] Thomas Hall, an Orange County freedman, agreed, contending that if married slaves were owned by separate masters each slave would go "by the name of the slave owners' family. In such cases the children went by the name of the family to which the mother belonged."[19]

After emancipation some freedmen took the names of their wives' owners, especially if they chose to live on that plantation after the war.[20] But most common was the experience of George Harris of Jones County. His father, Quash Harris, belonged to the Harris family who lived on the adjoining plantation. George and his mother, Jennie Andrews, were owned by John Andrews. After the war they all adopted his father's name: "We changed from Andrews to Harris."[21]

Once marriages were legalized, names chosen, and separated families reunited as much as possible, North Carolina blacks moved to form a free community. Next to the family, the church would emerge as the most important institution in the black community. Before the Civil War most North Carolina free blacks as well as slaves participated in religious services along with whites. They either sat in separate sections during the regular services or attended special services provided for them as members of the white-run churches. Moreover, after 1831, it was illegal for any North Carolina black to preach.[22] During the few years of Presidential Reconstruction, blacks began to break with the past. They left white churches in large numbers as black ministers quickly emerged not only as religious instructors but as community and political leaders as well.

The process was slow and the story from 1865 through 1867 is one of initial efforts. Very few sources are available on the history of the black church during this period, but it is clear that the church became a focal point of the black community. Mass meetings, socials, speeches following parades commemorating important events, and the two freedmen's conventions were all held in churches. Moreover, most ministers quickly emerged as political spokesmen, appearing before mass meetings, holding positions in the Equal Rights League and similar organizations, and serving as delegates to the two black conventions. Ten ministers attended the 1865 freedmen's convention, and seven participated in the 1866 meeting.

More important, blacks began insisting on their own churches. Initially many asked only to be treated equally within the established white churches, and to varying degrees white church leaders altered their views on religious education and church structure to meet black demands. Generally, however, blacks felt that white churches would not go far enough and they began instead to form their own churches. This trend, only a small ripple during Presidential Reconstruction, accelerated after 1867, until by the 1870s most churches in North Carolina were either all black or all white.[23]

After the war most white North Carolina churchmen maintained, as they had before emancipation, that blacks were innately inferior, ignorant, and shiftless. They were willing to give blacks religious instruction that taught them to be quiet, subservient, honest, and industrious, but most refused to promote the kind of education that would lead blacks to positions of leadership. Moreover, no white southern churches even considered integrated worship with blacks on a basis of equality.[24] Still, the southern Presbyterians, Baptists, Methodists, and Episcopalians all adapted somewhat to the freedmen's changed condition. These adaptations ranged from the most conservative stance—reluctant acceptance of the fact that blacks were free to leave white churches but offering no help or encouragement from the white body—to, for the nineteenth century, a very liberal position—that blacks should be well educated, that they should form their own churches with their own leaders, and that black church leaders should participate on an equal basis in overall church governance.

White North Carolina Presbyterians changed the least. They discouraged blacks from forming their own churches and refused to allow independent black churches to exist within their organization. Faced with these restraints, black Presbyterians left to form their own institutions, primarily under the auspices of the northern organization, although most such churches were not started until the 1870s.[25]

The Episcopal church handled emancipation and the role of blacks within its organization in a completely different manner. One major reason was the reunification of the northern and southern branches of that church in 1865. While other southern Protestant churches had split with their northern counterparts before the Civil War over the issue of the morality of slavery, the southern Episcopalians had established a separate organization in 1861 only out of the necessity of political disunion. This factor made reunification after the war an easier matter.

One result of this reunification was the establishment of a well-financed and extensive program of education for the freedmen. Under the auspices of the Protestant Episcopal Freedmen's Commission, founded in 1865 to provide "religious and secular instruction" for the freedmen, northerners and southerners worked together with a minimum of tension. The commission was especially successful in North Carolina under the leadership of one of its members, Bishop Thomas Atkinson, who continually argued the justice and necessity of educating the freedmen so that they could occupy positions of religious leadership. Influenced by his argument, the North Carolina Episcopal Convention of 1865 followed the lead of its national body and urged whites to accept the freedmen's new status and "to elevate the colored race as fast as it may come." To accomplish this end, the committee on the religious instruction of the freedmen proposed several resolutions which recognized, as no other southern white church group did, that blacks were truly free.

Episcopalians, like other southern churchmen, were unwilling to promote the social equality that they believed accompanied churches integrated on a basis of equality. But most northerners at this time did not believe that true freedom demanded integration and social equality. The various activities of North Carolina blacks during this period indicate that they agreed; they wanted equal treatment but did not demand integration. Nevertheless the Episcopalians went further than any other white southern church, and resolved that

> in view of the radical changes wrought in the colored man's political, and, to a large degree, social condition, it is advisable that there should be radical changes also brought about in his religious and ecclesiastical relations—that to reach him with the teachings and blessings of the Church, it is the sense of this Council, that separate houses of worship should be provided as soon as practicable, (the white people, in this, aiding the colored,) . . .—that there should be

separate Sunday schools and separate congregations—that colored superintendents and catechists should be secured and appointed when practicable . . .—that all colored congregations, when competent to form a parish, should have power . . . of electing their own pastors, and that the pastors may be either white or colored clergymen.

A second resolution asked the North Carolina clergy to seek out "at once . . . suitable colored men for catechist and Sunday-school teachers, and to give them, as far as possible, personal instructions to fit them for those posts." Another urged black Episcopal ministers "to come among their own people in this Diocese, and labor in their sphere with us." The committee further recommended that "steps be taken . . . for the education of colored young men for the ministry of the Church to their own people in our midst." Thus this committee paved the way for separate but equal parishes. The convention, however, postponed adopting these resolutions until the next statewide meeting.[26]

Still North Carolina Episcopalians were not satisfied with mere words. They translated their liberal rhetoric into action and established not only Sunday schools, which were the primary means of educating blacks in southern Baptist, Methodist, and Presbyterian churches, but also day schools. By May 1866 the North Carolina diocese had more schools and teachers for the freedmen than did any other diocese. It had established three parochial schools—in New Berne, Wilmington, and Raleigh—with six teachers and about five hundred students. Other day schools were also established, which were locally operated and supported. In Gaston County, for example, "the ladies of the family" of one of the principal owners of the High Shoals Iron Works founded two schools, one for white and the other for black children. Twice a week they instructed "a large number" of blacks in "the rudiments" of English and in religion. The two ladies also taught in two Sunday schools, again one for whites and the other for blacks. The church took perhaps its most significant step in 1867 when it established St. Augustine Normal School and Collegiate Institute in Raleigh to train black teachers and ministers. The diocese of North Carolina and the Protestant Episcopal Freedmen's Commission sponsored and jointly supported this new institution of higher education.[27]

Thus, with the help of the national General Conference, North Carolina's Episcopal church began what were for those times liberal programs, establishing separate black churches and educating a black ministry. Of course, the Baptists, Methodists, and Presbyterians also had separate black churches and ordained black ministers. But these religious groups did not admit their black churches and black ministers into their governing bodies. Only the Episcopalians accepted black ministers as well as lay delegates into the annual diocesan conventions on an equal basis.[28] Moreover, blacks who remained in white Episcopal churches—while they suffered certain reminders of their supposed inferiority—received the same rights of burial in the churchyard, marriage in the church, confirmation, baptism, and visitation by the minister as did whites. North Carolina blacks responded positively to these liberal programs as well as to the efficient and comparatively large educational system. Most black Episcopalians remained in the church and new black communicants joined in large numbers.[29]

North Carolina Baptists found a middle road between the Presbyterian and Episcopal solutions, encouraging blacks to form their own churches. The state Baptist Convention and many of the regional associations issued reports and passed resolutions recommending that blacks be allowed to withdraw from white churches and be encouraged to organize their own places of worship, if they wished.[30] Most black Baptists welcomed this option because they quickly realized that emancipation had not altered the inferior position they held within the white Baptist churches. They were still required to sit in the galleries or in the back of the church. They could not participate in church government. It was also clear that they were expected "to observe all the social barriers that existed between slave and master."

These factors, combined with the whites' encouragement, led to separation. Wilmington blacks formed the Orange Street Baptist Church in the summer of 1866. In November 1865 black Baptists in Chapel Hill started their own church, although they continued to use the white Baptist church building for their services and meetings until 1871. By April 1866 blacks in Murfreesboro had organized their own church, but they also used the white church for their services for a while. In November they built their own church, "for the erection of which our citizens of every class contributed cheerfully." The black minister they hired, L. W. Boon, noted that his church would temporarily stay within the bounds of the predominantly white Chowan Association. But he predicted that by May 1867 there would be twenty black churches with approximately three thousand members in that association. He proposed that at that time these black churches should form their own association, and asked for the "cooperation of the ministers of the Chowan Association, without whose aid and countenance he desires not to take a step."[31]

The Colored Baptist Church of Raleigh, with three hundred members in December 1866, had been established for "many years." But the members had worshiped in the basement of the city's white Baptist church when it was not occupied by the white members. In a petition to the state legislature on December 1, 1866, these blacks explained that they had "long felt the necessity of a separate house of worship, but the . . . kindness of the white bretheren, in connection with our poverty, has induced us to adapt ourselves to the situation without complaint." Since emancipation, however, they felt that their "religious enjoyment, and usefulness . . . would be greatly promoted, by having a separate organization, and distinct house of worship." But since they did not have the money "to purchase a suitable lot" they asked the legislature to grant them a half-acre or so of state property so they could build a church, "to be used & occupied by us, until such time as the State may need said lot for public purposes." This petition was signed by the eight "white officers" and the six "colored deacons" of the Baptist Church of Raleigh.[32] But this effort failed when the Joint Standing Committee of Public Buildings and Grounds recommended that the request be denied.[33] The legislature agreed, and no land was granted.

Over two thousand other North Carolina black Baptists chose to remain within the white churches.[34] It is impossible to discover why they did so, but perhaps, as in the case of the Raleigh blacks, lack of money was the cause. For blacks in the countryside, distance as well as financial difficulties were important considerations. Some, of course, might have been happy within the white churches. Many of these churches started Sunday schools for blacks, and white ministers taught some of them and their children to read and write.[35] But the trend toward separation in the Baptist faith, started during Presidential Reconstruction, continued. In May 1867 J. D. Hufman, a well-informed white minister, estimated that the white Baptist churches had "retained only a fragment of their 'very large' colored membership which existed at the close of the war." In

1867 black Baptists did form their own General Association, and held their first state convention in 1869. By 1872 the two races were entirely separated.[36]

The developments in the Methodist churches of North Carolina were very similar. Southern Methodists were immediately forced to face the issue of the separation of blacks from their congregations because of the already well-developed black Methodist organizations—the African Methodist Episcopal Church and the African Methodist Episcopal Zion Church. In 1866 the annual conference of the Methodist Episcopal Church of North Carolina received petitions from the Zion African Churches of New Berne and Fayetteville, asking that the white-owned buildings which the black churches were currently using be "conveyed" from the white to the black Methodist organization. The committee to whom these requests were referred rejected this appeal for the outright transference of property. But the conference did agree to abide by the rule of the General Conference, which said "that whenever entire churches and congregations shall have voluntarily left us and united with the African M.E. Church, the Trustees be advised to allow them the use of the house of worship heretofore solely occupied by them, as before they left our church."[37]

While these and other similar cases were easily solved,[38] the events at the Front Street Methodist Church of Wilmington during 1865 led to bitterness and suspicion between whites and blacks. The white minister, the Reverend L. S. Burkhead, set the tone when, after Union troops occupied Wilmington in the winter of 1864–1865, he denounced the freedmen for being "intoxicated with the bright visions of their own importance . . . , all filled with [ideas of] . . . social supremacy and political equality." He also verbally attacked a black army chaplain by the name of Hunter, who had delivered what whites saw as an inflammatory sermon to the black portion of the Front Street Church congregation. Hunter, a North Carolina slave before the war, was in 1865 a minister of the Methodist Episcopal Church of the United States and a chaplain in the United States army. He had told the black congregation that they were now free and, more important, that they were equal to whites and deserved all the opportunities and privileges to which every American was entitled. That same afternoon Burkhead wrote that Hunter had preached a "'pure anti-slavery gospel,' dashed with the radical spirit of political intrigue," and that he had unsettled all of the freedmen's "former principles and ideas of subordination." Moreover, he continued, "some of the class leaders . . . seemed already in imagination to be walking the streets of the capital of the nation and listening to their own silver-toned voices dispensing the 'glad tidings' of the Greeley and Sumner gospel to the Congress of the United States."

In response to these attacks the black members of the church petitioned General Schofield, then the commander of the occupying federal troops in North Carolina, explaining that they were "under the jurisdiction of the M. E. Church, South, whose teachings are in opposition to the interests of the Government of the United States," and asking permission "to transfer" their "relation to the A.M.E. Church of the U.S." They told Schofield that they also wished to replace Burkhead with Hunter and asked him to give them "possession of our church property" and to "protect us in the worship of God according to the dictates of our own consciences." Burkhead retorted by accusing Chaplain Hunter of manipulating the congregation for his own ends.

Schofield ordered a compromise. He ruled that the black members of the congregation would use the church for half the day, "when the pulpit will be occupied by such minister, white or colored, as the colored members may select." Whites would use the church for the rest of the day. But members of both races could attend the services of either minister, white or black. Burkhead was furious. He claimed that the order was "enough to try a second cousin of Job" and predicted that the decision would "kindle the spirit of envy, hatred and revenge; and thus arrays the negroes against the whites in bitter controversy which must necessarily tend to greatly damage both parties."[39]

Given Burkhead's feelings, it is not surprising that this compromise failed to end the disquiet. At the opening of his service on June 18, Burkhead "made some remarks . . . against colored persons, whether soldiers or otherwise, presuming to take seats with the 'superior' class in the lowest part of the house." A white observer felt that these remarks were "altogether uncalled for, and alike insulting to the colored soldiers and their [white] officers present," and pointed out that there was only "one colored man seen below and he a well-dressed soldier, behaving as respectfully as any person." The *Wilmington Herald* agreed that Burkhead would have been wiser if he had spoken privately to the "offending" black soldier. But it also argued that "there must be taken into the act . . . the hostility the blacks first showed in this Church" by attempting "to eject the whites entirely," thus creating "a strong feeling against them; and then the natural prejudice of the white people against association with the blacks" also had to be considered. The tensions at the Front Street Methodist Church did not diminish until October 1865, when the black members bought another building for their exclusive use.[40]

White members of the Fifth Street Methodist Episcopal Church of Wilmington obviously agreed with the attitudes expressed by Burkhead and the *Wilmington Herald*. In January 1866 members of the African Methodist Episcopal Zion Church asked the board of the Fifth Street Church for the use of their church for half of each day. The board refused by a unanimous vote, arguing that such an arrangement "would be detrimental to the peace, comfort and best interests of our church." The board, its pride hurt, could not understand the freedmen's desire for their own church and felt it necessary to point out "that colored people separate from our church without any provocation on our part; that the history of the past shows how earnest and constant our labors have been for their salvation; and that, notwithstanding they are not now under our spiritual guidance, we, nevertheless, feel the same earnest desire for their good moral deportment, . . . and final salvation." Moreover, they continued, if blacks stayed, "our ministers would take the same care of them *now* as heretofore."[41]

Despite such pronouncements of good will, blacks rejected this paternalistic approach and continued to protest their inferior status within the Methodist Episcopal Church, South. Throughout 1865, Wilmington's Reverend Burkhead continued to complain that every Sunday some blacks tried to sit in that portion of the church designated for whites only. He noted, however, that on each occasion he was successful in getting them to move to the gallery. In Salisbury the *Carolina Watchman* reported that in May 1866 "an ill-advised negro woman tested . . . her supposed privilege under the 'civil rights bill,' to seat herself among the white people." Although the minister stopped the service to tell her that a seat was "provided" for her in the gallery, thereby causing her to leave the church, the *Watchman* was disturbed by her "insubordinate" behavior. Noting that "our churches are built with galleries for the accommodation of colored members," it claimed that the gallery seats were just as comfortable as those on the first floor and that the black woman should have been satisfied with "the place appointed for her color."[42]

Most blacks, however, chose another form of protest; they simply left the white church organization. The tabular statement issued by the annual convention of North Carolina Methodists in November 1866 showed an increase of about 2,400 white members over 1865. But black membership declined by over two thousand from the previous year and by almost seven thousand from the 1860 figures. On the other hand, the A.M.E. and the A.M.E. Zion churches enjoyed rapid growth in North Carolina. By 1869 the A.M.E. Church of North Carolina had fifty ministers and 7,431 members. By the end of 1865 the A.M.E. Zion Church of North Carolina had 7,267 members belonging to fifty churches, thirty-five of which were newly founded or had switched from the Methodist Episcopal Church, South during 1865.[43]

The resolutions adopted by the Wesley Chapel African Methodist Episcopal Church of Raleigh may explain why most North Carolina black Methodists changed affiliations. On April 16, 1865, this church group held a meeting "to take in to consideration the propriety of trans-furing our Church to the A.M.E. Church and resolve our connection with the Methodist E. Church South." These black congregants explained that they took this action because the white church had seceded from the Methodist Episcopal Church twenty-one years earlier "for the purpose of perpetuating Slavery." Accusing the southern church of having "taught rebelion," they explained that they were "compelled to liston to her ministers till the coming of the Fedarel Army, [and] now we Desiar to dispence with the Services of men whos fidelety to the government by us is doubted in order therefore that we may be able to worship God according to the dictates of our conscances."[44]

Still, from the scant evidence available, it seems likely that these black churches tried to create and maintain good relations with North Carolina whites. The 1865 Convention of the A.M.E. Zion Church of North Carolina resolved that "whereas, Moses was not permitted to lead the children of Israel into the promised land because he called his brethren rebels, . . . and as we are ministers of the gospel of peace, therefore *Resolved*, That it be our duty to avoid all irritative expressions both in our private and public discourse, that we may be wholesome examples to our congregations." Another resolution echoed the same theme when it noted that "*Whereas*, For the preservation of peace it is necessary that all just laws should be obeyed; therefore—*Resolved*, That we will at all times counsel obedience to lawful authority, and impress upon our people the necessity of honesty and industry, that the lands may be cultivated, the wastes built up, and that the desolate parts of the land may bud and blossom as a rose." A third resolution thanked the Methodist Church, South for "the favors we have received" from many of its ministers, "who have extended the friendly hand and cheered our heart when we were ready to faint."[45] Blacks were also grateful to the many other whites who also supported their fund-raising projects.[46]

Still, while they desired aid from and harmony with whites, black Methodists were determined to promote their race's best interests. They argued "that as this is our native land, here we design to stay," and promised, "as patriotic citizens," to work for the well-being of all the people.[47] But such efforts on the part of blacks to achieve racial harmony would not work. Most whites would see any proclamation claiming that blacks were citizens as threatening to the southern social order and would not consider such claims as promoting anybody's "well-being" but the freedmen's.

The A.M.E. Zion Church of North Carolina also tried to advance black interests through its educational efforts, directed at training young black men and women "to fill important stations" in the church. The 1865 convention recommended that the local churches encourage "those now capable by appointing them as superintendents and teachers in our Sabbath Schools," which were "the nursery of the church" out of which would come "the material . . . to organize the Army of Reserve to carry forth the hallowed crusade of mercy and grace."

The convention's committee on education proudly reported that "when compared with that period when we could only look through a glass darkly, education is now in a flourishing condition." And the figures back up this claim. Within seven months of emancipation the church had 145 teachers instructing 2,834 students in its sabbath schools. But these achievements were not enough. The committee on education exhorted ministers to "keep the importance" of education "constantly before the people; otherwise we can not expect the blessings of this favorable opportunity to be fully realized." It also noted that day schools should be established as soon as possible and black teachers hired when available.

Finally, the delegates applauded a proposal to build a manual labor school in North Carolina.

The convention also noted some problems with the church's educational efforts. After thanking whites for the aid they had already given to promote these educational endeavors, the delegates, in "an appeal . . . to the Benevolent Public," asked for additional help. They explained that while their members "will go forth . . . to organize churches, . . . to gather the lost sheep of the House of Israel, . . . [and] to organize both Sabbath and day schools wherever it is possible," they could not do so effectively because "there are great masses of . . . [freedmen] who have no books nor means to obtain them." They asked for donations "either of money or books" from those "whose hearts overflow with benevolence toward this long-oppressed people."[48]

While black churches began to emerge as a center for religious worship, educational instruction, and community pride, other community activities also expressed the new spirit of independence. Blacks soon organized a social life for themselves. Many cities had Negro bands, fire companies, and lodges. Schools sponsored parades and exhibits, and black citizens sometimes held balls and dances.[49] While these organizations and activities may seem relatively insignificant, their existence demonstrates that blacks were quickly creating their own free society. They also organized self-help groups like the burying society in New Berne.[50]

Another important element in the formation of community cohesiveness is a newspaper. While no blacks started newspapers, a few whites did attempt to publish newspapers to serve the black population. The *Journal of Freedom*, published weekly in Raleigh by northerner Edward P. Brooks, was "devoted to the interests of the Freedmen of the South and the establishment and maintenance of Equal Rights for All Men, regardless of class or color."[51] The 1865 freedmen's convention passed a resolution urging "the colored population of the State" to support the paper.[52] But this endeavor failed and the paper survived for only one month, from September 30 to October 28, 1865. In November 1865 the Reverend James Sinclair, a native of Scotland who had moved to North Carolina before the war as a Presbyterian minister and had served in the Confederate army before joining the Union army as a chaplain, launched a second attempt to begin a newspaper for blacks. Sinclair published a prospectus in the *Wilmington Herald* for "The Southern Freedman." This paper, which he planned to publish in Wilmington, was to be "devoted to the interests of the . . . colored freedmen now in the South," espousing "the religious as well as the secular rights of the race."[53] But Sinclair was even less successful than Brooks, for there is no evidence that the paper ever began publication.

Blacks were far more successful in forming politically oriented groups to promote their interests. Throughout North Carolina they organized equal rights leagues under a variety of names. These associations were dedicated to working peacefully "for a repeal of all laws, state and national, that make distinction on account of color," and to "demand of the lawful authority protection for our property, schools, presses and churches." These organizations, often supported by the more socially oriented groups, held parades and meetings, passed resolutions, and sent petitions to protest discrimination and to demand equality.[54]

The most popular activities sponsored by these groups were the organization of demonstrations and speeches honoring significant days in their history. As has been shown previously, blacks organized many such celebrations in 1865, and they continued this tradition in 1866 and 1867. Each year they commemorated the anniversary of the Emancipation Proclamation. In 1866 large, orderly parades were reported in Wilmington, Fayetteville, Halifax, and New Berne. In 1867 newspapers wrote of celebrations in Wilmington, Raleigh, Goldsboro, and New Berne. The fire companies, lodges, bands, schools, church groups, and equal rights leagues all participated. Prominent blacks delivered speeches and choirs and bands sometimes performed after the parades.[55]

Blacks were the only North Carolinians reported to have celebrated the Fourth of July in 1866. They did so in at least four cities—Raleigh, Charlotte, Tarboro, and Wilmington.[56] Several newspapers, while pointing out that the gatherings were orderly and the participants well behaved, generally resented such Fourth of July demonstrations. The Raleigh *Sentinel* explained: "The colored people of the South may celebrate the day with zest and real delight, for they alone, of the people of the South, truly enjoy that liberty. But so long as military surveillance, the Freedmen's Bureau, the Civil Rights bill, and a threatened constitutional amendment which robs the . . . Southern people of the rights they enjoyed under the old Constitution, are held over us as a rod, the celebration of the Fourth of July could only serve as a reminder of better days gone!"[57]

Blacks held many other meetings to celebrate other important dates in their history or the successes of certain organizations. Wilmington blacks had several such meetings, along with parades.[58] Blacks in Raleigh met in June 1866 to celebrate the first anniversary of the United Brotherhood, an organization devoted to the elevation of the black race. Membership in the brotherhood was opened to "all good men—every man who has respect for himself as an individual and as a citizen, and that has the interest of our race at heart—every man that appreciates honesty, industry, sobriety and charity." Those attending the meeting resolved not to recognize "any person as a good citizen or as worthy of the respect and support of good men, who will encourage . . . any course of conduct . . . or of obtaining a living, which does not have a tendency to elevate our race as a people."[59]

On other occasions blacks met to hear speakers visiting their city. In January 1866 black Wilmingtonians gathered to hear James H. Harris, the black leader from Raleigh who played a prominent role in the 1865 freedmen's convention.[60] Four months earlier, about one hundred blacks in Wilmington, "regularly organized as a meeting," hosted the Reverend Cheeseborough, a black minister serving as a chaplain in a black regiment stationed "in the vicinity of Newbern." Cheeseborough irritated whites by accusing President Johnson of having only southern white interests at heart and claimed that the head of the Freedmen's Bureau had visited the South only to conciliate whites. Blacks, he maintained, must be allowed to sit as jurors if they were to get a fair trial, and must gain the right to vote and hold office. He also told blacks to band together to "resist or defend themselves against the measures now enforced everywhere, both North and South." And he boldly advised: "If a white man injures or kills one of you, . . . kill two or three white men for it." After the report of his speech appeared in the *Wilmington Herald*, a Freedmen's Bureau officer arrested Cheeseborough. After admitting that "his remarks were indiscreet," the minister was given the choice of imprisonment or leaving the city forever. He chose the latter option.[61]

In April and May of 1866 Raleigh blacks met several times to debate a controversial issue: whether or not they should send "North to obtain a Physician for the colored people." This issue was raised because some felt that Raleigh doctors charged very high prices. The committee appointed to look into the situation recommended "that some steps be taken to obtain a Physician from the North, and that the colored people pledge themselves to give him their entire patronage." James H. Harris, however, who had been out of town during the preliminary meetings, spoke out in opposition to the report, arguing that Raleigh doctors were good and did not discriminate against blacks in their fees. The meeting then rejected the committee's recommendations.[62]

In New Berne and Goldsboro, blacks convened to praise the Freedmen's Bureau. The Goldsboro meeting, held in May 1866, attacked the report by Generals Steedman and Fullerton that was critical of the Bureau in North Carolina. They drew up a petition to send to Congress, asking that the Freedmen's Bureau be continued, claiming that blacks could not get justice in the civil courts. This petition explained that "from a life-long experience as slaves of the men who now administer the laws, we cannot convince ourselves that equal justice will be meted out to us by them; but, on the contrary, we have in a year's experience of freedom, every reason to believe that without the freedmen's bureau, or some similar protection, we shall not be permitted to live even in peace, and our condition thus becomes really worse than when we were slaves and did not expect justice." The petition also asked "that the protecting influence of the freedmen's bureau be continued, in order that the young ladies now teaching our children may be induced to remain and continue their labor."[63]

New Berne blacks also met in May to praise the work of the Bureau and to denounce the investigation by Steedman and Fullerton. They charged that the investigation was designed to make "political capital in favor of the President's Policy." Indeed, Johnson had sent the generals throughout the South on an inspection tour of the Bureau hoping that they would write a negative report that he could use against the radicals in Congress. The New Berne blacks resolved that so long as North Carolina refused to grant them

> the right of Suffrage (the only peaceable means of protecting our own interests); so long as the punishment inflicted on a colored man for crime (or pretended crime) is different from what would be inflicted on a white man for a similar offence; so long as colored men if necessitated to be abroad after a certain hour at night are subject to arrest[,] search and the forfeiture of weapons (if they have any) while white men can walk at all hours without molestation; in

a word so long as we are not made equal before the law, we consider the Freedmen's Bureau an indispensible necessity.[64]

In August New Berne blacks again met, this time to express "their appreciation of the faithful administration of Colonel Wiegel," superintendent of the Freedmen's Bureau stationed in New Berne, who was being transferred. Many politically prominent New Berne blacks attended. Amos York presided; J. W. Hood and George Price served on the committee on resolutions. All three had attended the 1865 freedmen's convention. The meeting praised Wiegel for possessing those qualifications necessary to a good Bureau agent—"wisdom, sound discretion and purity of intention, and a moral courage sufficient to face the frowns and intimidation of the openly vicious [whites], and to resist the temptations of flattery."[65]

The largest political gathering held by North Carolina blacks during Presidential Reconstruction was the statewide convention of the North Carolina Equal Rights League of Freedmen, which met in Raleigh in October 1866. This meeting was planned at the 1865 freedmen's convention when it formed the league. The officers of that league published a call "to the Colored people of North-Carolina" in the Raleigh *Standard* in August, reminding them that the 1866 meeting would be held in Raleigh in October and explaining that the league was formed "to look after the interest of the Colored People of the State." Auxiliary leagues were also formed "to promote the cause of Education, and to look after the suffering poor." The league officers pointed out that while blacks appreciated the work done by northern benevolent societies, "we must learn to rely upon ourselves, and the world is looking to us for a demonstration of our capacity to perform the part of useful, intelligent citizens." Counties were to be represented at the convention on the same basis as they were in the state legislature. "In Counties where there are Leagues, the Counties are to be represented by the Leagues." The purpose of the convention was to "adopt such measures as will best promote our interests."[66]

As in 1865, blacks in several counties held mass meetings to select delegates to the convention.[67] Forsyth County blacks, gathering in Winston, listened to the five candidates who vied to represent them. Alexander Vogler spoke of the importance of education and promised that if elected he would work to establish schools in the area. C. Jerry Blum, who could "read well and is moderately learned," spoke against "'having a poor house, for freedmen, in the county.'" Peter Fries, who was labeled "too impudent and saucy" by the Salem *People's Press*, denounced the wrongs committed by whites against blacks. He also promised to push for schools. Lewis Hege, the candidate elected to represent Forsyth County at the convention, was described by the *People's Press* as "the only one of the candidates whose talk merited the approval of the white persons present." It praised Hege for having "good sense, for a negro," and for not "put[ting] on airs." Hege told those attending the meeting that blacks must help themselves by working hard.[68]

There was a hotly contested race between Dennis Best and Monroe Edwards for the Greene County delegate seat to the convention. These men held "a regular canvass" and then blacks had a regular election. During the canvass the candidates spoke at several public meetings, discussing "general politics and practically every conceivable" issue. Best won the election. The Raleigh *Sentinel* criticized this sort of campaign; it praised the idea of a convention to promote "the cause of education," but advised blacks "to avoid politics as they would a viper."[69]

At the other county meetings, blacks passed resolutions that clearly showed their concerns and priorities. Some urged blacks to work hard and to be good citizens; two spoke of the importance of education; four stressed the need for economic opportunities. Blacks meeting in Raleigh on July 28 passed rather mild resolutions, praising the freedmen for educating themselves and for being "not only industrious, but well disposed."[70]

At the New Berne meeting on September 8, the resolutions were more specific and constructive. First, those attending resolved that "the attainment of wealth and education is highly essential to the well-being of our people, without which we can never be elevated to the level of our more favored fellow-citizens," and they urged all blacks to find gainful employment "as will insure them at least a comfortable living." They also suggested that blacks consider the opportunities offered by the Texas Cotton Company, which was recruiting black laborers for jobs in Texas; by "the proposal of Mr. Clark, of Beaufort county, who offers 1,500 acres of land to colored settlers on very liberal terms"; by the Reverend E. H. Hill, a New Berne black minister, "who offers a large track [*sic*] of land in the upper part of this county, for three years, rent free, to persons who will clear it up and cultivate it"; or by "other landlords who may be induced to let their land on good terms." They made these suggestions because they believed that "there is no surer means of obtaining wealth and respectability than by agriculture." Another resolution called for the construction of "buildings for public schools wherever possible, and the establishment of a high school in Newbern for the qualification of teachers."[71]

Rowan County blacks met near Salisbury on August 4. The chairman, S. Ellis, stated that the meeting was needed "to show the colored people the duties which devolve upon them . . . , their marriage relations, paying taxes, working upon the public roads, &c." Along with electing a delegate to the convention, the gathering heard a few men deliver speeches and a committee of twelve, drawn "from different parts of the county," presented several resolutions. One pledged that "if any man is known to work under fifty cents and board within the county of Rowan, he will have to abide the consequences, or for less than a dollar a day and board himself."[72]

The Salisbury *Union Banner* disapproved of this meeting, claiming that "these proceedings exhibit a restlessness, as well as great ignorance, on the part of the negro." It praised Rowan County blacks for generally abstaining from "public demonstrations, such as public meetings and gatherings," which, it argued, were "profitless and injurious to them as a class." Then, in language reminiscent of a paternalistic slaveowner, the *Banner* maintained that such meetings

> ingender [*sic*] bad feeling and excite prejudice. . . . The Southern people are their best friends. They are well acquainted with their habits. They know their nature and their necessities. Among the Southern whites they live and must continue to stay. Whatever blessings they may hope to derive from their freedom must be secured through and by the consent of the Southern whites. . . . To them they must look for protection and co-operation in every measure which has for its object their welfare and moral or political elevation. And in order to secure the favor and encouragement of whites, they must act in such a manner as to deserve them.

The *Banner* argued that blacks must fulfill their contracts, be sober and industrious, and abstain "from all public demonstrations, mass meetings, and idleness." "This," the *Banner* maintained, "will do more to secure them happiness, raise the price of their labor, and give them peace and plenty than all the mass meetings they can hold can possibly do." And it warned blacks that if they tried to raise the price of labor by organizing themselves they would turn whites against them and "the whites will refuse to employ them altogether."[73] The *Banner* could not or would not understand what blacks clearly saw: to be truly free, blacks must be secure from such threats and from their complete dependence upon white employers.

One hundred ten delegates from sixty-one counties met in Raleigh on October 2. Seventeen had also attended the 1865 freedmen's convention. John Randolph, Jr., of New Berne, a leading member of the 1865 convention, was also elected again in 1866, but he was unable to attend.[74] Representatives came from all over the state, unlike the 1865 meeting when delegates came primarily from the eastern and central counties.[75]

In other ways, however, the 1866 delegates were quite similar to those who attended the 1865 convention. Most were native North Carolinians; of the sixty-nine whose birthplaces can be identified, sixty-two were born in North Carolina. Three others were born in Virginia, one in South Carolina, and one in Georgia. Only two native northerners, one from New York and one from Massachusetts, attended the 1866 meeting. One native North Carolinian had been educated in the North. Also like the 1865 representatives, most delegates to the 1866 gathering had probably been slaves before the war. Only ten can be identified as having been free. Seven had definitely been slaves, but forty-eight others can be assumed to have been slaves.[76]

The literacy rate among the delegates to the 1866 convention was also similar to that of the 1865 representatives. Of the sixty-nine delegates who can be identified, forty-one (or almost 60 percent) were literate according to the 1870 census, compared to approximately 57 percent for the 1865 convention. Another seven 1866 delegates could read but not write. The 1870 census listed twenty-one as not being able to read or write.

The occupational and residential patterns of the 1865 and 1866 delegates were also similar, although there was a slightly higher percentage of farmers among the latter group. In addition, an even higher percentage lived in rural areas—forty-one of the seventy-three whose residences can be discovered. Seventeen 1866 delegates were farm laborers and another thirteen were farmers. There were twenty-one artisans,[77] a millwright, three grocers, a marketer for a seminary, six laborers, and one who worked in a railroad warehouse. Three were teachers and seven were ministers. Two of the delegates, John S. Leary of Fayetteville and James E. O'Hara of Goldsboro, later became lawyers. Leary was the founder and the first dean of the Shaw University Law School. In 1868 O'Hara became the first black man to be admitted to the North Carolina bar.[78]

Slightly over 35 percent of the 1866 delegates can be found to have owned some property, compared to 33 percent of the 1865 representatives. In 1866, of the sixty-four delegates on whom such information can be found, twenty-five owned no property, twenty-one owned both real and personal property, twelve owned only personal property, and six owned only real property. Of the thirty-nine property owners, seven held estates valued at $100 or less, ten had property valued at between $100 and $500, fourteen at under $1,000, and eight owned property worth over $1,000.

Nineteen delegates—more than 17 percent of those who attended the 1866 convention—held elective office after 1868. Two of these, James O'Hara and John Hyman, served in the United States House of Representatives, the former for two terms, the latter for one. The remainder were elected to the state legislature or to one of the state constitutional conventions.

Despite the similarities in the backgrounds of the delegates to both conventions, the mood in 1866 was far different from that in 1865. The 1866 convention adopted several resolutions that were politically oriented and radical in nature. North Carolina white leaders had hoped that such a development would not occur. This convention was referred to in the Raleigh *Sentinel* and the Raleigh *Standard* as the "Colored Education Convention." According to their reports, its primary purpose was supposed to have been the promotion of black educational needs. The *Sentinel* praised this goal, and argued that the convention was "called purely to consult upon the best plan of organizing and inaugurating a feasible system of Education for our colored population." This, it said, was a "laudable" object, because "it has no political aims or ends." But the *Sentinel* feared that many blacks, both throughout the state and at the

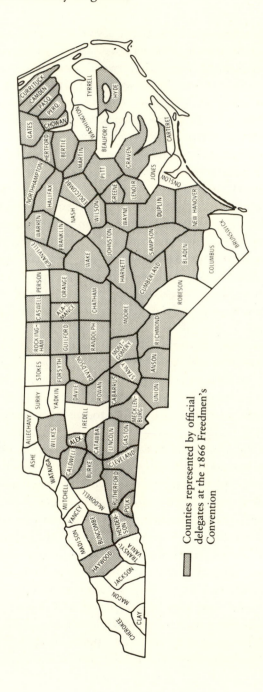

Counties represented by official
delegates at the 1866 Freedmen's
Convention

Map 4. 1866 Freedmen's Convention

convention, did not understand this purpose, and the paper warned that the introduction of politics at the meeting would damage the harmony between whites and blacks.[79]

When the convention opened at the African Methodist Church of Raleigh on October 2, it appeared that a conservative approach would prevail. James H. Harris, a native of Raleigh and chairman of the committee that wrote the moderate address to the state's constitutional convention in 1865, was chosen president. James Bowman of Fayetteville suggested that the convention invite various "distinguished [white] citizens of North Carolina." Some delegates objected, but those who argued that it was necessary to try "to form a test of sincere friendship between the races" carried the day. Dr. H. J. Brown, delegate from Hertford, then spoke on "the subjects of Education and Equality before the law." Several other delegates delivered speeches, "making good and earnest appeals to the people to consider the object for which they were assembled [i.e., education, not politics]," and urging the delegates "faithfully to discharge their duty towards God, towards their fellowmen, and towards themselves."[80]

The next day, Governor Worth addressed the convention "on morality, education, and religion." He urged blacks to be industrious, sober, and honest, and to acquire knowledge and wealth. He promised he would do everything he could to protect them "in all" their rights. But he warned them: "I shall be equally ready to have those punished who do wrong." He also told them that their late masters had kindly feelings toward them, and that all whites "feel that they owe you a debt of gratitude for your quiet and orderly conduct during the war." He closed, echoing the theme of many other whites, by warning blacks "not to meddle in governmental affairs. . . . Avoid politics. Practice industry."[81]

William A. Graham, a former North Carolina governor, United States and Confederate senator, and vice-presidential candidate, wrote a letter to the convention that repeated Worth's themes. He praised the convention's efforts "to educate your people," but warned the delegates not "to establish seminars for the higher branches of learning." He advised them instead to direct their attentions "to primary schools." Like Worth, he also cautioned them to be industrious, sober, and truthful.[82]

But the delegates felt they were capable of more than work and a primary school education. On October 3 Dr. Brown again addressed the convention, this time "on Phrenology and Ethnology." Denouncing Dr. Josiah Nott's claims that blacks were inferior, he argued that blacks were "superior to the American Indians, and in every respect equal to . . . [the] Anglo-Saxon." "According to science," he claimed, "no two races . . . were so much alike as the Caucassian [sic] and the negro." They had "the same imitative, moral and intellectual faculties." He cited the accomplishments of Henry Highland Garnet and other prominent blacks as examples of the kinds of achievements of which blacks were capable. If blacks seemed inferior, he concluded, it was only due to slavery and "therefore it is the white man's shame."[83]

John Randolph, Jr., of New Berne, writing that he regretted being unable to attend the convention, told his fellow blacks that they should consider not only the educational needs and "the laboring interests of our people," but also "our political rights." He concluded: "It must be remembered that these are peculiar times in which we live, and in all your counsel and deliberations, show yourselves 'as harmless as doves, but as wise as serpents' to the end that we all may be benefitted."[84]

The convention then got down to its real business. First, it adopted a constitution for the Freedmen's Educational Association of North Carolina. The purpose of this association was "to aid in the establishment of schools, from which none shall be excluded on account of color or poverty, and to encourage unsectarian [sic] education in this State, especially among the freedmen." The association was also to "assist the educational associations in counties, towns or captain's districts, to obtain teachers, and in all other matters that circumstances shall make desireable." Membership in the association was open to any adult who favored these objectives and paid the one dollar annual dues. Each locality was instructed to form an auxiliary league, with a president, a vice-president, a secretary, a treasurer, and a five-man board of trustees. The board of trustees was "to provide one or more school houses, keep them in good repair and supply fuel." It was also to "provide a pleasant home for teachers, and pay their salary so far as able."

The Committee on Business then presented more politically oriented resolutions that the delegates rapidly adopted. One hailed "the passage of the Freedmen's Bureau Bill, Civil Rights Bill," and the Fourteenth Amendment. Another thanked Charles Sumner, Thaddeus Stevens, Benjamin Wade, Lyman Trumbull, and Horace Greeley, as well as Fredrick

Douglass, Henry Highland Garnet, "and other beacon lights of our race" for the work they had done. The delegates also demanded the right to vote. They noted cogently that just as "the reconstructed States regard taxation without representation as unjust and not in conformity with a Republican form of government," so too do "we native born colored citizens of North-Carolina, regard the same principle as applicable to us in every relation, unjust and directly in violation to our sacred rights as American citizens." The convention also passed resolutions urging blacks to establish a policy of economic power. It advised "the colored people . . . to form themselves into joint Stock companies, wherever practical; also, that they respect and patronize each other in their various branches of business."

The delegates then passed resolutions criticizing certain events which had occurred in North Carolina. One protested the apprenticeship practices, whereby black children had been "ruthlessly taken from" their parents and bound out without their consent. Another complained of the "outrages" prevalent in several counties where blacks had been killed or robbed. Pointing out that no one had been arrested for committing these outrages, the convention urged "colored people in every county, district and village throughout the State [to] form themselves into auxiliary leagues, which leagues must be connected with the State organization . . . and whose duty it shall be to receive reports of outrages from auxiliary leagues, or from the people . . . , and communicate them to headquarters, and such newspapers throughout the country as it may deem proper, so that the government and the world may know the cruelities inflicted upon us, and of the disadvantages under which we labor."[85]

Two North Carolina newspapers criticized these resolutions. The Charlotte *Western Democrat* praised Governor Worth's speech and condemned the convention for taking "action on political subjects." It warned: "The colored people cannot benefit themselves by meddling with politics." The Raleigh *Sentinel* concurred, arguing that these resolutions "approving the action of Congress [and] impugning the integrity and fairness of the Judicial and Executive officers of the States, . . . will go far towards diverting from these colored people that feeling of sympathy and kindness which was entertained towards them."[86]

But the freedmen refused to heed this advice. On the third day of the convention, in apparent support of the resolution accusing whites of committing outrages against blacks, delegates from several counties made statements about "their treatment in the counties in which they reside." Some of this testimony was positive. Delegates from Camden, Anson, Gates, Guilford, and Pasquotank claimed that in those areas there existed "a feeling of perfect love and harmony between the two races." Harmon Unthanks of Guilford, a former slave who later became a leader in North Carolina's Republican party, pointed out that in his neighborhood, "the daughters of Gov. Morehead was [sic] earnestly engaged in teaching colored." Edmond Bird of Almance claimed "that the only prejedice [sic] existing against the negro is only entertained by the lower and ignorant classes of whites, whilst the intelligent and better class are well disposed to help the negro." Thomas Farmer of Wilson noted that while blacks had "suffered greatly from injustice, . . . things begin to wear a bright future."

But the situation in many other counties was described as deplorable. Delegates from Lenoir, Richmond, Montgomery, Burke, Bertie, Sampson, and Forsyth counties told of the ways in which blacks were "shamefully treated by the whites." In Richmond County, "money and fire arms" were taken from blacks "and colored laborers are most cruelly whipped on plantations." In Montgomery County a black man was killed for "trespassing on the premises of a white person." Two blacks had been "shot down" recently in Burke County. In Bertie and Sampson counties, "colored men were cheated out of their labor, children were taken and bound without the consent or consultation of their parents." Also, in several counties blacks were in abject poverty, without schools or churches.[87]

On October 5, the closing day of the convention, William Holden addressed the delegates. He urged both blacks and whites to cultivate and to strengthen "the general good feeling between the two races," and explained that they had to "mutually sustain each other." The black community needed to learn from whites in the arts and sciences, and in the areas of history and government. Blacks also depended on whites for land and houses, while many whites needed blacks to cultivate their farms. Blacks might also be needed to defend the country against foreign enemies. To fulfill these mutually sustaining functions, Holden urged blacks "to procure homes, . . . [and to be] industrious, temperate and economical. Labor was the first consideration." He told them that they "had no time to waste at public gatherings." They should also *educate their children*." He felt that blacks were "capable of much greater mental improvement than they had thus far reached," and noted that black children were "apt to learn." In turn, he said, whites should grant blacks "all their civil rights." But he told blacks that no one should think of social equality, and he urged them "for the present to keep out of politics."[88]

The convention listened politely and then went about its business, passing several additional resolutions and approving an address and a petition. One resolution urged every delegate to "return home, to form, or cause to be formed, an Equal Rights League." In petitions "to the Legislature of North-Carolina" and to "the Congress of the U.S.," the delegates demanded "the right of suffrage, in common with other citizens of the United States, in consideration of our loyalty, citizenship and merit."

In an "Address of the Freedmen's Convention to the White and Colored Citizens of North Carolina," the delegates presented "our grievances, our sufferings and the outrages heaped upon us, because of our helpless and disqualified position for self-defense, resulting . . . from no greater cause than our long and unjust political disfranchisement." They asked, "in the spirit of meekness, *is taxation without representation just?*" And they argued: "History and conscience answer no!" They cited several examples of loyal service that blacks had rendered to the United States, not only "to the general government, in the bloody struggle through which we have just passed," but also during the American Revolution and in the War of 1812. Arguing from historical example, they explained that white Americans "have taught us one good thing . . . : 'That all men are born free and equal, and that they are endowed by their Creator with inalienable rights. . . . That to secure these rights, governments are instituted among men, deriving their just powers from the consent of the governed,' &c." They pointed out that blacks—men and women, adults and children—had been "beaten with clubs, robbed, shot and killed . . . , and the authorities regard it not." They argued that blacks needed the vote in order to protect themselves, and maintained that they deserved the right to vote "by merit. . . . We believe the day has come, when black men have rights which white men are bound to respect. We intend to live and die on the soil which gave us birth . . . with all . . . [its] faults. . . .

Will you . . . treat us as human beings, with all our rights? It is all we ask."

Then the officers of the Freedmen's Educational Association of North Carolina and of the state's Equal Rights League were elected to one-year terms. James E. O'Hara and James H. Harris, both native North Carolinians, were elected presidents respectively of these two organizations.[89] The delegates then adjourned to return home to carry out their work.

Probably the most striking feature of this convention was that it was much more radical than the 1865 meeting. In 1865 the resolutions and the address were couched in vague, moderate terms and entirely neglected the issue of political power and judicial rights. But in 1866 the central themes were black suffrage, full equality before the law, and self-help through education and economic power.

Why did this change occur? One factor was surely the actions taken by the Republicans in Congress in passing the Civil Rights and Freedmen's Bureau Acts and in submitting the Fourteenth Amendment to the states for ratification. The delegates to the 1866 convention were certainly encouraged by these events, which probably led them to make additional appeals to Congress. The resolutions they passed were addressed to the members of Congress as well as to North Carolina legislators. Also, by listing the "outrages" committed by whites upon blacks, they were not merely expressing their rage; they were publicizing their troubles, hoping that northerners would adopt other necessary policies.

But even if Congress had not passed legislation that blacks favored, the actions of white North Carolinians probably would have caused black radicalization. The 1866 convention frequently cited white offenses against blacks to justify their resolutions, while in 1865 the delegates had been willing to wait to see how whites would behave. When blacks convened in 1866, whites had already acted: they had passed the Black Code; they had committed outrages; they had treated black laborers unfairly. Understandably blacks would wait no longer for legal and political rights. Their attempt at a moderate course in 1865 had failed to persuade whites to treat them justly.

In late December 1866 and early January 1867 some North Carolina blacks again held mass meetings, this time to elect delegates to the "National Colored Loyal League" convention to be held in Washington, D. C., beginning January 10, 1867. The only meetings reported were held in Raleigh and High Point.[90] At the Washington convention, James H. Harris was elected deputy president. Like the 1866 freedmen's convention, this meeting passed resolutions declaring "that the government has no more right to deprive a man of his vote than of trial by jury; . . . that the colored race have the right to the ballot because they are citizens, tax-payers, and patriots." It also proclaimed "that all laws which make a discrimination on account of race or color are unconstitutional and void." During his stay in Washington, Harris, along with another black man, had an hour's interview with President Johnson. Harris told the president that blacks were not safe in North Carolina "and that they will never be fully guaranteed in their rights as citizens without the power to vote."[91]

A few black North Carolinians disagreed with the resolutions passed at the 1866 North Carolina freedmen's convention and at the national conference requesting the right to vote. In January 1867 fifteen freedmen from Warren County sent a memorial to Congress requesting that blacks *not* be given the vote. They explained that they "do not expect or desire to vote or even to be equal to white folks." In fact, they said that they were certain that they were inferior to whites: "The Asp . . . will complain that his maker had not given him strength equal to the Elephant, courage equal to the Lion, sagacity equal to the Ape. . . . [So too] the African [will] . . . complain that his maker had not given him fair skin and superior mind of the European." But blacks must learn, they argued, to accept their inferiority. Because the black petitioners claimed to believe that they were inferior, they asked Congress "to restrain Mr. [Thaddeus] Stevens and his co-workers in their unconstitutional efforts to make black white, the Asp an Elephant, or the Colored race equal to the White." They also requested that blacks be allowed "to work and not vote." Universal black suffrage, they contended, "would demoralize both races, the White would work weeks before the election[,] shut up the blacks giving them meat and drink and take them to polls to vote as they would make them." Five of the fifteen freedmen who signed this petition did so with their marks.[92] There is no other information about this petition or the petition-ers, so it is impossible to ascertain whether they were acting in response to white pressure. It should be noted, however, that Warren was a very repressive, secessionist county, and that this is the only document by blacks expressing such sentiments. Moreover, because none of the signers could be located in the 1870 census, it is possible that this petition was a fake.

Most black North Carolinians applauded the passage by Congress in 1867 of the Military Reconstruction Act, granting them the vote and inaugurating the era of Congressional Reconstruction. They held meetings throughout the state to organize and prepare for their entrance into the body politic.[93] But the few reported speeches delivered at these meetings were far from radical. Silas Barnes, a speaker at a Halifax meeting, maintained "that the negro's duty is to labor." He argued that "politics was the rock on which the Union was dissolved" and he advised his race "to steer aloof from it." He also said that the black man's best friend was the white southerner: "Give me . . . an educated gentleman; he is our friend by instinct." He asserted that "he loved his old master and felt towards him as if he had been his father."[94]

There is no way to know how representative Barnes's comments were of black attitudes, but James H. Harris—by 1867 one of the most prominent blacks in the state—first told his fellow blacks that the passage of the Military Reconstruction Act was an event to celebrate, but then urged them to work at being good citizens by educating themselves, laboring diligently, and obeying the law. He warned them that "while we maintain all our rights, and abate nothing of our manhood as a people, let us do nothing to re-kindle the slumbering fires of prejudice between the two races. Remember, we are on trial before the tribunal of the nation and of the world, that it may be known . . . whether we are worthy to be a free, self-governing people."[95]

Thus blacks faced Congressional Reconstruction hopefully but cautiously. In 1865 they had courteously petitioned whites for equal economic and educational opportunities and had hoped this moderate policy would encourage whites to treat them fairly. But by 1866 it was obvious to them that North Carolina whites would not give freedmen an equal chance. Therefore, the 1866 delegates demanded full equality and the right to vote. These rights were necessary, they argued, to protect themselves against white abuse. In 1867 they gained the vote and equality before the law. They were then ready to start anew, to work with whites for the betterment of both races.

But other problems plagued both blacks and whites throughout Presidential Reconstruction. One of the most serious was the labor situation. In both the 1865 and the 1866 freedmen's conventions, the delegates constantly stressed the necessity of industry, economy, and sobriety. In

1866 they also emphasized the importance of joining together for economic security and economic power. Whites, too, in their political assemblages and in the legislation they enacted, were primarily concerned with labor and the economy. A new economic system had to be forged. But, as was the case with politics, whites and blacks often had different visions of how this new system should develop.

5 Forging a New Economic System

God in his wisdom put the negroes in the south to do the menial work.—Sarah Ann Tillinghast to her brother, May 6,1866, William Norwood Tillinghast Papers

White people seem to entertain strange notions of the relations of labor to society, some think that the only difference between freedom and Slavery is that then the negroes were obliged to work for nothing[;] now they have to pay for what they used to have for nothing, not recognising the right of the negroes to personal liberty, personal security and private property.—Report by Dexter Clapp, October 10, 1865, Narrative Reports, Freedmen's Bureau Papers

My mistress never said anything to me that I was to have wages, nor yet that I was free. . . . But I don't [plan] to work any longer than to Christmas [1865], and then I'll ask for wages. But I want to leave the ferry. I'm a mighty good farmer, and I'll get a piece of ground and a chunk of a hoss, if I can, and work for myself.—Black ferryman to John R. Dennett, September 12, 1865, in John R. Dennett, *The South As It Is*, pp. 121–22

FEW PROBLEMS INVOLVED in the transition from slavery to freedom were more complicated than those concerned with forging a new economic structure. Hardships existed simply because the Civil War had been fought on southern soil. General Sherman's troops had trampled lands and burned homes in the southeastern counties of North Carolina. Lack of livestock, land deterioration caused by soldiers of both armies, and simple neglect added to the difficulties. Moreover, the slaves' initial response to emancipation created a labor shortage as many congregated in cities and towns or wandered through the countryside testing their new-found freedom.

But these complications, caused by the war and its immediate aftermath and aggravated by poor weather conditions, were greatly compounded by the legacy of North Carolina's antebellum attitudes. Neither race could escape the past. Blacks mistrusted whites and wanted to assert their independence. Most whites, on the other hand, retained their prewar racial views.

In private letters and newspaper editorials, North Carolina whites continually asserted their belief that blacks could do only agricultural or menial labor. Because most believed that the former slaves were naturally lazy, they also maintained that the freedmen would not work unless whites forced them to do so. They complained that rather than seeking employment blacks were congregating in towns and indulging "in dissipations." Laws were needed, they said, to "compel negroes . . . [to] go to the country for work." And the North Carolina General Assembly acceded to these wishes by enacting the Black Code.[1]

Numerous whites argued that blacks had to be forced to work, not only for the obvious economic reasons but also as a means of social control. They contended that idle freedmen acted with insolence, engaged in political activities, and talked "of schools [and] equality with whites." The Raleigh *Sentinel*, for example, charged that vagrant blacks "join the societies, and follow the processions, and huzza for liberty." They even called each other "Mr. and Mrs. . . . rather than go to the country and work on the farms."[2]

There was certainly some substance to the frequent charges of black idleness. Most whites who wrote these complaints spoke from first-hand experience and cited specific examples to prove their claims. Other sources also noted that thousands of blacks left their plantations upon learning that they were free. But it must also be remembered that immediately after emancipation many blacks felt that they did not have to work, especially not for their former masters. They viewed work under labor contracts as essentially the same as the old slave system. By their temporary idleness, many of these freedmen believed they were asserting their independence. Alex Huggins of New Berne explained: "Twa'nt anythin' wrong at home that made me run away. I'd heard so much talk 'bout freedom I reckon I jus' wanted to try it, an' I thought I had to get away from home to have it."[3] But they also soon realized that they had to acquire economic security. By January 1866 most were back on the farms.

White North Carolinians noted this change. The number of complaints of blacks not working declined continually after January 1866. More important, the number of comments by those citing firsthand experience dropped even more drastically than did the more impressionistic newspaper reports. Of equal significance is the fact that almost the same number of whites commented that blacks were working well. In fact, at times whites contradicted themselves. Sometimes they complained that blacks would not work, but on other occasions they complimented blacks on their industriousness. For example, as early as May 1865, David Schenck, a reluctant unionist if not a die-hard secessionist, admitted that while he expected all his former slaves to leave him, he was not uneasy about finding other laborers, "as there are many 'freedmen' hunting labor." In fact, he declared, "I am half inclined to believe that after the social revolution is fully accomplished, we will be the gainers by the change. . . . The negroes now seem . . . to be a good deal alarmed especially as there are so many . . . unable to procure labor, since the return of our soldiers to their homes, and not many [Negroes] are leaving their homes and those that did are returning and working for small wages."[4]

By 1866 the number of favorable comments about the freedmen's work was increasing and continued to do so throughout 1866 and 1867. The Raleigh *Sentinel* was pleased that most of the freedmen who originally "flocked to the towns" had returned home and were laboring diligently. Charles Pettigrew, a wealthy planter, felt "the negro is doing remarkably well considering the very great change in his position." He even admitted that he did not think that white people "would have borne so great a change any better."[5]

One leading commercial entrepreneur from Wilmington not only believed that blacks were willing to work, but blamed his fellow former masters for any idleness the freedmen had exhibited. He maintained that if whites paid blacks promptly and treated them fairly, they would be "good and faithful servants." He argued that "the difficulty between the negro and the planter arose from the fact that the planter was unwilling to accept his altered position. He would not demean himself to treat with the negro upon terms for his labor."[6]

Most whites were unprepared to admit that the problems of adjustment might be at least partially theirs. Instead, they blamed the Freedmen's Bureau or northerners in general as well as blacks for any labor difficulties they encountered.[7] Many argued that the Bureau, by preventing whites from reestablishing "their old relations to the negroes," prevented the creation of a stable labor force. The *New Berne Times* contended that Bureau agents "wholly unacquainted with the negro character, and having sentiments and feelings adverse to those entertained by Southern people," discouraged planters from hiring the freedmen "because they cannot do so without subjecting themselves to the dictations and restrictions of the Bureau." "V" of Warren County, in a letter to the editor of the Raleigh *Sentinel*, spelled out these views more fully. He charged that blacks "take pride in going to the Freedmen's Bureau and reporting white people for the most trivial matter, to be tried by some ignorant and prejudiced Lieutenant, or probably a low abolitionist and negro worshipper, who shows more respect for the evidence of a mean, lying, roguish and rascally negro, than for the evidence of a truthful and respectable white man."[8]

Because these comments by North Carolina whites clearly reflect prejudiced attitudes, perhaps the Freedmen's Bureau, with its active involvement in labor affairs and in adjusting labor relations, is a more accurate source for establishing the willingness of blacks to work. In its supervision of labor the Bureau was, as we shall see, fairly evenhanded. It did not always side with the freedmen; sometimes it was quite sensitive to the needs of whites.

The Bureau's first step was to issue regulations, guidelines, and circular statements about the new labor system. On April 28, 1865, General Schofield issued General Order No. 32 explaining to both white and black North Carolinians that slavery was dead and that the freedmen now had to be paid for their labor. Several Bureau agents in the field also made similar pronouncements. In addition to issuing general guidelines, the Bureau actively worked to promote a viable labor system. It not only told blacks that they had to work hard and obey their "masters'" orders, but it also admonished them not to "give . . . impudence." Instead, the Bureau told blacks to maintain "a respectful and polite demeanor" toward whites. The Bureau promised that it would protect freedmen who followed this advice, but warned that those who failed to do so would "be punished."[9]

To enforce this policy, the Freedmen's Bureau initiated programs to encourage, if not force, blacks to work. At the close of the war the Bureau had established camps and had issued rations to destitute blacks as well as whites. Many whites had protested that these camps encouraged idleness among the freedmen, but generally blacks worked hard in these camps and the Bureau steadily reduced the number of freedmen on governmental assistance. By 1866 only a few camps remained, and the people still living there were, by and large, either the "old and infirm" or young orphans. Even this population worked hard enough in the camps to be independent of governmental aid.[10]Moreover, the Bureau made it clear that it would not support able-bodied freedmen who could find work outside the camps.[11]

Some officers who obviously believed that this order was inadequate cooperated with local white officials to force blacks to work. Several, with Colonel Whittlesey's approval, turned black vagrants over to local authorities who ordered them to work on public projects. Whittlesey also warned blacks that if they violated their contracts or were idle, they would be fined, imprisoned, or forced to work on the public roads or in the workhouses.[12]

The Freedmen's Bureau also informed blacks that they would not receive land from the government. During 1865 many freedmen believed that abandoned lands would be divided and distributed among them. Most white employers and Bureau agents felt this was the main reason former slaves were reluctant to sign labor contracts for 1866. Consequently the Bureau issued several proclamations explaining that there were to be no land grants.[13]

In conjunction with these pronouncements, the Freedmen's Bureau also returned abandoned land and other property to former rebels. General O. O. Howard reported in December 1865 that "nearly all the [North Carolina] farms transferred by treasury agents as 'abandoned' have been, under orders, restored to owners."[14] This policy was carried out despite the fact that it was often unfair to the freedmen. Major Wickersham reported that he had several cases where whites presented a legal title to land "occupied by Freedmen who claim to have purchased it but being slaves could have no title." Even in these cases the land was restored to the whites.[15]

It appears, then, that the policies of the Freedmen's Bureau favored white employers in their efforts to secure a reliable labor force. The Bureau, however, also engaged in work designed to help blacks. Throughout 1865 it furnished freedmen with transportation to available jobs. More important, it supervised most labor contracts written between the freedmen and their white employers to ensure that they were fair. But its most significant work was to investigate all cases of reported abuses by whites against the freedmen. Because of this close involvement in labor activities, Bureau agents became competent to judge how well the new labor system was working, and their conclusions differed significantly from those of many North Carolina whites.[16]

According to almost all Bureau agents,[17] blacks—even as early as 1865—were willing and eager to work. In his quarterly report of October 15, 1865, Colonel Whittlesey noted: "Contrary to the fears and predictions of many, the great mass of colored people have remained quietly at work upon the plantations of their former masters during the entire summer. The crowds seen about the towns in the early part of the season . . . returned to their homes, so that but few vagrants can be found." In fact, he claimed that there were more white vagrants than black, and concluded: "It is the almost uniform report of the officers of the bureau that freedmen are industrious." Whittlesey's report of December 1865 reiterated these opinions, although he did admit that some freedmen were reluctant to make contracts. But this, he said, was because they had heard rumors that they were to receive land. He predicted, correctly, that their attitude would change once they found that these stories were false. O. O. Howard, reporting on conditions in North Carolina as of November 1, 1866, noted that there were "very few complaints . . . made against the freedmen for refusing to work. . . . The freedmen . . . have been almost universally at work and supporting themselves."[18]

But even though most blacks willingly worked, they did not share equally in the benefits of the emerging economic system. White employers developed a number of devices, in addition to the restrictions of the Black Code, that were used either to intimidate blacks or to keep them subservient.

At first some masters avoided telling their former slaves that they were free. John Bectom, living on the King plantation near Fayetteville at the end of the war, noted that many masters, including his, told "the slaves to go to work that they were not free, that they still belonged to them." But, he continued, one by one they left anyway.[19]

Once this device became ineffective, many planters tried to avoid paying their laborers. "Thousands" of blacks, according to Colonel Whittlesey, went to their closest Bureau agent to file charges against their employers regarding wages. In Warren County alone, in a single month, 150 freedmen protested when their employers refused to pay them. Throughout August 1865 Rowan County agents handled an average of twenty-one cases a day, and they predicted that September would be worse. During December 1865 the assistant superintendent at Morganton handled 193 such cases. The agents in the Western District, from the surrender through December 1865, settled 2,087 cases of labor disputes. Freedmen from every part of the state filed countless similar complaints.[20]

Even the few agents who felt that whites were trying to treat blacks fairly qualified their statements. Clinton A. Cilley, superintendent of the Western District, concluded that while "perhaps, two thirds of the Whites are willing to do well by their former slaves [and that] at least three fourths . . . are willing to employ the Blacks," "not more than two thirds are willing to give them fair prices." He continued: "When I say two thirds of the Whites are willing to do well by the Blacks, I mean they are willing to do so, under the advice and authority of the Bureau. . . . There are not one hundred men that I know of in this District who would deal out what I call justice to the Blacks, unless for the Bureau. The feeling of mastership, and the conviction that Blacks have few rights that a white man is bound to respect, have not yet been eradicated from the minds of the planters." Like many other agents, Cilley concluded that if the Bureau were removed from the state "the Blacks would be no better off than before the war."[21]

While some agents believed that the situation was improving in 1866 and 1867 and that there was "a growing disposition on the part of the planters and people generally to deal fairly and justly with the Freedmen," most still argued that without the presence of the Bureau blacks would not be paid.[22] And while the number of cases of nonpayment did decline during 1866 and 1867, hundreds of blacks still filed complaints.[23]

Hundreds of whites also whipped or threatened blacks in other ways in order to force them to work or to behave "properly" or to deprive them of their property. As in the cases dealing with nonpayment, the freedmen themselves went to the Bureau officers to file charges about these abuses. Occasionally they did so in groups. A petition received by the superintendent of the Eastern District from twelve freedmen of Gates County recounted typical abuses. The blacks complained that "the white-man" used threats and acts of violence to compel them to work "at his price." They asserted, "We wish to work and take care of our selfs and familys and benefit the Contary all we can and live upright just and honorable but if this be the case how can we . . . [;] we hav . . . no protection and no privilege." A black man told a newspaper correspondent for the *Philadelphia Inquirer* that while the blacks did "well enough in town," they had "mighty hard times" in the country, where whites beat and abused them for the "least little thing." And because whites no longer had an economic stake in the black citizen's welfare, they would readily kill one if he misbehaved.[24]

Three Freedmen's Bureau agents, after returning from "an official visit to Fayetteville and vicinity," wrote that whites "exercise the authority of masters over these people and punish them at their will with such severity as to them seemed fit. It is even reported that negroes have been killed" by this cruelty. John R. Dennett, the northern reporter for the *Nation* on tour in the South, noted that during the first half of September 1865 the office of the assistant superintendent of the Freedmen's Bureau at Salisbury heard eleven similar complaints of abuse. Most freedmen charged that their employers had whipped them. One man claimed that he was told to leave the plantation on which he had worked or receive one hundred lashes. Another had been whipped seventy-two times, and still another was whipped so severely that his back was "all raw."[25]

General Thomas H. Ruger, commander of the Department of North Carolina, complained that in Sampson County "a portion of the Slaveholders" were abusing the freedmen in another way. Endeavoring "to repossess themselves of the negroes again," a "few" went to the county police to gain assistance in forcing their former slaves to return to their old plantations. The police hung freedmen by their thumbs until they promised to return. Ruger also claimed that the "county police contend that the negro has no right to hold anything as property and as such they are robbed of all they have by their former masters." Finally, he maintained that the practice of hunting blacks "down by dogs and carrying [them] back is more common now than it was when they were slaves."[26]

More mild-mannered whites tried to intimidate blacks with verbal threats. Many told blacks that they would import white laborers from the North or from Europe to replace the freedmen if they refused to work. The *New Berne Times*, for example, warned the freedman that if he "begins to neglect his work, or make demands for a higher price than is stipulated in his contract, . . . [his] employer [will] turn him adrift and put a white man in his place."[27] This call for white immigrants was not mere talk. Several North Carolina whites actively sought to promote immigration, although they were generally unsuccessful.[28] Still others believed that in order to save the South from economic and social disaster, blacks would have to be colonized if they could not be forced to work.[29]

But no action was ever taken to promote colonization, and blacks loudly opposed such rhetoric.[30]

The labor contract blacks were required to sign was probably the most effective means white employers used to ensure themselves a subservient labor force. Throughout Presidential Reconstruction most freedmen were engaged in agricultural production. They were paid either monthly wages or a portion of the crop. In both cases, contracts could be written with either the employer supplying equipment and food or the employee providing his own rations. While these contracts varied in particulars, there was a general pattern, and those supervised by the Freedmen's Bureau varied little from those written without its approval.

Examination of a few of these contracts provides a good overall view of how the new economic system worked. All contracts stipulated the wage or the employee's share of the crop. They also listed those supplies to be provided by the employer and those to be provided by the employee. The contract between J. J. Battle of Edgecombe County and four freedmen for the year 1866 is typical of those stipulating a monthly wage with rations. It noted that Battle would furnish his laborers "with comfortable quarters, and the amounts of money and rations per month, which stands opposite their respective names." In this case a male received $13 per month plus sixteen pounds of bacon and a bushel of meal. Females earned $7 a month, twelve pounds of bacon, and a bushel of meal.[31]

A typical contract for shares, approved by the Freedmen's Bureau, is that between P. P. Agostini of New Hanover County and two freedmen for the year 1867. In this case the freedmen supplied "all seeds, tools, horses and all things necessary for the proper cultivation thereof and subsist themselves." In return they received two-thirds of the crop plus all the vegetables they "raised for the use of their family." The employer provided material to build a house, along with fuel and a mule. In a contract between W. S. Meachum of Anson County and a freedman and his family for 1866, the employer provided "a horse or mule" to plow the land while the employee had "to furnish himself and family clothing and provisions." The laborer in turn received half of the crop.[32]

All contracts for wages and many for shares also clearly specified exact duties and working hours for the laborer. In this area as well as in other categories, however, the contracts for wages were almost without

exception more restrictive than those for shares. For example, the Freedmen's Bureau contract for wages stipulated that the freedmen would "do
all kinds of labor common to farms of the country, [and] . . . to work
ten hours per day." Wage contracts not approved by the Bureau were
even more specific. The contract between David Barlow of Edgecombe
County and eight freed people for the year 1866 provided that the laborers
would "perform creerfully [sic] any kind of plantation labor, that may
be required of them." They were "to begin and leave off work . . . by
some signal from the manager." From the first of May through the first
of August they worked from "before sun rise . . . until after sun sets,"
with two hours off "in the heat of the day to take dinner." They were
also allowed only every other Saturday afternoon off.[33]

Whites also inserted provisions to ensure that their laborers would
fulfill the entire year's contract. Of course, this was rarely a problem
with sharecroppers, whose payment would not come until the crop was
harvested. But a clause was devised for those working for wages that
was equally effective, if not more so, and certainly more restrictive and
demeaning. In almost all contracts, including those approved by the Freedmen's Bureau, the laborer received only half of his monthly wage per
month. The employer retained the balance until the end of the year.[34]

Employers also added several sections requiring their workers to be
obedient, hard-working, and orderly. Most contracts, both for wages
and shares, allowed the employer to discharge a laborer either with or
without giving him his back wages if the employer felt the freedman had
misbehaved, worked improperly, or in any other way violated his contract.
When such contractual provisions had been approved by the Freedmen's
Bureau, however, the employee could appeal to a Bureau agent if he
believed that he had been unfairly deprived of his wages. Most contracts
for wages also allowed employers to deduct from earnings time lost due
to sickness, idleness, or absence without leave. A few contracts for shares
also had similar provisions. The contract between Henry T. Clark and
five freedmen for the year 1866, for example, provided that "when ever
any [laborer] shall fail in his duty or lose his time he shall pay . . . at the
rate of 40 cents per day, which shall be assessed against his share of the
crop." The contract between W. S. Meachum and his laborers specified
that "if any crop, on account of . . . negligence, idleness or loss of time,
is injured," the employee would "make good the damaged [sic]."[35]

Several contracts also specified how the freedmen were to behave. Some merely noted that the laborers must "be respectful in their deportment." Others added a provision requiring employees not to fight or act in a "disorderly" manner. A few also prohibited freedmen from "assembling or gathering" on the farm without the employer's consent.[36] With all these stipulations, it is not surprising that some blacks were suspicious of the contracts, "supposing the article of agreement to be more binding on them than the employer."[37] Others, obviously with some justification, believed they were binding themselves "as slaves for the time being."[38]

Another problem the freedmen faced was the general inadequacy of wages. In 1865 the average monthly wage in North Carolina was about $9 for males and $6 for females, including board. The average share was from one-fourth to one-half of the crop. During 1866 and 1867 wages rose slightly, so that by the end of Presidential Reconstruction males earned about $11 a month with board. Females, however, still averaged only $6 per month. The average share remained the same.

There were some regional variations. Wages in western North Carolina were the lowest in the state, generally ranging from $8 to $10 a month for males and from $5 to $6 for females; shares were from one-fourth to one-third of the crop, depending on whether or not the freed people boarded themselves. In the Charlotte subdistrict, however, where there was a greater demand for labor, shares were as high as one-third of the crop with provisions or one-half without rations. Around Tarboro, "one of the best cotton raising regions of the State," and in Edgecombe County, in the central part of the state, wages were also higher because of the great demand. In 1866 and 1867 freedmen earned from $13 to $15 a month plus board in these areas. But in nearby Johnston County men earned only $8 and women only $4 per month plus board.[39]

Despite these variations, all wages were low. The northern journalist Sidney Andrews argued that these earnings were "utterly insufficient for anything more than bare support."[40] Apparently some freedmen not only agreed but tried to do something about it. In 1865 a group of blacks met in Washington, North Carolina, to object to their low salaries and to agree not to work for less than $1.50 per day. Another group from Rowan County met in August 1866 for the same purpose. They resolved "'that if any one of our race is known to work under fifty cents and board per day, within the county of Rowan, he will have to abide the consequences, or for less than a dollar a day and board himself.[']"[41]

Others protested their low pay in another way; they left North Carolina for other states where wages were higher. The Wilmington *Journal* reported that in 1866 thirty-two hundred North Carolina blacks left to work in Massachusetts, Connecticut, and other New England states for $20 a month.[42] More commonly, black laborers moved to other southern states. According to newspaper accounts, Freedmen's Bureau records, and other sources, "Negroes by 10 of thousands" had left North Carolina for wages as high as $300 a year plus traveling expenses in Georgia, Florida, Arkansas, Mississippi, and other states farther south and west. In fact, David F. Caldwell, a wealthy North Carolina planter and politician, wrote in January 1867 that the "flow southward" was "so great . . . that many of the *Negroes haters* [sic] among the proudest portion of our people are beginning to fear that we will have no *labouers* [sic] left."[43]

These reports are highly exaggerated. North Carolina's population increased from approximately 990,000 in 1860 to almost 1,110,000 in 1870 while the increases for Georgia, Florida, Arkansas, and Mississippi were less. Still, enough blacks must have left seeking better pay to prompt these accounts.

A minority of freedmen could sometimes earn higher wages by working in areas other than agriculture. In 1865 about one-third of North Carolina's black population worked in nonagricultural occupations. In fact, five times as many blacks as whites worked in these occupations.[44] Many worked on the rivers or docks. One black pilot, considered the best on the Cape Fear River, earned $15 a month, which was more than any other pilot earned, white or black. Turpentine hands averaged the very high salary of $16 a month plus board. Blacks in the fishing and lumber industries were earning from $1.25 to $3 per day. Mechanics in the Western District averaged $2 a day, while farm laborers received only 75¢, both boarding themselves. The Wilmington and Manchester Railroad advertised for 100 to 200 laborers "to rebuild and keep up the track." It was hiring both whites and blacks at $12 a month plus rations and a "shanty room furnished." Some blacks in western North Carolina earned from $2 to $3 a day working in the gold mines. But this was not steady work, and they could not expect to average such wages on a yearly basis.[45]

Most nonagricultural laborers, however, earned no more than farm hands. An eighteen-year-old girl, for example, worked as a nurse for only $5 per month plus board. Teenaged males in the Wilmington area were employed as either house servants or field hands for the same wage—$7 per month plus board. One group of black stevedores earned only $10 per month plus rations in 1865. In September they went on strike, demanding an increase of $5 a month. Another group of stevedores, earning 15¢ per hour "for stowing cotton," went on strike, demanding 25¢. The consignees refused these demands and hired whites instead. The *Wilmington Herald* argued that 15¢ was "a very good price" and maintained that the strikers were "poor" "crazy" "fellows" to think they could get "such fabulous prices as they ask . . . , while labor is so cheap and so much in the country unemployed."[46]

White employers argued predictably that blacks were earning a very good wage. In fact some felt that the freedmen should work for less. Major H. D. Norton, assistant superintendent for the subdistrict of Morganton, contended that "there seems to be a desire among the whites to keep down the price of labor." The Wilmington *Dispatch* argued that blacks should work merely for enough to buy "a sufficiency of food and clothing." The Agricultural Society of New Hanover County resolved not to pay "prime hands" more than $10 per month or one-third of the crop, with "the laborer furnishing his own rations and clothing."[47]

It should be noted that North Carolina's prewar wages for white farmhands were the lowest of any state in the Union. The average monthly wage for white farm workers in the state in 1860 was $10.37 with board.[48] This was about the same average wage paid to the freedmen after the war. Also, one piece of evidence indicates that white laborers were earning no more than blacks in the postbellum period.[49] After Reconstruction, in 1889, wages in North Carolina went even lower, with men earning $6 to $10 per month and women from $4 to $5 a month. In this case, however, the report of the North Carolina Bureau of Labor Statistics did show that black farmhands were earning less than whites.[50]

Whites and blacks also had different attitudes toward the method of payment. Most blacks preferred to work for shares. As one freedman explained to *The Nation*'s correspondent, John R. Dennett, he preferred to lease land because under the sharecropping system he felt more independent. As we have seen from an examination of the contracts, those written for shares were less restrictive than those for wages. Whites on the other hand preferred to pay blacks a monthly wage rather than to make contracts for a share of the crop. In fact, Dennett claimed that only a few landowners would lease land to blacks because most wanted to keep blacks "in such a condition that they could be hired as laborers at low wages." Indeed, he believed that whites "preferred to let a 'no-account white man' have a plantation rather than rent it to Negroes."[51]

Whites, however, claimed that they preferred wages because this was a more efficient system for both parties. A committee appointed by the Spring Garden and Rocky Point Farmers Club, for example, after investigating "the subject of labor," reported that "it is better for the employer and employed, that the negro should work on farms by the year at stipulated wages" rather than for shares. A meeting of the Agricultural Society of New Hanover County in November 1866 also announced that its members preferred the wage system to sharecropping. They explained explicitly that the wage system "produces system and good order on the farm, avoids all the usual causes of wrangling and dissatisfaction among the hands," and "it must be better for the laborer . . . to have . . . wages fixed and certain, and not dependent on the vicissitudes of the season as well as of price &c."[52] Of course, the society was right—from its own vantage point. But by denying the freedmen the risks involved in working for shares, whites also denied them the opportunity to make enough profit in boom years so they could save, buy their own land, and gain economic independence and security.

Many Freedmen's Bureau agents agreed with North Carolina whites. General O. O. Howard, reporting on North Carolina in 1865, claimed that "the freedmen work more faithfully for money than for a share of the crop."[53] Agents in the field opposed sharecropping for another reason. George S. Hawley, assistant superintendent at Murfreesboro, believed that the freedmen who worked for wages were "best prepared for the winter, having saved from their earnings, sufficient to support themselves and families." On the other hand, those who worked for shares had to spend "a large part of their produce in paying for provisions upon which to live during the season."[54] J. F. Conners, assistant superintendent for Johnston County, thought that the number of freedmen working for shares would be less in 1867 than in 1866 because of "the many failures on the part of the freedmen in croping [*sic*]" due to the "loss of team and lack of provisions to carry them through the farming season."[55] These losses reportedly were due in large part to thievery. Conners noted that "if the freedpeople could keep mules and stock they would get on well, but there is no security for them against thieves."[56]

In these examples the problem seems to be less the sharecropping system than the choice made by the freedmen to board themselves. John R. Edie, superintendent of the Western District, noted: "Great difficulty has arisen" among freedmen who boarded themselves. Indeed, he continued, "4/5 of the laborers have run out of provision and the owners of Lands are unable, or unwilling to sell, or otherwise furnish provision." Yet one Bureau officer reported that many freedmen who had worked for wages in 1866 were going to sharecrop in 1867, "seeing the good fortune which has rewarded a few of the most industrious and thrifty of those who have cultivated on shares."[57]

As we have seen, many blacks also distrusted written wage contracts and disliked hiring out for a year at a time. They were willing to have written yearly contracts for shares, because these contained few restrictions and provided the opportunity—or at least the hope—of eventual financial independence. When employed for wages, however, the freedmen preferred to work either by the day or the month. Whites, on the other hand, preferred written, yearly wage contracts to assure themselves a more stable labor force.[58]

The different attitudes held by these whites and blacks stemmed from two sources. First, as employers white landowners obviously wanted to bind blacks to their farms as tightly as they could and to pay them as little as possible. Their desire for cheap, reliable, subservient workers merely reflected their economic interests. Only reluctantly did they pay the freedmen just wages or rent blacks land where they could work more independently. Moreover, some denied blacks licenses to open stores "on the grounds of non residence" while whites received licenses under similar conditions.[59] Here again, whites wanted to maintain a dependent rural black population; they opposed giving blacks opportunities for independence in either rural or urban communities.

Probably of equal importance, many whites clung to the old patterns and attitudes developed under slavery. They believed that it was necessary to control the black population for the good of society. Situations where the blacks worked under restrictive wage contracts, often in gangs with overseers, were as close to slavery as whites could manage. In the special situation of the South, these two factors—economic and socio-racial—were organically and inseparably connected. The desire to keep wages low and contracts restrictive and binding was buttressed by the desire for social control and white supremacy.

Blacks, on the other hand, wanted to be independent. Many resisted any labor system that reminded them of slavery. The freedmen had been shown by the example of their white masters that land ownership and economic independence were keys to respect and manhood, and they looked for the means to gain this respect. This is most clearly evident in the desire of many freedmen to buy their own land. Captain Horace James, superintendent of the Eastern District, asserted that for blacks "the ownership of real estate is their strongest incentive to industry." General Sickles reported in 1866 that the freedmen were "anxious to acquire land for themselves."[60] In the same year, the cashier of the Freedmen's Trust and Savings Company concluded that any black man who had money was "buying . . . land."[61]

Some blacks attempted to translate these dreams into reality by pooling their resources. In May 1865 one group rented a large rice plantation near New Berne so they could work on their own. The white owners might not have rented this land to them, providing them with the opportunity to gain economic independence, if they had thought the blacks could succeed. But as Whitelaw Reid, a northern correspondent touring the South, maintained, they were certain that the freedmen would fail. Instead, however, these blacks did "exceedingly well."[62] In August another group of freedmen from Lenoir County formed a joint stock company to raise $10,000 by January 1, 1868, to purchase "homesteads" for themselves. The money was to be acquired by assessing the 250 members of the company $48 per year, to be paid in $4 monthly installments.[63] They also held weekly business meetings "in which they discuss the best ways of promoting their mutual prosperity." They also established a store, "on a joint-stock basis," that was prospering.[64]

White landowners generally opposed these and other attempts by blacks to gain economic independence. In addition to poor pay, restrictive contracts, and a reluctance to lease land, some whites also used fraud as a means to keep wages low and blacks dependent. In April 1866 a white southern minister in the Goldsboro area reported that the Bureau agent there was in league with at least two and possibly three "rebel" farmers to cheat the freedmen. He cited one detailed case to illustrate his charge. One white man, he claimed, had employed twenty or thirty freedmen and women at $2 to $10 per month for the year. At the end of the first month, he told his laborers he had no money with which to pay them. Instead, he gave "them an order on a Store to get Such goods as they want, and one of these working hands got an order to get a pair of Shoes for himself and wife, . . . and he had to pay $7 for the two pairs."[65] The account books of A. H. Arrington show that he provided his laborers with calico, shoes, and food as well as luxuries such as brandy and snuff and then deducted the cost of these provisions from their wages. When he settled accounts at the end of 1866, he owed nine of his laborers, for an entire year's work, sums ranging from $1.22 to $43.52, with the average being $16.92. Five of his laborers owed him money, ranging from $2.55 to $64.88, with the average being $30.15.[66]

The experience of freedwoman Dilly Yellady's family was equally frustrating. After the war her family moved to Halifax County and began to work for shares. Despite years of hard work, moving annually from one plantation to another, they "made no money. The landlords got all we made except what we ate and wore. They would always tell us we ate ours up."[67]

These cases indicate that some whites were developing a new device to keep their black employees poor and economically dependent. In January 1867 the *Standard* confirmed that some farmers were beginning the "evil practice" of keeping "little stores or supplies of whiskey, calicoes, . . . and the like, with which they tempt ignorant colored people, and in which they pay them a part of their wages." It advised the freedmen to "avoid these little, one-horse whiskey shops . . . [and] to trade . . . where they get the best bargains." It explained to the freedmen that they did not have to buy their supplies from their employers and that "they should be on their guard, lest at the end of the year they find themselves in debt for things which have been little or no benefit to them."[68]

The clearest attempt on the part of some whites to establish a labor system as close to slavery as possible was the abuse of the apprenticeship system. Before the war North Carolinians had used apprenticeship "as a means of controlling free black children." Almost immediately after the war many planters adopted this same strategy to gain not only cheap labor but also to control the freed children and, on occasion, their parents as well.[69]

Before the North Carolina General Assembly passed an apprenticeship law in March 1866, the Freedmen's Bureau tried to set up certain guidelines for apprenticing black children. In July 1865 Colonel Whittlesey wrote one of his assistant superintendents that minors who "have no parents to provide for them" should be bound out "when good homes can be found." But he also suggested that the children "should have some voice in the selection of their guardians." Whittlesey ordered another assistant to bind out children with parents only "with the consent of their parents." Those without parents could be bound out only "with the consent of an officer of this Bureau." In November, however, he amended these guidelines when he told the superintendent of the Western District that he could "bind out children without the mother's consent, if she is clearly unable to support them." But above all, until the legislature acted, Whittlesey insisted that the Freedmen's Bureau supervise apprentices.[70]

Yet Whittlesey favored binding out young blacks because he felt that they could benefit from a just apprenticeship system: "By means of the apprenticeship system, comfortable homes have been provided for a large number of orphans and other destitute children." He admitted, however, that he was also "very suspicious of it," because of the danger that it would foster "the old ideas of compulsory labor and dependence. Still, with proper safeguards," he believed it could be "useful as a temporary expedient."[71]

Whittlesey's ambivalent opinions on apprenticeship led to confusion among the agents in the field, who themselves held differing opinions about blacks and the appropriateness of apprenticeships. This confusion led to "inconsistent, subjective, ad hoc decisions." Bureau officials disagreed over whether parental rights should always have precedence over those of a white planter who might be able to better support and educate black children. They also held differing opinions on whether apprenticeship contracts, once made, should be upheld under all circumstances because of the sanctity of contracts.[72]

The inconsistent signals from Bureau officials made it easier for many white North Carolinians to ignore the "safeguards" Whittlesey had ordered his agents to impose. Most county courts began to apprentice black children in 1865. In February 1866 several freedmen from Gates County, in a petition to the Bureau, claimed that whites had taken their children and had hired "them out to who they cuse [sic]." The Duplin County Bureau agent maintained that whites there "frequently" had black children apprenticed to them, claiming that they were orphans, "whereupon we find both parents are living and will take better care of the children than the new masters." In March the superintendent of the Southern District reported that in Sampson County the "county Court has been engaged in apprenticing children to their former masters . . . without respect to the wish of the parents or condition of children." In fact, the county police were even seizing children from the adjoining counties and bringing them to Sampson to be apprenticed, despite the fact that many of these minors were already employed at good wages. The superintendent believed that this was being done in part to overcome the scarcity of labor in that county.[73]

In March 1866 the General Assembly enacted, as one section of the Black Code, regulations on apprenticeship. Black children were to be bound out in the same manner as whites and were to be treated in the same manner as white apprentices. Three discriminatory provisions, however, were inserted. In binding out black children, former masters were given preference. Further, the county courts had the power to bind out black children "when the parents with whom such children may live do not habitually employ their time in some honest, industrious occupation." There was no such provision for white children. Moreover, black girls were bound out until the age of twenty-one, whereas white girls were apprenticed only until they were eighteen.[74]

The Freedmen's Bureau objected to this law. In May Colonel Whittlesey ordered his agents, "in all matters pertaining to the Apprenticeship of 'Freed-Children,'" to be "guided by the State Laws in force, in respect to the apprenticeing [sic] of *white* children." And in October General Robinson, the new assistant commissioner, told Governor Worth that his agents had been ordered not to allow the courts "to make any discrimination between Whites and Blacks, in the apprenticing of children." In addition, "no child, whose parents are able and willing to support it can be bound without the consent of the parents. Children over fourteen years of age will not be bound out as apprentices under any circumstances." In response to this pressure, Worth asked the General Assembly in November 1866 to remove the law's discriminatory clauses, which it did.[75]

Throughout Presidential Reconstruction, and especially in 1866, however, countless abuses of the apprenticeship system continued. The superintendent of the Southern District, Allan Rutherford, reported in September 1866 that several county courts in his district were "taking Colored Children away from their parents and binding them as apprentices to their former Masters." Two days later he again wrote of this practice, adding that girls eighteen years of age and older and boys, sixteen and seventeen, "who were earning good wages," had been apprenticed against their parents' wishes: "In some cases [the children] have been confined in the County Jail until such time as they could be removed to the plantations of their masters." He believed that "the whole proceedings have been conducted as if they were still Slaves, and unless a stop can be put to it, Slavery will be re-established to all intents; they having the labor of all the young Freed-people, without the expence of providing for the old and infirm."[76] Daniel L. Russell had several black children, some as old as eighteen, apprenticed to him in a similar fashion, kidnapping them from their parents and keeping them in jail until they were bound out to him. General Robinson felt that this action looked "like a reestablishment of slavery under the mild name of apprenticeship."[77] The superintendent of the Western District reported twelve similar cases during the last half of 1866. There were also several such cases in the Central and Eastern Districts.[78]

The minutes of the county courts throughout North Carolina show clearly that these examples were not isolated cases. Thousands of black children were apprenticed during 1865 and 1866. Guion Johnson in *Antebellum North Carolina* selected five counties, typical of various sections of the state, and listed the number of children apprenticed in the years 1801–05, 1831–35, and 1851–55.[79] The figures in table 5 summarize Johnson's findings. Table 6 shows the situation in these same counties for the year 1866. In four of the five counties apprenticeships increased to varying degrees. But most noteworthy is the fact that the greatest increase in apprenticeships occurred in Edgecombe County where

Table 5. Antebellum North Carolina apprentices

County[a]	1801–5	1831–35	1851–55	One-year average
Carteret	59	28	29	7.7
Pasquotank	39	101	67	13.8
Edgecombe	69	53	25	9.8
Cumberland	61	92	106	17.3
Orange	83	79	66	15.2
Total	311	353	293	63.8

[a]Average for the five counties for one year in the periods 1801–5, 1831–35, and 1851–55: 62, 71, and 59, respectively.

labor was scarce and wages high. In Cumberland, on the other hand, labor was plentiful and wages low, and there the number of apprenticeships decreased.[80]

In addition to the increase in the number of apprenticeships in Johnson's selected counties, even greater abuses occurred in a few counties that Johnson did not study. In Jones County, for example, the court apprenticed seventy-six black children in 1866. But the most shocking situation existed in Sampson County, where, during the November 1865 term, the court apprenticed 218 black children. In the February 1866 term it bound out an additional 261. Two-thirds of these minors were found to be illegally bound, according to the standards issued by General Robinson in October 1866. Also it is important to note that during the May, August, and November 1866 terms, after the Freedmen's Bureau ordered most of these apprenticeships cancelled and started supervising apprenticeships carefully, the court bound out only sixteen children.[81]

Several other significant facts are apparent from the county court records. First, in the twelve counties where fairly complete records are available, sixty-two of the 777 apprenticed black children were sixteen years of age or older. Four were mothers who were bound out with their children. Sampson County again was the worst offender; of the 453 children apprenticed in two terms of its court, forty-five were over sixteen years old. Further, the vast majority of those apprenticed were bound out not to learn a trade but to "learn farming," a skill in which many were already quite competent due to their slave experience. Finally, most were bound to their former masters. In her analysis of apprenticeship

Table 6. Apprentices in North Carolina in 1866

County	Number of apprentices	Comparisons with antebellum figures
Carteret[a]	10	Increase
Pasquotank[b]	22	Increase
Edgecombe[c]	57	Very great increase
Cumberland	7	Decrease
Orange[c]	16	Slight increase or about the same
Total	112	Increase

[a]Court records are clearly incomplete as the court canceled two apprenticeships in 1867 that were not previously listed.
[b]All are labeled "negro."
[c]Most are designated "negro," a few are designated "white," and the remainder have no racial designation.

records Rebecca Scott also found that most those apprenticed were old enough to work. She too concludes that "labor rather than a public welfare function was primary in child indenture."[82]

Many blacks, either in groups or individually, actively protested these abuses. The delegates at the 1866 freedmen's convention passed a resolution bitterly complaining about the "ruthless" apprenticeship system.[83] In February 1866 twelve blacks from Gates County petitioned the Freedmen's Bureau to stop whites from taking their children. In April freedmen from Hertford, Bertie, and Gates counties sent a similar petition to the Bureau.[84] Many black parents also complained individually to Bureau officers that their children had been bound out without their consent.[85] After investigating these cases, the Bureau canceled many of these indentures.[86]

Finally, in January 1867 the North Carolina Supreme Court heard a case involving two black girls, Harriet and Eliza Ambrose, who had been apprenticed to Daniel L. Russell without their parents' consent. The parents had filed suit with the aid of the Freedmen's Bureau. The court, in voiding the apprenticeship contracts, delivered a strong censure against those who would violate due process of law: "The Constitution and the laws of the country guarantee the principle, that no freeman shall be divested of a right by the judgment of a court, unless he shall have been made party to the proceedings in which it shall be obtained." Blacks were now free. Therefore, in the name of justice, they could not be deprived of their rights "of property or person, without the privilege of being heard." Thus no child, black or white, could be bound out until due notice had been given and then only with the "consent of the parent or next of kin, and when the child is present in Court." All apprenticeship contracts made contrary to these principles were pronounced null and void.

One might wonder, given the general attitude of most North Carolina whites toward the freedmen as described throughout this book, why the state's highest court overturned the Robeson County Court and strongly defended black rights. First, the men who composed the Supreme Court— Chief Justice Richmond Pearson, William H. Battle, and Edwin G. Reade— were among the state's most distinguished members of the bar and all had a profound respect for the law. Battle, for example, although a Democrat during Reconstruction, opposed the Ku Klux Klan's illegal activities. In other ways, too, these justices were not typical of the state's white population. While all three had been unionist Whigs before the war, only Battle became an active Democrat during Reconstruction; Reade became a Republican while Pearson, technically neutral, supported Grant's presidential candidacy in 1868.

More important, it should be noted that the court merely defended the principle of due process. One would expect that the leading jurists in the state would have that much respect for the law. Even North Carolina's Black Code guaranteed blacks minimal legal rights, and many whites did have a sense of fair play and opposed the more extreme abuses of freedmen's rights that this case reflects. Even so, however, the court carefully avoided criticizing Russell, the planter to whom the Ambrose girls had been apprenticed, or the Robeson County judge who had granted the apprenticeship contracts. It should be remembered that Russell had kidnapped several black children and kept them in jail until the county court bound them out to him. Still, the Supreme Court described the case in highly diplomatic language: "The humane and intelligent judge, who heard the cause, would never have remanded the petitioners to the custody of the defendant, if he had supposed that he had the right to look behind the order of binding, not so much perhaps for any fault in the defendant as because there was no propriety in taking them from the society and services of their parents and friends to bind them to any person."

After this ruling many other black parents went to court to get their children's apprenticeship decrees reversed. Freedmen's Bureau officers also brought illegal apprenticeship notices to the courts' attention for cancellation, and endeavored to make sure "that no new indentures were executed except in conformity with the laws."[87]

While serving as apprentices many black children were abused by their "masters." Governor Holden appeared to encourage this behavior when he argued publicly that black children who were apprenticed should be whipped "as a wholesome stimulant . . . if they are not working as they should."[88] Many masters agreed. One Brunswick County freedwoman, for example, complained that her child had been treated "with great cruelty," "tied up to a tree by his thumbs—having been first stripped—and . . . then beaten with sticks for a long time." Allan Rutherford, the superintendent of the Southern District to whom this complaint was made, ordered the justice of the peace in Brunswick County to investigate. Another example of abuse emerged when one member of the General Assembly charged that near Tarboro two black girls had been apprenticed to their former master, a man whose wife had previously ordered their mother to be whipped to death. He claimed that the girls were now neglected, "nearly starved and not half clad; the only garment they wore, while picking cotton in the inclement weather of December, was a straight gown, short in the skirt, and with short sleeves, with neither shoes, stockings, nor bonnets."[89] These white North Carolinians apparently had not yet adjusted to the fact that blacks, including apprentices, were human beings.

While black laborers were poorly paid and sometimes abused, most still worked hard. Consequently by 1866 North Carolina's economy was doing surprisingly well, especially considering the economic dislocation caused by the war and the social revolution wrought by the Emancipation Proclamation and the Thirteenth Amendment. Statements on agricultural production show generally good harvests. By 1866 favorable reports flowed in from most parts of the state. As early as April the Raleigh *Sentinel* told its readers that the "prospects" for the cotton crop "in regard to the labor of the freedmen, is flattering." It observed that "a larger crop . . . than usual" was seeded. In August it noted that "judging from the quantity seeded and from the general condition of the crop," the cotton crop would be "larger and of a better quality than in 1860, unless the picking season should be too wet." The *Carolina Watchman* of

Salisbury noted that the newly harvested wheat crop was "nearly an average yield," oats were "uncommonly heavy," corn "exceedingly fine," and vegetables "most abundant."[90] Specific accounts from many counties throughout the state echoed these optimistic reports, claiming that more acres of corn, cotton, tobacco, and other agricultural products had been planted than ever before. Business was also booming on the Cape Fear River where the Wilmington *Dispatch* reported that things were "again flush." In fact, it claimed that "business on the river has increased to such an extent . . . that several lines are unable to meet the demands upon them for transportation, and are building new boats to enable them to meet the requirements of the public."[91]

In many of these reports the good prospects were in part credited to the hard and steady labor of the freedmen. These comments by the Wilmington *Journal* are typical: "As a general rule, . . . the freedmen . . . are working with much industry."[92]

In some areas of North Carolina, however, harvests were not good. But this was due to bad weather rather than to the lack of a reliable labor force. The Raleigh *Sentinel* reported that the corn crop would probably be only a third of its normal size because in many parts of the state "the crop has been literally burned up by the drought and heat." This was especially true in the Piedmont region. Throughout most of this area and as far west as Wilkes, Burke, Henderson, and Transylvania counties, the cotton, corn, and wheat crops were "almost a total failure." Also, in Onslow County there were poor prospects due to a drought. But in the southeast, in parts of Sampson, Robeson, Cumberland, and Duplin counties, the problem was just the opposite; here heavy rains and severe hail storms ruined most of the cotton and corn crops.[93]

Because of poor weather conditions, both whites and blacks in some areas experienced grave hardships. Many complained of a lack of bread. State representative L. S. Gash reported that 209 families in Henderson County alone were "destitute of the means of subsistence," without bread or meat. Conditions in Transylvania County were not much better. In Union County, at least a hundred destitute families were without bread, and at least fifty were "in a state of immediate, absolute want." One hundred thirty-five citizens of Stanly County, in a petition to the General Assembly requesting aid for the destitute, explained that widespread poverty existed despite the fact that "they [had] labored industriously and economised as well they could," because of "the unprecedently severe drought." They explained further that the poor could not be cared for by the wealthy as "in times past" because "now the wealthy have become poor."[94]

But even in these areas many whites admitted that it was the weather, not the freedmen, that caused this suffering and deprivation. Letters from the affected regions reported that most blacks were working "quite as well as we expected, and are generally peaceable and quiet."[95] The Freedmen's Bureau officer stationed in Morganton noted that some whites there did complain that the crop was small because the freedmen were "negligent and lazy," but he argued that "the drought . . . is the *real* cause."[96]

While bad weather conditions exacerbated hardships in some parts of North Carolina, there were poor people throughout the state. A detailed study of poverty was done from December 1866 to February 1867 after Colonel James V. Bomford, then head of the Freedmen's Bureau in North Carolina, offered to distribute rations to the destitute. The General Assembly, in accepting this aid, ordered Governor Worth to write the chairmen of the warden courts in each county "in order to ascertain the extent of the destitution." Worth asked each chairman to supply him with the "number of destitute in their respective counties." After receiving their responses, Bomford estimated that the state had 3,550 poverty-stricken whites and 1,995 destitute blacks. Most were widows with children or the old and infirm.[97]

These figures, however, underrepresent the total number of those in need of aid. Several counties did not submit full reports because they did not need total federal assistance; they claimed that they were able to provide for most, if not all, of their poor. The chairman of the Halifax County Court of Wardens, for example, informed Worth that there was "a commendable disposition on the part of the Blacks to support their own poor," despite the drought and the resulting "short crop." This, he claimed, was due to their "good management and strict economy." The chairman of the Alleghany County wardens reported only paupers, all white, whom his county was able to support due to its "abundant" crops. The chairman of the Lincoln County wardens listed only those who were truly "destitute"; he omitted "a greater number who are really not destitute [but] still . . . are in a situation that requires relief." Beaufort County reported only those who were not already receiving aid from the county. The chairmen of Granville, Guilford, Union, and Rowan wardens courts did not include those who were in their poorhouses.[98]

Strikingly, though, almost twice as many indigent whites as blacks were reported in this survey. There are several possible reasons for this. First, one might assume that the Freedmen's Bureau was already taking care of poor blacks. This, however, was not the case. The Bureau had gradually diminished rations to both refugees and freedmen after January 1, 1866, when all persons who were able to work were refused aid.[99] After October 1, 1866, General Howard forbade the issuance of any rations.[100] One could also explain the difference in the number of needy whites and blacks by simply pointing out that there were twice as many whites as blacks residing in North Carolina. However, before the Freedmen's Bureau discontinued the issuance of rations, more than ten thousand blacks received this aid.[101] This would seem to indicate that there were probably more needy blacks than the chairmen of the wardens courts reported.

The chairmen of the wardens courts most probably listed more white than black indigents either because these courts did not concern themselves with the freed people's plight or because they felt blacks could tolerate more poverty without aid than could whites. Two sets of facts support these suppositions. First, in many cases, the wardens of the poor clearly refused to care for indigent blacks.[102] In fact, one black man from Columbus County complained that freedmen were taxed while their poor were still excluded from the poorhouse.[103] Hertford County blacks were also taxed "without receiving aid from the County Wardens for their poor and helpless."[104] Some counties did provide some aid to indigent freedmen, although in every case where figures are available they cared for fewer poor blacks than whites.[105]

Other facts indicate that there were more needy blacks than the survey showed. F. A. Fiske, superintendent for education of the Freedmen in North Carolina, reported in October 1866 that there would be "considerable suffering among the Freedmen . . . owing to insufficient crops and the failure of many of the Freedmen to obtain for their labor remunerations enough for the support of their families."[106] More significant, the Freedmen's Bureau's records listing rations issued during 1867, after the chairmen's survey was made and after the issuance of rations was resumed, show that blacks were supplied with more rations than were whites, although the differences between the two groups was not great. This could be due to the fact that the county wardens of the poor were caring for white indigents but not for blacks. Thus probably more blacks than whites in North Carolina during Presidential Reconstruction were poor enough to need outside aid, although the difference between the groups was small. But most surprising is that the number of those needing aid remained low, probably no more than 10,000 in a population of 1,000,000.[107]

Despite poverty among some elements of the population, it appears that the labor system—at least from the point of view of white landowners who were making profits from a successful crop throughout much of the state—was working well. Where crops were poor, the weather was to blame. In those areas where there were poor, most were cared for, especially if they were white. Most important, North Carolina succeeded in creating a labor system that would survive well into the twentieth century, a system that bound blacks to the land through poverty, restrictive contracts, debt, and violence. Some whites spoke out for black rights; the North Carolina Supreme Court struck down one of the worst abuses. Still, most white employers worked to create a system that would further their own economic interests.

Blacks fought this new system that they saw as reminiscent of slavery. But while most worked hard, their wages were so low that they were forced to live on a level of bare subsistence. Few were able to accumulate enough money to buy their own land and thereby gain some economic independence. While many blacks protested these inequities, most whites refused to listen. As was the case with legal and political rights, the two races had different interests and different goals. But it was the white employer who was in control, so it was his views that generally prevailed. The same fundamental clash of attitudes and interests can be seen in the areas of law, order, and justice.

6 Crime, Violence, and Justice: A Quest for Law and Order

The negroes persist in living a life of dissipation, idleness and vagrancy, depending upon robbing and stealing for a living.—"C" of Lenoir County in Raleigh *Sentinel*, March 22, 1866, p. 3

I fear the chance for *Buffaloes* and *Negroes* to get Justice done them by . . . our [Currituck] *County Court* will be but slim.—Affidavit from Samuel Dowdy in a letter from S. H. Birdsall to the Assistant Commissioner, August 7, 1866, Letters Received by the Assistant Commissioner, Freedmen's Bureau Papers

ALL SOCIETIES OBVIOUSLY strive to maintain order through a system of laws. North Carolina was no exception. But as with politics and labor, blacks and whites often had different perceptions of the criminal justice system and how it should operate. Influenced by their antebellum experiences, their racial biases, and their economic positions, both groups tended to have different fears and different goals.

The major fear which initially pervaded the white community was of black rebellion. In antebellum days whites continually feared slave rebellions, and this apprehension did not end with emancipation. In fact, especially during the early months after the Civil War, many were obsessed with the idea that a black rebellion would occur. As early as July 1865 Governor Holden received a request from the most "prominent and influential men" of Hertford County, asking for the right to form an armed militia "as a measure of protection against domestic violence and internal disorder." They explained that "the sudden emancipation . . . of men ignorant, credulous and prejudiced . . . may justly arouse apprehensions for the future safety of an unarmed people from whose control they are now released." Moreover, they "feared that under the teachings of wicked men, plans of insurrectionary violence and insubordination may be suggested, which can only be repressed by the presence of a sufficient military force ready for instant action when the emergency demands." While they assured the governor that such a force would "only [be] used to preserve the public peace and restrain social disorder," one must wonder what these terms meant when such prominent men placed fears of "insurrectionary violence" and "insubordination" on the same level.[1] Such a force might have served to quiet the fears of whites, but one can also imagine how the fears of blacks would have been intensified.

During the following months Governor Holden received similar requests from officials in Hyde County and in Wilmington.[2] In December the state Senate Committee on Military Affairs asked General Ruger for permission to form an armed militia "to more effectualy [sic] suppress any insurrectionary movement on the part of Free Negroes should they attempt it." Ruger refused because of "the general quiet conduct of the freedmen (to guard against the acts of whom, I understand to be the chief reason for such arming)." Consequently whites continued to be apprehensive about the possibility of a black insurrection.[3]

Many believed that such a rebellion would occur around Christmas, once the freedmen discovered that they were not going to receive free land. The editor of the *New Berne Times* was only one of many whites who claimed that there was "a partially, or fully organized plot of rascality on foot among the recently freed negroes." He based this conclusion on "reports" and "inklings" he had heard after blacks had been told that the property of their former owners was not to be divided among them, as well as on the "natural tendency of the negro's mind when he sees his hopes disappointed."[4] Despite the fact that several Freedmen's Bureau agents investigated these reports and rumors and found them all to be without substance,[5] and despite the fact that no rebellion occurred that Christmas, white apprehension continued.

Throughout 1866 many still claimed that blacks were arming or drilling, or otherwise plotting violence against whites. These rumors generally were accompanied by calls to disarm blacks and to arm whites.[6] In many cases blacks actually were disarmed. The mayor of Wilmington, for example, disarmed one freedman and fined him "for laughing in the street." The Freedmen's Bureau ordered the mayor to return the gun. In

June 1866 the mayor of Goldsboro embarked on a program of disarming all blacks in that city. The same was true in New Berne, Winton, and in several counties along the Virginia border.[7]

While fear of insurrection was the most extreme form of the paranoia that enveloped much of the white population, their apprehensions surfaced in other areas as well. Plagued with the notion that blacks were "criminal" types, many whites felt that the freedmen were more inclined to live by thievery than by honest work. The Charlotte *Western Democrat*, for example, claimed: "We never had the least idea that many negroes would work if they could get a living in any other way." It maintained that blacks were engaged in stealing, for "their idea is to live in idleness and eat and sleep." Because of this widespread assumption numerous whites, in the press as well as in private correspondence, accused the freedmen of committing most of the thefts that occurred in the state.[8] Some also argued that blacks stole not only because of their alleged innate laziness and criminality but because they were influenced by a "radical breed of dogs who teach ignorant blacks that negroes ought to have and are entitled to the same rights and privileges, in both Church and State, as the whites." Many not only attacked northerners living in the South generally, but singled out Freedmen's Bureau agents for encouraging black thievery.[9]

Several North Carolina whites suggested various methods to reduce alleged black thievery and associated crimes. Some felt that the reinstitution of a civilian militia and the removal of the Federal army would help.[10] The Raleigh *Standard* and the Charlotte *Western Democrat* suggested that blacks convicted of theft should be hung or shot.[11] Others believed that stringent laws would be sufficient.

But just as the fear of insurrection was ill-founded, the belief in the basic criminality of blacks is not substantiated by the facts. It is true that a good deal of crime was committed by both blacks and whites in North Carolina after the Civil War, ranging from petty larceny and thievery to murder, arson, and rape. But this is not surprising. Social disorder occurs after any war, and the Civil War was especially devastating with emancipation adding to normal postwar dislocation. Racial antipathies, economic competition, and black poverty also stimulated crime.

It is impossible to discover exactly how high the crime rate was in North Carolina and who was responsible for the crimes that did occur.

Most reports are at best incomplete; many are impressionistic, based on rumor and exaggerated by prejudice. Federal, state, and local records nevertheless provide some clues. The report of Thomas H. Ruger, adjutant general of the Department of North Carolina, is the only statewide summary that consistently gives racial designations. Ruger listed "outrages by blacks against whites" and by "whites against blacks" in North Carolina from June through December 1865. In his catalog of crimes committed by whites against blacks, he reported the following: fifty-six cases of assault and battery; seven assaults with a deadly weapon; twenty-nine larcenies; thirteen murders; two kidnappings of black children; and three attempts to commit rape. The number of crimes by blacks against whites were listed as twenty-six assault and batteries, forty-five larcenies, one murder, seven arsons, one attempt to commit rape, and five rapes.[12]

While the report was "complete of all cases brought before a Military Commission, and may be regarded as accurate, so far as high crimes are concerned," Ruger warned that his figures were low. He noted that "it has been impossible to procure material for [a] thoroughly accurate report of minor outrages, owing principally to the fact that no complete record has been kept by the agents of the Freedmen's Bureau." He maintained that "cases of simple assault, and of more or less of [sic] cruelty by the Whites towards Blacks" remained unrecorded. Ruger also wrote that the report's figures on cases of larceny committed by blacks were probably low.[13] Still, it appears from these statistics that blacks were more likely to steal while whites were committing more serious crimes, involving physical assault on blacks. Even before Congressional Reconstruction and the prevalence of Ku Klux Klan activities to intimidate and control blacks, it appears that some whites engaged in violent activities while many blacks, perhaps feeling that their former owners owed them something, stole.

The report of the assistant commissioner of the Freedmen's Bureau in North Carolina on outrages committed in July 1866 again shows this tendency. In that month only one freedman was listed as having assaulted a white person. At least forty-nine whites, however, reportedly assaulted, whipped, shot, or falsely imprisoned blacks. And the number of "outrages . . . by whites against colored persons," including "assault and battery, rape, church-burning, arson, and murder," were said to be increasing daily.[14]

The reports from Freedmen's Bureau agents in the field, upon which these statewide summaries are based, show that in every area of the state the same pattern prevailed: white crimes against the freedmen exceeded the number of crimes blacks committed against whites. In addition, whites committed most of the crimes of physical abuse, while the freedmen generally were responsible for petty larceny and robbery.[15]

For the pattern of crimes after 1865 one must turn to the records of the state courts. Several problems, however, exist in analyzing these sources: only those cases that came to trial are listed—the actual crime rate was certainly much higher; there is evidence, to be discussed later in this chapter, that some authorities arrested blacks more readily than whites, causing an inherent racial bias in the statistics; the records, like those of the Freedmen's Bureau, are incomplete; and the race of a criminal was not always designated. Sometimes from other evidence, such as newspaper accounts or reports from Bureau officers, the race of the accused can be determined. Also, while the race of the defendant was not always given in the court minutes it would sometimes be listed in the docket, or vice versa. By cross-checking all the sources, the race of most of the accused was determined. Elsewhere it was assumed that those not designated as blacks were whites, for the purpose of the following computations. While there is probably some error because of this assumption—certainly some who were counted as white were black—the number of possible errors is so small that it does not seriously affect the general pattern described here.

For the years 1865 through 1867, fourteen counties had complete county court records. These show that 502 whites and 136 blacks were convicted of misdemeanors and felonies. Only seven superior courts have complete records; these show that for the same two-year period 248 whites and sixty-eight blacks were convicted of various crimes. This means that less than one percent of the white population (based on the 1860 census) and less than one-half of one percent of the black population in these counties were brought to trial for crimes during Presidential Reconstruction.

Another set of court records confirms this finding. Fifty-eight superior courts clerks submitted full compilations of trials in their counties from 1865 through August 1867. These reports were submitted in response to a request by Governor Worth for the following: (1) the number of felony convictions in the county for the past two years; (2) the number actually punished; and (3) the punishment inflicted. These documents, too, have their limitations. Most reports did not list the race of the accused, so only the total numbers can be used. Moreover, many clerks reported trials for both county and superior courts; others did not specify whether their figures were only for the superior court or for both courts. Nevertheless, the records indicate the level of court activity. Of the fifty-eight counties answering the questionnaire, five had no felony trials. For the remaining counties there were 1,124 convicted felons, of whom 635 were punished, most for larceny.[16] Guion Johnson's *Ante-bellum North Carolina* provides statistics for comparison. For the five-year period 1811–15, with thirty-six superior courts and twenty-eight county courts reporting, 779 felons were convicted. In 1839, in thirty-nine superior and county courts, 682 felons were convicted.[17] Considering the increase in population by 1865, one might conclude from the preceding information that the crime rate in North Carolina dropped in the postbellum period. The clerk of the superior court for Pasquotank County certainly believed that this was the case there, for he claimed that "there has been less crime in this county in the past two years than there has been for many years previous."[18]

But one needs to be cautious about these data. As will be demonstrated later, many of the state's criminals were never caught and brought to trial; this is especially true of those crimes where blacks were the victims. And despite the statistics presented, most segments of North Carolina's population believed that the state's crime rate was high. Only eleven North Carolina newspapers during the two-year period of Presidential Reconstruction commented on the peaceful conditions in the state, and when they did so, they expressed surprise. Because whites feared that emancipation would bring crime, violence, and perhaps insurrection, they saw quiet conditions as news. An article in the Salisbury *Union Banner* was typical of such reports. In November 1866 it observed that "our city was never more quiet and peaceable. There is a total absence of the many serious violations of law and order." It also wrote that for Rowan County as a whole there had been "no capital offense committed" since the surrender. Admittedly surprised, the *Banner* conceded that "when the negro population was turned loose upon the community, heedless and unadvised with respect to the duties required of them under the law, it was natural that we should feel much apprehension for the security of life and property, and the quiet of the community; but, fortunately, this portion of our population have behaved remarkably well, . . . and it is our boast now that there has not been a rape, murder or arson committed in the county, during all the clash of authority and demoralization subsequent to the surrender of the Confederate forces."[19]

These reports of peace and quiet were the exception, though, as the vast majority of sources available argued that the reverse was true. Writers bemoaned the prevalance of almost every sort of crime: horse stealing, burglary, highway robbery, riots, rape, arson, and murder. Thievery was the most common complaint. Stories of robbery and associated crimes abound in North Carolina's newspapers, including those that occasionally commented on how peaceful conditions were. Individual North Carolinians and Freedmen's Bureau agents made similar comments, and many others decried the total collapse of law and order. G. F. Granger's letter to Thaddeus Stevens in January 1866 was typical of these reports. He wrote: "Thieving—Highway robbery—Riots—Affrays . . . are indulged in as pastimes [sic]. . . . Rape . . . Arson—& all sorts of frauds are more than common— . . . Plunder prowls abroad over the land—Murder stalks abroad at noonday."[20]

While many such reports either blamed whites and blacks equally for the high crime rate or did not accuse either race, the press was frequently quicker to report those crimes committed by blacks. Throughout Presidential Reconstruction newspapers were filled with articles about blacks allegedly committing thefts and burglaries.[21] But contrary to white fears, the press was able to find only a handful of incidents where blacks physically attacked whites. These stories charged blacks with four cases of attempted rape, five cases of rape, two cases of murder, and several cases of assault.[22]

Obviously, there were criminals—both black and white. And even if the crime rate during Presidential Reconstruction was somewhat lower than during the antebellum period, as the records analyzed previously might indicate, the lawlessness that did exist was sufficient to generate continuing fears and to create hardships and resentments. Theft was probably the most serious problem. Blacks frequently stole, especially from whites. But in numerous cases blacks were the victims of white thievery. The Freedmen's Bureau records as well as North Carolina's newspapers cite hundreds of such cases. In 1866 in the subdistrict of

Goldsboro, for example, the Bureau agent there wrote that "the frequency of thefts and violence committed against the freedmen . . . [by whites] since civil government was restored, is becoming truly frightful." In fact, he claimed that "many of the freedmen complain that they have less protection now in their persons and property, than they had before they were set free." Many of the robberies were thefts of horses and other farm animals. Typically, blacks were beaten during these robberies.[23]

Blacks were often helpless to do anything about these crimes. Many were afraid to report the robberies or search for their stolen property for fear that they would be killed.[24] Besides, reporting the robberies often did no good. Captain George Glavis argued that "whenever an offense is committed against a freedman, the offender is sure to escape unpunished; to my knowledge not one has been convicted." To support this claim Glavis noted that during a short period of time there had been fourteen cases of white crimes against blacks in his area, including murder, rape, and theft, but "not one [person] had been arrested or even molested."[25] In Duplin County the civil authorities had failed to arrest the "bands of white ex Rebels" who were roaming around, "clubbing and ill treating colored men and run[ning] off their stocks." The Duplin County police captain bluntly told one black man "'that none of his men would go [catch mule thieves], that they . . . were under no obligation to hunt property for niggers.'"[26]

In a few cases the Freedmen's Bureau even charged the police with robberies and beatings. Wiliam Beadle, superintendent of the Southern District, asserted that the Duplin County police were "armed enemies . . . , particularly against the rights and property of the Freed people." Colonel Whittlesey wrote that the police of Johnston and Sampson as well as Duplin counties "are not only inefficient, but are often engaged in robbing freed men and others who sympathize with them." Allan Rutherford claimed that several members of the Wilmington police assaulted an eighty-five-year-old black man and stole his property. When the men were finally brought to trial, the justice of the peace dismissed the case, arguing that the policemen "could not be sufficiently identified" since the only witness was the black victim.[27]

In addition to individual thieves or small groups of robbers, North Carolinians—especially blacks—had to face several bands of organized gangs. The largest of these groups were labeled "Regulators."[28] They operated primarily in the southeastern part of the state during 1866 and 1867, and according to many reports generally preyed upon blacks. Allan Rutherford, superintendent of the Southern District, wrote, for example, that these bands roamed his area with impunity, "stealing horses mules and stock from the Freedmen . . . , and making threats against their lives if they complained." "Burgaw," a native white writing in the Wilmington *Journal*, reported that "Regulators," operating "with impunity," were "committing all manner of depredations upon the freedmen, stealing their mules, money, &c., and exciting terror wherever they go. . . . It is believed that their field of operations extends from Newbern to Wilmington, and will increase, and that some of the lowest scum of society in all these counties are joining the band."

The civil authorities found themselves incapable of capturing these Regulators. Their task was complicated by the fact that the band members often either blacked their faces or were unknown to their black victims. Moreover, whites were "either in collusion with them, or purchase[d] their security by a quiet acquiescence." Rutherford argued that because of this immunity, "their organization and number has greatly increased so that in some sections citizens fear to speak of the matter to their neighbors or friends, not knowing but that they may belong to them."[29]

Many Freedmen's Bureau agents believed that whites who robbed blacks, and authorities who ignored these crimes, did so chiefly because they were determined "to prevent niggers from owning stock or land" and because they believed "that a Freedman should not be allowed to own property." One native white agreed that many of his fellow citizens contended that "the negro has no right to hold anything as property." Thus, he continued, blacks "are robbed of all they have by their former masters, even to turpentine that they have made. . . . The negroe's [sic] crops where they have rented land and made farms . . . is claimed and now being used by sons of their old masters."[30]

While the difficulty of retaining their property, their crops, and their farm animals created a great economic hardship for blacks, a bigger problem was their fear of physical attacks by whites. The Freedmen's Bureau papers as well as other sources are filled with hundreds of accounts of violence committed against blacks, including assault and battery, assault with deadly weapon, and murder.

Whites attacked blacks for a variety of reasons. Generally, these assaults occurred when whites felt blacks were not acting properly. Dennett, quoting a Freedmen's Bureau officer, maintained: "'It's the first notion with a great many of these people, if a Negro says anything or does anything that they don't like, to take a gun and put a bullet into him.'" The provost marshall and Freedmen's Bureau officer in Greensboro agreed that "cases of assault [against blacks] . . . are very numerous, and almost always without sufficient cause." He concluded that while some white North Carolinians "appeared honestly anxious to treat their Negroes kindly," most did not. Thus he feared "that the withdrawal of the Federal troops would be the signal for a reign of violence and oppression."[31]

Other records support these charges and beliefs. A Freedmen's Bureau agent reported that one black man was badly beaten by a crowd for going to the agent after the crowd had verbally abused him and after one of them had "struck him a violent blow." Several whites wrote that many blacks "were beaten severely" in a near riot in Concord "for no better reason . . . than that they were 'too sassy and stubborn.'" Edwin Fuller, a prominent planter, recorded that a group of students and villagers in Chapel Hill attacked blacks for holding a political meeting. Another influential white politician lamented that several other whites in Chapel Hill "maltreated an old black man . . . for trying to exhibit some magic lantern pictures which were of an abolition tone in some instances." This is just a sampling of hundreds of such reports.[32]

Many blacks were also murdered for similarly insignificant reasons. One white citizen of Montgomery County, for example, killed his black employee for using "offensive language" and for singing "lewd songs." Several citizens, including the Montgomery County sheriff, petitioned Governor Worth to pardon the white man who was spending six months in jail for his crime. Their rationale well illustrates the general white attitude that physical abuse was justified as a means of social control. These citizens argued that the white man's release "would . . . exercise a wholesome influence on both races." If the court's sentence were allowed to stand, they argued, it "will have the effect of making the whole negro population believe that they can offer any indignities they are inclined to towards the white race and that any assault made by the whites for a redress of wrongs will be severely punished in our Courts and their own insolence protected as well as justified." At least Governor Worth did not agree with these contentions; he refused the request for a pardon.[33]

Murders, however, continued. The *New Berne Times* wrote of a black soldier killed in Morehead City for taking "rather more liberty than an Anglo-Saxon . . . likes to submit to." The local Caswell County Bureau agent reported that a freedman there was shot by his former overseer after reporting to the owner of the land on which he was working that the overseer had stolen part of his crop. An army officer in Concord claimed that several white men killed several blacks and wounded others because the freedmen had assembled to hear a Bureau officer "speak on topics touching their welfare." A correspondent for the Philadelphia *Inquirer* contended that the Duplin County police, along with some leading citizens, murdered four blacks in order "to create a panic among the negros [sic] and then drive them from the county" without "their share of the crop."[34]

It is impossible to verify all, or even most of these hundreds of reported incidents of physical abuse, for most such cases never got to court. Freedmen's Bureau agents and army officers throughout the state complained that when whites assaulted or murdered blacks, even when the assailant had been identified, the civil authorities did little; the criminals either remained free or were finally tried by the Freedmen's Bureau or by a military court. General Ruger, for example, wrote in August 1865 that while there were "several cases of Homicide of freedmen by whites . . . , in no case . . . was any arrest made by the magistrates or civil officers, and no attempt had for investigation."[35] Similar reports, citing many specific instances, continued to flow in from military authorities and Bureau officers throughout 1866 and 1867. Hugo Hillebrandt, assistant superintendent in Kinston, thus concluded that blacks had no redress to the civil courts, which only encouraged whites to commit more outrages against them.[36]

Not surprisingly, then, many blacks felt that white officials offered them no protection. Speaking in Wilmington in May 1866, three freedmen expressed this attitude well. These blacks were chosen by those attending a mass meeting to represent black opinion to Generals Steedman and Fullerton, whom President Johnson had sent to the South to investigate the Freedmen's Bureau. The first speaker, Elias Halsey, maintained that blacks had "no protection at all, and . . . [were] exposed to danger night and day." He claimed that it did not matter how a man conducted himself, for "if he is a colored man, he is exposed to danger." At this point, "cries from all parts of the house" cheered in agreement. The Freedmen's Bureau, Halsey said, was the black man's only hope. "Remove this refuge, and you will see that we have lost our protection. We might just as well be in the open field, and the hail beating down as big as hen's eggs on our heads."

William McLauren argued that even in the city, "if a colored man should happen to touch a white man in passing on the street he would be called a 'damned troublesome nigger.' The children of whites are taught to insult the colored people and call them 'niggers.'" No matter how blacks behaved, he said, they were "all liable to insult. (Cries of 'That's so.')" And if blacks replied to these insults, they were "imprisoned and have twenty dollars to pay for release, or be in jail till the white man be willing to let us out." Thus, McLauren argued, if the Freedmen's Bureau left, "a colored man would have better sense than to speak a word in behalf of the colored man's rights, for fear of his life." G. P. Rourk concluded that if the Bureau were removed blacks would be "at the mercy of those who hate" them.

McLauren also predicted that if the Bureau were abolished, "in less than two weeks you will have to allay a riot in Wilmington." He explained that "there is such prejudice in the hearts of the white citizens that they would pick a fuss for no reason at all. The white man would abuse the black man, and the black man would say something against it, and there would soon be a general riot."[37]

Even with the presence of the Freedmen's Bureau, tensions between the races sometimes provoked what North Carolina newspapers labeled "a riot" or "a row." Twelve such incidents were reported during the period under study. Some were only sketchily outlined. The *New Berne Times* wrote of "a row at Kinston" in December 1865, which, it admitted, was just a rumor. The story it had received was that whites had "mobbed the negro school house" and that in retaliation blacks had "attacked the down train" for Kinston. No other details were given.[38] In either Greensboro or Goldsboro, "a row" started after a white barber refused to shave a black soldier. The soldier "became very abusive and cursed" the barber, whereupon the barber beat the soldier. The soldier drew his pistol. At that point "a number of men . . . interfered and this resulted in some shooting and a grand chase after the negro."[39]

Several newspapers gave a detailed report of an election day "riot" in Concord, which many blamed on the drunkenness of both blacks and whites. The Salisbury *Union Banner* argued that the blacks, "undoubtedly under the influence of liquor," were "very insultin—using such words as these—We came here to vote—we will be d—d if we don't vote. We are free; the bottom rail will soon be on top, &c." The *Banner* admitted, however, that the "whites were neither entirely sober nor faultless." Two "intoxicated" whites started the incident when one of them waved a pistol "in a menacing manner." They then "got into some difficulty with the negroes," the gun accidentally discharged, a crowed gathered, and "the riot began." It ended with the "whites running the negroes out of town." Several people, white and black, were injured.[40]

Two northern observers told a slighty different story. Dennett contended that the only cause of the riot was that the blacks were "too sassy and stubborn." Andrews believed that the attack on the blacks was "wholly unprovoked." Furthermore, not only were the county militia ineffective, he said, "but some of its members actually joined in the brutal assault upon the blacks." Federal troops stationed in the area, after investigating, arrested six or seven white men.[41]

In February 1867 an incident in Wilson resulted in the death of one white man, who was shot by another white by mistake, and the wounding of one black. As the *Wilson Carolinian* reported it, the "disturbance" grew out of a confrontation at the railroad station between a Mr. Pate and "a drunken negro who was indulging in boisterous and obscene language in the hearing of some ladies." A group of whites went to the station to arrest the black man but were met there by some armed blacks. The blacks fired first; the whites returned the fire, wounding one black man. The blacks then dispersed, with the whites in pursuit. Pate was shot by one of his own men in the melee. Several blacks were arrested and "any danger of a serious outbreak was promptly checked."[42]

A very different version of this incident, based on second-hand information, appeared in the Wilmington *Dispatch*, which illustrates clearly how rumors got started, fed by white fears of black conspiracies. The *Dispatch* correctly reported that Pate was mistakenly shot by one of his own men and that one black man had been wounded. But there the similarity in the stories ended. The *Dispatch* claimed that the incident started in front of Pate's home when Pate asked a black man, who was using "obscene language" that the women in Pate's house could hear, to move. The black man left, but returned that evening with thirty armed friends "to punish Mr. Pate." A group of whites discovered the plan and came to Pate's rescue, whereupon "the negroes formed in regular line of battle, and fired upon the citizens, who returned their fire and finally repulsed them." The *Dispatch* asserted that this was all part of an "organized" plot: "Their original plan was to burn the warehouse of the Wilmington and Weldon Railroad, and to burn other houses at the other end of the town, and while the citizens repaired to these fires, to break into the stores and houses in the center of the town, and commit robbery and other depredations." This plot was supposedly revealed to whites by a black man working for the railroad and thus the "original purpose" was defeated. The *Dispatch* also claimed that the man who reported "the conspirators" was shot by them "for having betrayed them."[43]

Perhaps it was because of this kind of mentality that several incidents occurred in Wilmington between whites and blacks, or perhaps William McLauren, the freedman who spoke at a mass meeting about the hatred of white Wilmingtonians for blacks, was correct. In any case, five racial disturbances took place in Wilmington from 1865 to early 1866. Some were minor, but in an apprehensive environment each incident was probably seen by whites as an antecedent to the black rebellion they expected. Blacks most likely saw each incident as a further example of white efforts to intimidate, control, and reenslave them. Press coverage of the events only served to heighten the tensions.

The first reported conflict occurred in July 1865 when allegedly, "a saucy negro soldier accosted a market man from the country . . . with a demand in the name of the Provost Marshall to pull off the grey jacket and brass buttons the marketman was wearing." Supposedly a white officer, hearing the marketman claim that he was unaware that his dress violated the law, took the black soldier "by the coat, gave him a continual kicking until he reached the opposite street and then drove him to his regiment." There the incident ended. But it was enough to provoke the *Wilmington Herald* to state that this was just one of many "frequent . . . collisions between the blacks and white" and to remind blacks that "their emancipation from slavery has not made the whites their slaves. . . . Indeed . . . the whites still are the priviledged class. . . . If the blacks . . . presume too far and demand too much, they will surely accomplish their own destruction."[44]

In August a "row" between the city police and a black soldier occurred, allegedly instigated by the black man who was described as "greatly under the influence of liquor." One policeman and the black soldier were wounded. The military forces arrested them both, but released the white man after investigating the incident. About two weeks later there was another "disturbance between the police and colored troops," but no one was injured. Again, it was reportedly started by a drunken black soldier. Two more similar incidents occurred in December. During a fire in March 1866 "a row" broke out "between several negroes of a colored Fire Company and several white men . . . , in which one negro was severely bruised on the head." The city officials restored order; no arrests were reported.[45]

Most of these disturbances resulted from blacks asserting their independence, either by insisting on their minimal civil rights or by resisting white abuse. The whites involved in these "rows" obviously resented this new black assertiveness. It should be remembered that before the war North Carolina law upheld the right of whites to defend themselves physically against black "insolence." As the North Carolina Supreme Court ruled in the 1850 case of State v. Jowers, "insolent language" either from a slave or from a free black was equivalent "to a blow by a white man." Therefore white retaliation was deemed to be justified.[46]

Racial antagonisms such as these, stemming in large part from antebellum experiences along with economic conflicts, led to the violence and crime North Carolinians witnessed during Reconstruction. The inability of either the military or civil officials to deal effectively with this crime only led to further violence. Whites resented the presence of the military and the Freedmen's Bureau while blacks had little regard for civil officers. Thus neither exhibited much confidence in the criminal justice system as a whole. Blacks looked to the military for help, but it provided only sporadic security. Whites, on the other hand, sought aid from civil law enforcement agents and the civil courts.

There were several levels of civil courts in North Carolina during Presidential Reconstruction. In the towns and cities, mayor's courts tried misdemeanors ranging from drunkenness, disorderly conduct, and disturbing the peace to vagrancy and petty theft. On the county level, justices of the peace had the power "to restrain evil-doers, rioters, and disturbers of the peace." Their jurisdiction, however, was limited to cases where the penalty was less than $100. Above them were the county courts, where three or more justices of the peace tried a wide variety of cases, including most civil cases, criminal cases where penalties were over $100, and all cases of petty larceny, assault and battery, breaches of the peace, "and all other crimes and misdemeanors," where, upon conviction, the penalty did not "extend to life, limb, or member." County courts also served as the governing bodies of the counties. The superior courts, composed of eight judges who rode the circuit, had jurisdiction over "all pleas of the State and criminal matters," either by original jurisdiction or on appeal from the county courts.[47] The state Supreme Court stood at the apex of the structure.

In addition to these civil courts, military commissions tried civilians until July 1866. They heard cases involving both blacks and whites, the bulk of which concerned labor disputes. But they claimed jurisdiction over all cases where blacks could not testify in civil courts or where the penalties for blacks and whites, as provided by state law, differed. Despite these jurisdictional claims, however, the military and the Freedmen's Bureau were too understaffed to deal with most criminal cases. The records of the Bureau and those of North Carolina's courts show clearly that blacks were generally tried in civil courts after 1865. The military's role was mainly to keep a watchful eye on the courts' proceedings to prevent cases of obvious abuse.[48]

Nevertheless Governors Holden and Worth and most other native whites objected to this official arrangement, claiming that it was not only unconstitutional but also subversive to peace and good order. Worth argued that "confusion, idleness, vice, crime and jealousy, and irritation between the two races, are consequences of the existing order of things."[49] Not until July 1866, however, after the state convention amended North Carolina's laws so that no discrimination against blacks existed legally, did the Freedmen's Bureau officially turn over all cases, except claims for wages where the Bureau had witnessed the contracts, to the civil courts.[50] General Robinson, assistant commissioner of the Bureau at the time, then reported that there was "a fair administration of justice on the part of the civil courts, and [that he] believed that after sufficient time had elapsed for an adjustment of the new relations subsisting between the two races, mutual confidence would be restored."[51]

Other Bureau agents shared Robinson's optimistic outlook. In Sep-

tember 1866 John R. Edie, superintendent of the Western District, observed that "there are at present but few complaints of injustice towards
Freedmen by the Whites." He maintained that the civil courts were dis-
posing of those cases recently turned over to them by Robinson's order
"with impartiality." In the same month Stephen Moore, superintendent
of the Eastern District, also reported that cases tried in his area "have
generally favorably [sic] to the negro." H. H. Foster, assistant superintendent of Duplin, Onslow, and Sampson counties, after attending "all the
courts," noted that there "seemed to be an earnest idea of the Court and
the Bar that the Freedmen should have all the protection of the Law."
Lieutenant Hawley, who visted the Bertie County court in May 1866,
argued that blacks were "ably defended."[52]

Of course, most North Carolina whites also claimed that blacks
received equitable decisions in the state's courts. They often cited cases
of blacks being acquitted and whites being convicted of abusing blacks,[53]
and Governor Worth seemed to be working to maintain this image of
impartiality. He denied, for example, a petition from several leading
white citizens of Craven County, including three state legislators and the
county sheriff, requesting pardons for six "young men" who had been
imprisoned for assaulting a black man. The petitioners maintained that
the whites were "of the most respectable characters, and that the colored
man greatly provoked the neighborhood by his thefts and abuses." They
argued that the imprisonment of the white youths, who had severely
whipped the black man, "has had a pernicious effect" on the community.
Worth, in explaining his denial of the request for clemency, argued that
the whites should not have taken the law into their own hands.[54]

Blacks, on the other hand, often felt they could not get equal justice
in North Carolina's courts. At their conventions and in their meetings
blacks complained loudly about injustice in the courts.[55] Others protested
individually. For example, one black woman bitterly resented the fact
that her white employer, who hit her twice over the neck with a broom-
stick, was only fined a penny and costs by the Alamance court. The court
accepted the man's explanation that he was justified because the woman
had contradicted something he had said to her.[56]

Others agreed that many blacks faced discrimination in court. Allan
Rutherford, superintendent of the Southern District, believed that white
men were acquitted of assaulting freedmen because the courts were still

following the doctrine established in *State v. Jowers*, which proclaimed, as Rutherford saw it, "that . . . insolence from a negro is equivalent to a blow from a white man" and that any white man is the judge of "what are 'insolent' words."[57] Lieutenant George Hawley contended that while the judge and lawyers "manifested a willingness to mete out impartial justice to the negroes, magistrates and jurors, and petty officers of the court, are still to a great extent, governed by their old prejudices against the black man, in administering justice in cases where they are concerned." He argued that "fair minded men, on other subjects, often express a wish to have a negro whipped on the mere suspicion of larceny, and without the formality of a trial." Even Superior Court Judge Edward J. Warren on circuit duty in Elizabeth City, admitted that "an obstinate jury . . . refused to convict a man for killing a negro" even though he had given the jury "explicit instructions to do it." The *Western Democrat* observed other similar cases and concluded that "a jury is not the safest tribunal before which" a black man could go. "It would be much better for *him* if he could be tried before a few sensisble and experienced Justices who would not be influenced by the past."[58]

Thus opinion in North Carolina was divided as to how fairly the courts treated blacks. Black citizens, many Bureau agents, and some native whites believed the courts were biased; most North Carolina whites argued, along with some Bureau agents, that they were impartial. An examination of the court records is not definitive either. First, because the records rarely indicate anything but the general category of crime, it is impossible to ascertain the seriousness of a crime within that category. There is also no way to determine whether the accused received a fair trial and was convicted on sound evidence or whether he was frivolously arrested and convicted on hearsay or other flimsy evidence. Consequently, while obvious cases of discrimination appear in North Carolina's court records as well as in other documents, general trends are difficult to determine. But computing the average penalty for a general category of crime and identifying categories where an unusually large number of blacks relative to their proportion of the population were tried and convicted demonstrate that in some counties blacks apparently did not face gross discrimination; elsewhere, abuses were widespread.

Only scattered records are available from the mayor's courts. In Salisbury the docket of only one session exists. In this case at least there was no apparent discrimination, as the two whites and one black convicted of being drunk and disorderly were each fined $5 plus costs.[59] The proceedings of New Berne's mayor's court from July through October 1865 exhibit no overt pattern of discrimination, with one possible exception. During these months, when the cases were reported daily, thirty-three whites and forty-six blacks were tried on a wide variety of charges including being drunk and disorderly, gambling, assault and battery, theft, and vagrancy. The penalties were generally the same for both races. Two blacks and one white, for example, were convicted of vagrancy. One of the blacks was sentenced to two days of labor on the streets, the other to seven days of labor. The white man was given fourteen days of labor. After a raid on a house of prostitution, eleven people were convicted—the two proprietors, three prostitutes, and six "frequenters," two of whom were black. There was no discrimination in the sentences; all the frequenters were merely "reprimanded, and discharged," the proprietors fined $50 each, and the prostitutes fined $10 each. There was also no mention of the interracial mixing at the establishment, an act that would certainly seem to violate southern social barriers. The only possible case of discrimination the records show was when two blacks were "bound over to keep the peace in the sum of $200" after using "threatening language toward citizens."[60]

The court record for Wilmington reveals the same general trend. Between September 1865 and January 1866 very few cases came before the court. In fact, on September 18, 1865, the *Wilmington Herald* commented that the record of the past week had been so "dull" that the number of cases on the criminal docket "would hardly justify its [the court's] continuance were it not a necessity."[61] Of those cases heard, whites and blacks alike were tried and convicted of being drunk and disorderly and fined similar amounts. A policeman was given a thirty-day suspension for being drunk and shooting at a black man. In May the Wilmington *Dispatch* reported a fight between a white and a black. It maintained that the white man was drunk, falling "easy prey to the brutality of the negro, who, after knocking him down, . . . kicked him about the head and face." Yet each man was fined $10 in the mayor's court.[62]

On the other hand, the records indicate at least some racial bias in Wilmington's administration of justice. On November 1, 1865, six blacks brought thirty-five barrels of resin to town. Because they were not able to give "a satisfactory account of its title," the city confiscated the resin until the blacks could prove it was theirs, since, as the *Wilmington Herald* argued, "There is a strong belief that it has been stolen." The court discharged the blacks because there was no evidence of theft. Still, they were obviously penalized by the confiscation of the resin, and the dictum of innocent until proven guilty was ignored in their case. A second example occurred when a black man was confined to jail for one day, "charged with giving insolence" to a white woman. He was released only because the woman failed to appear to support the charge. On another occasion the mayor's court fined a freedman $10 after he had spent a night in jail, because he objected to three policemen searching him in such a way that "he took them to be robbers." The mayor's court fined another black man $25 and sentenced him to five days in jail for "getting on a 'bender' and playing the braggadocio towards the police."[63] Generally, the fine for drunk and disorderly conduct was $10 with no imprisonment. While one cannot be certain, it appears that in these latter three cases blacks were punished for being "uppity" to whites.

Other data suggest another kind of discrimination in Wilmington. During January 1866 nine blacks and only one white (in a town that was about half black and half white) were convicted of petty thievery. Since the press did not report penalties, no conclusions can be drawn about the fairness of the sentences. It is possible that there was an increase in crime among blacks during the hard winter months. But a suspicion lingers that blacks were more readily accused of theft than whites. This suspicion is reinforced by a report from Allan Rutherford, superintendent of the Southern District stationed in Wilmington, attacking a statement by the mayor, A. H. Van Bokkelen, in which he maintained that blacks were always given the right to introduce testimony, and that he judged all cases "fairly and impartially after hearing *all* testimony." Rutherford disagreed, being "well-convinced" that in all cases "where colored men are concerned, the fact of their being colored men, is so strong against them that it requires a great amount of evidence to overcome the presumption of their guilt."[64]

While there are no available records of the Charlotte mayor's court, the assistant superintendent there, A. W. Shaffer, cited one specific occurrence and concluded that that trial, "like the trial of other colored persons on complaint of whites, was an unmitigated farce, he [the black defendant] having been given no time or opportunity for defense." Shaffer accused the city officials, "from the Mayor down," of being "the worse kind of men to promote peace and good feeling between the two races. The police force particularly are perhaps the most injudicious selection . . . being in the main ignorant, bigoted, and irresponsible."[65] It appears then that while blacks stood a fair chance of receiving equitable treatment in some mayor's courts, the cases of discrimination were numerous enough to indicate that blacks could not be certain that this would always be the case.

As with the records of the mayor's courts, those of the county and superior courts are also difficult to analyze. The minute docket, which is the major available source, lists only the name of the accused, the class of crime with which he was charged, and the sentence imposed. The docket does not show the magnitude of the crime, and while it identifies most black defendants by race, other evidence shows that it did not always do so. In some counties there was no racial designation for any defendant. In other counties, where blacks were usually labeled as such, it is impossible to be certain that the absence of racial designation means that the defendant is white. Cross-checking several sources, however, usually confirms the race of most of the accused, and elsewhere it was assumed, for the following analysis, that those not labeled black were white. While this probably creates some error, the number so mislabeled is probably so small that the error does not seriously affect the conclusions.

Given these cautionary provisos, one does find that in many cases there was no apparent discrimination. In most areas the number of blacks tried for crimes was in proportion to their percentage of the total population. Furthermore, many blacks were found innocent, regardless of the seriousness of the crime. In the Edgecombe County Court, for example, seven blacks and eleven whites were tried for larceny. One of the blacks and three of the whites were found innocent. Of the five blacks and twenty-one whites tried for assault and battery, two whites and two blacks were found not guilty. In the Rowan County Court, of the two blacks tried for assault with intent to commit rape, one was adjudged not guilty and the other was only found guilty of assault and fined $10 plus one month in jail. In the Mecklenburg County Superior Court, of the two blacks tried for murder one was found innocent; the other was hanged. The one black tried for arson in the Rowan County Superior Court was found not guilty. In the Wake County Superior Court two blacks and three whites were charged with murder. All were acquitted of that charge, although one of the blacks was convicted of man-slaughter and the other, along with one of the white men, of felonious slaying.[66]

In many counties the penalties for whites and blacks convicted of similar crimes appear to have been the same. In Wake County, for example, the county court required both blacks and whites to work on the public roads "under the same rules." In the superior court a white and a black man were convicted of felonious slaying. The white was fined $1,000 and sentenced to twelve months' imprisonment. The black was given only a $25 fine plus a year's imprisonment. The Mecklenburg County Superior Court permitted two freedmen charged with burglary, the sentence for which could be as severe as hanging, to plead guilty to larceny, for which they received thirty-nine lashes each. The court gave whites similar punishments for simple larceny such as stealing mules, cotton, or a watch. The Charlotte *Western Democrat* argued that such proceedings clearly demonstrated the "merciful feelings for the freedmen exhibited by the North Carolina courts and juries."[67]

There were, however, many cases of clear discrimination in the courts of North Carolina. In fact, enough such cases occurred that in November 1866 O. O. Howard noted that the Freedmen's Bureau officers in the state had been required for many months "to attend the sessions of the county courts . . . to protect the interests of freedmen."[68] These cases of discrimination took many forms. First, it appears that in several counties blacks were arrested and convicted more readily than whites. This suspicion first arises from the imbalance in the numbers of blacks and whites convicted. The Cabarrus courts, for example, convicted twenty-three blacks and only eight whites while the population of the country was approximately eight thousand whites to four thousand blacks.[69] In Jones County, with a population about equally divided between whites and blacks, fifteen blacks and three whites were convicted in the superior court.[70] The records show similar disproportions in the courts of Forsyth, Lincoln, Montgomery, Person, Rowan, and Sampson counties.[71]

Moreover, whites received favored treatment in many courts, partially because blacks were often not allowed to testify. In March 1866 Colonel Whittlesey wrote to O. O. Howard that while the state legislature had repealed "all previous acts upon the subject of negro testimony" so that no legal distinction on account of race persisted, judges still practiced discrimination. He therefore concluded that a black man had "very little chance of getting his due before the Civil Courts of N.C."[72]

This view is supported by several specific cases. In May 1866 Richard Dillon, a Bureau officer, after observing the proceedings of the Carteret County Superior Court, reported that there was "systematic exclusion of negro testimony." In December 1866 Lieutenant Hawley contended that in his district of Hertford and Craven counties "no case has been tried before a civil court, in which a freedman has recovered damages, or received redress, when opposed to a white man." He added that in cases where freedmen had been assaulted "the evidence of colored men is either not sought, even when very essential, or if presented, fails to be considered sufficient cause for indictment." He also charged the courts with refusing or neglecting to call black witnesses, "though their names, and statement of circumstances have been particularly brought to the notice of the Solicitor or Clerk." In other cases grand juries refused to issue indictments against whites even when the testimony of white men confirmed charges made by blacks. Similar situations occurred in the courts of Guilford, Cumberland, and New Hanover counties.[73]

This type of discrimination also existed in civil cases. C. W. Dodge, Bureau agent at Plymouth, charged that magistrates exhibited no desire "to give justice to the freedmen, especially, in the matter of wages, judgment being given almost invariably in favor of the white man."[74]

Blacks also faced different types of penalties, especially corporal punishment and binding out for court costs. The Freedmen's Bureau later stepped in to halt both these discriminatory practices. As to corporal punishment, until 1866 the penal code allowed for whipping or standing in the pillory as well as fines and imprisonment for felonies, including larceny.[75] Many courts throughout the state ordered both whites and blacks to receive corporal punishments.[76] Many North Carolinians vigorously defended this practice. The Raleigh *Standard*, noting that both whites and blacks were whipped, maintained that "when a person, black or white, is guilty of stealing, he deserves to be whipped." It argued further that since the state had no penitentiary or houses of correction and no money with which to build them, criminals had either to be whipped or set free. The Charlotte *Western Democrat* felt that whipping was an effective way to reduce "stealing and deviltry." The Raleigh

Sentinel also supported the practice. The *New Berne Times*, however, argued that these punishments were "barbarous."[77]

But this debate had been going on since the antebellum period.[78] What concerns us here is the difference between the treatment of blacks and whites. Despite the many counties where both whites and blacks were whipped, in several others there was discrimination. At least in Catawba, Cumberland, Jones, Edgecombe, Columbus, Nash, and Rutherford counties, blacks were whipped while whites were merely fined. This was probably the case in many more counties where records are incomplete. For example, Captain C. W. Miles, assistant superintendent in Rockingham County, complained that there were "some very severe cases of whipping" in his area. Colonel Whittlesey also maintained that this practice was quite widespread. While admitting that "the law makes no distinction on account of color," he argued that throughout the state, "in the practical application, colored men are publicly whipped, and white men discharged on the payment of a small fine, or giving bonds for future good conduct." He asserted that blacks viewed this trend "as a revival of slavery."

At the end of 1866 corporal punishment generally ceased in North Carolina by General Order No. 15, issued by General Sickles. In some areas, however, blacks were still whipped illegally. Stephen Moore, superintendent of the Central District, cited five cases of blacks being whipped, one of them twice, while no whites had been whipped in the two months since Sickles's order had gone into effect. Allan Rutherford, superintendent of the Southern District, reported that while the order was being obeyed in Bladen, Cumberland, and Columbus counties, freedmen were still being whipped in Sampson, Duplin, and New Hanover counties.[79]

No common characteristics appear to have distinguished those counties where both blacks and whites were whipped from those which discriminated. Often neighboring counties practiced different policies. Counties throughout the state, including those with large black populations and those with low percentages, practiced discrimination; others with similar populations in similar areas treated blacks and whites the same.

The practice of binding blacks out if they could not pay their fines or court costs was even more reminiscent of slavery than was the procedure of public whippings. This binding out was done under a provision of a March 1866 law entitled "An Act More Effectually to Secure the Maintenance of Bastard Children, and the Payment of Fines and Costs on Conviction of Criminal Cases." This was one of the laws that was debated along with the Black Code, but that, as written, did not mention race. It provided that in all cases where a person fined or sentenced to pay court costs could not pay, the court could sentence that person to no more than twelve months in the house of correction, or it could give that person the option to "bind himself as an apprentice to any person whom he may select, for such time and at such price as the court may direct."[80]

The courts never applied this law to whites, but they bound many blacks, several without their consent. This practice probably stems at least in part from antebellum laws and court decisions. Before 1840 white and black vagrants could bind themselves out in lieu of court costs. In that year, however, this option was modified for whites to a fine and imprisonment, while blacks could still find themselves penalized into "a continuous form of servitude, little better than slavery."[81] The Revised Code of 1854 allowed a white convicted of any offense to swear that he was a pauper, whereupon he would be released from his obligation to pay costs. No such provision was enacted for blacks.[82]

After the war a few county courts allowed both blacks and whites to take the oath of insolvency, as provided in the 1854 Revised Code.[83] In many more cases, however, the postbellum courts hired blacks out. Such practices were generally confined to sections of the state where the black population was large and demand for labor was great. Another indication of a connection between labor shortages and this "apprenticeship" system is the fact that, in those cases where figures are available, blacks were often bound out for exceedingly long periods of time. It should be remembered that the average salary for a laborer was about $10 per month. Also, while court fees probably varied from county to county, and while statistics for what these fees were are nearly nonexistent, in Sampson County at least the county court finance committee recommended no more than $10 in court costs for minor offenses and a maximum of $25 for "all aggravated cases such as larceny or felonious stealing" and the like.[84]

With these data in mind, it is reasonable to conclude that the binding out practices of some North Carolina courts were outrageous. Courts in at least eleven counties "apprenticed" blacks in a way which indicates that they were more concerned with obtaining cheap labor than with dispensing justice.[85] This practice was most widespread in New Hanover County, where in 1865 and 1866 at least twenty blacks were bound out for the payment of fines and costs. The court sold two at a public auction, for a period of one year each, to pay their $40 fines. The eighteen others were confined in jail "for non-payment of Jail Fees" until they agreed to bind themselves out, despite the fact that many of them had been acquitted of the charges against them and the others had already been whipped as their punishment for crimes. As Allan Rutherford, Bureau superintendent of the area, complained, "many poor Freedmen" had been incarcerated "for months, on account of non-payment of Jail Fees, and as their fees are continually accumulating, I see no reason why their imprisonment should not be perpetual unless they choose to regain their liberty by selling themselves to some planter for a term of years."[86]

In Sampson County, while only two cases of "selling" were reported, the circumstances surrounding them indicate that here also there was an economic basis to this practice as well as collusion between the civil authorities and the planters. In one case the captain of police for the county arrested a freedman named Irwin "on a charge of being Lieut. of a Co. of freedmen, who were going to 'rise' of which Co. Virgil Crumke, freedman, was alleged to be Capt." But Irwin was the only one arrested. He was jailed for forty-eight hours and then released, "chargeable with costs to the amount of over $28.00." He paid $11 of these fees, but to pay the balance "his services were sold" by the police captain to a friend of his, Trixon Cooper, for one year "—the latter refusing to release him upon his paying the balance—which Mr. John Everett[,] a farmer of this Co., would advance to Irwin." Cooper also tried to force Irwin's wife to work for him "by threats & false representation." Both Irwin and his wife wanted to go to work for Everett, but in flagrant disregard of the 1866 law Irwin was given no choice; he was forced to work for Cooper. At the same time another freedman, Nick Butler, was arrested for "drawing a pistol on a white man." He too was held in jail for two days and was then released without a trial, without a conviction, and yet sold for a year for jail fees of $13. Major Wickersham ordered the arrest of "all parties concerned" in both these cases, so they could be brought to Wilmington for trial.[87]

Many native whites were appalled at such blatant abuses. The *Wil-*

mington Herald argued that these practices demonstrated "that there yet is wanting a readiness on the part of our people to accept 'the situation' fully," and deplored the fact that some whites refused to comprehend "the fact that the negro is now absolutely free." The *Sentinel* agreed; pointing out that such practices had been "promptly reversed by . . . U.S. Authorities," it noted its "surprise" that "the thing should have been repeated." It maintained that "the war freed the colored race," and that their freedom now had to be maintained.[88]

Nevertheless, more "sellings" occurred. The Craven County Court bound out one black man for two years for a jail fee of $83.80. A black mother convicted of larceny in Davidson County was sold for a year for the payment of court costs, leaving "a helpless child" uncared for. In Forsyth County six blacks, all convicted of larceny and all having received whippings of fifteen to thirty lashes, were bound out for about a year each to pay court costs. The Rowan County Court "apprenticed" six blacks for terms ranging from six months to eleven years for fines of no more than $10 plus court costs.[89] Numerous similar cases occurred in Hyde, Iredell, Alamance, Johnston, and Wake counties.[90]

This "apprenticeship" system, binding out blacks for fines and court costs, is similar in some respects to the peonage system that developed after Reconstruction. Aided by the corruption or acquiescence of local law officers and court officials, some North Carolina planters found a new way to ensure themselves cheap labor. As Pete Daniel notes in his thorough study of twentieth-century southern peonage, "the distinction between peonage and slavery was often blurred."[91] The same was true of the "binding out" system employed by some courts in 1866 and 1867.

Court discrimination occurred in many other ways. Penalties for blacks were often harsher than for whites. In Wake County, for example, the court sentenced one black convicted of assault and battery to be placed in the stocks four separate times for a total of eight hours, fined $200, and jailed for one year in the workhouse. He was the only black convicted of assault in the county during this time. Unfortunately, the details of this case are unknown, but the penalties imposed on thirty-five whites convicted of this crime ranged from one penny to $40 in fines, the average being about $5. None was placed in the stocks; none was sent to the workhouse.[92]

Some blacks also had a difficult time convincing juries that it was they who had been abused. One Rowan County black man accused six whites of coming to his home one night, beating him, and shooting him as he tried to escape. Three or four white witnesses, however, claimed that the whites did not beat the black man and that no shots were fired. In fact, the witnesses swore that there were no firearms in the crowd—a highly unlikely claim for that period. The black man was arrested, tried, and convicted of perjury, for which he received thirty-nine lashes and was forced to stand for one hour in the pillory, as well as to pay a fine of $1 plus costs.[93] No one asked what these three or four white witnesses were doing at this black man's home at night. The white men were believed, and the black severely punished for daring to accuse whites of a crime.

Other juries sometimes convicted blacks for what seems to be not "keeping their place." Several freedmen were imprisoned "for over six weeks" in the Wake County jail, "half starved and nearly suffocated on account of the air and the stench of accumulated filth . . . for language uttered which their former masters termed insulting." In Buncombe County a black man was put in jail after he "cursed" a white woman.[94]

Justice for blacks in North Carolina courts was uncertain at best, and what is important in a criminal justice system is consistency and dependability. While blacks in many counties received a fair trial with no overt discrimination in the arrest, the trial procedure, or the penalties, many North Carolina courts practiced various forms of discrimination and committed injustices. While no consistent pattern emerges, more cases of discrimination, as well as more violence and crime, seemed to occur in the southern and eastern parts of the state where the black population was most numerous and where plantation slavery had been most widespread before the Civil War. Here also whites had a greater need for labor.

While many blacks demonstrated courage and independence by reporting crimes, retaliating against white mobs, and resisting insults, their rewards for these efforts were meager. Resistance sometimes led to riots; the reporting of crimes often resulted in more violence—and sometimes death. Blacks could not consistently rely on the state's law officers or its court system to protect either their lives or their property. The legal system often supported the white elite's racial views and economic needs. Violence, supported by biased law officers and court systems, helped perpetuate racism and black poverty to the social and economic advantage of many southern whites.

7   A "Mania" for Learning:
The Freedmen's Quest for Education

The Freedman . . . "has got a disease for learning." It is a mania with him.—*Journal of Freedom* (Raleigh), October 14, 1865, p. 2

[Educating blacks] puts notions of equality into their heads that wholly unfits them for any kind of servitude.
—A Morganton woman named McAvery to Mrs. R. L. Patterson, February 21, 1866, Patterson Family Papers

NORTH CAROLINA BLACKS sought economic independence, security in their lives and property, and equitable justice in the state's courts; these ingredients were necessary if they were to achieve "true" freedom. They realized, however, that one additional ingredient was necessary to success in America; this was education. Northern educators in the South as well as Freedmen's Bureau agents continually commented upon the freedmen's passion for learning. For example, Harriette Pike, a white northerner teaching blacks in Wake County, wrote that the freedmen's "delight" at her opening a school knew "no bound. Old and young are eager to learn." She cited a few examples. "Very often" she observed "mothers in the midst of their children trying to learn from *them* what *they* have learned during the day." She also found "men and boys who have to work in the cotton-fields from sunrise till dark, sitting under a tree studying a Primer during the few moments of rest they are allowed after dinner."[1]

Blacks organized in many areas to raise money to build schools, buy books, and pay teachers.[2] In Warren County a group of freedmen met in July 1866 to raise "a School to educate our poor ignorant children." In April 1867 "a large number of Freedmen" in Burke County organized "to solicit funds for the education of our indigent brethren."³ At both the 1865 and the 1866 freedmen's conventions the delegates stressed the need for blacks to educate themselves and their children, and the 1866 conclave adopted a constitution for the Freedmen's Educational Association of North Carolina. This association was "to aid in the establishment of schools" throughout the state.⁴

Whites, on the other hand, were divided on the subject of educating the freedmen. Some spoke out in support of black education. One wealthy North Carolinian, in a speech to blacks in Raleigh, urged them to establish schools and asserted that success would come through knowledge and hard work. Another planter believed that the state should support schools for freedmen "by a tax upon the black population." Some newspapers also applauded black educational endeavors. The Raleigh *Standard*, for example, praised the work of two black schools in Raleigh. The *Wilmington Herald*, lauding an exhibition by black school children, argued that the education of blacks had "the sympathy and respect of the community. The blacks will be all the more profitable members of the community when they shall be educated in the elements of the English language and mathematics."⁵

Whites sometimes even actively aided black education. Most white churches started sabbath schools for blacks, planters often requested teachers for their employees, and some native whites even engaged in teaching the freedmen. The *Charlotte Times* maintained that the whites in that town, "far from throwing obstructions" in the path of black education, were doing "everything . . . to assist and advance" the work done at the several black schools in the city. Most whites in New Berne, Pineville, Goldsboro, Lumberton, and Monroe also reportedly aided and encouraged black schools.⁶

Many other whites, however, fought any type of education for blacks. A white minister in Statesville reported that about half of the citizens there refused to sign "a paper" which argued "that the freedmen sh'ld have a school."⁷ Freedmen's Bureau agents throughout the state wrote of numerous other instances of white opposition to black education. In September 1865 Major Charles Wickersham, superintendent of the Southern District, found "almost the entire Community opposed to educating the Blacks." The assistant superintendent at Elizabeth City wrote that the flourishing school there might close because of "the bitter feeling against it." The white citizens of Greensboro actively "discourage[d]" the Society of Friends' school for blacks there.[8]

A few whites even threatened or used violence to prevent blacks from gaining an education. Some threatened or actually burned schoolhouses, while others attacked teachers. In New Hanover County, for example, three white men dragged a northern teacher, Thomas Barton, three or four miles into the woods to beat and rob him. They called him a "G–d d—d Yankee Nigger school teacher," and told him: "The niggers were bad enough before you came, but since you have been teaching them, they know too much and are a damn sight worse." The men then gave Barton five days to leave town; he did.[9]

Most whites, however, probably took the middle road position best described by Nathaniel McLean, a minister and member of the North Carolina General Assembly from Lumberton. Writing to Samuel S. Ashley, the assistant superintendent of education for the Southern District, McLean argued that while "no opposition will be made" to Ashley's work, neither would there be "any demonstrations of *delight*." He cautioned that "if those [northern teachers] placed amongst us will act *discreetly* and evince a *harmonizing* spirit, our people in Robeson will judge & treat them accordingly—A due observance of law and order, an improvement in morals, a *decent* respect for the rights and opinions of others—properly inculcated and impressed on the minds of the Freedmen will be the surest passport to the attainment of the objects aimed to be accomplished."[10]

Others who halfheartedly supported efforts to educate blacks did so for specific reasons. Many believed that only native southern whites should instruct blacks, for they could then design and control the curriculum. They argued that instruction for blacks should be aimed at creating a peaceful, hardworking black population that knew its proper place in southern society. This group felt that a "proper" education would instruct blacks on how to work diligently, thereby increasing their usefulness to their white employers. Education, they contended, should consist of instruction in social duties and responsibilities.[11]

An editorial in the Fayetteville *News* presented a similar view. The *News* insisted that southern whites held no prejudice against blacks "beyond that which is common to all people, filled with a consciousness

of superiority." It maintained that despite emancipation, "the curse pronounced upon the decendants of Ham . . . will remain . . . , to fix a gulf
between them and the Caucasians. . . . His shackles may be striken
off . . . but still—'A servant of servants' will he be to other nations; 'a
hewer of wood and drawer of water;' in all that pertains to excellence,
advancement or perfection in knowledge, . . . immeasurably inferior."
Still, southerners had "not only the moral duty, but the practical interest . . . to strive for the establishment of the right schools of instruction"
for the freedmen. They should "fix upon some means of fitting them
[blacks] for the manner of life which they are destined hereafter to follow."
The editorial claimed that northern teachers were "instilling into their
minds false ideas, and instructing them day by day to the accomplishment
of their own ruin." An education sponsored by southern whites would
avoid these pitfalls. The *News* then concluded with a clear defense of
education as an instrument for social control:

> It has been objected by many that the acquirement of the mere
> rudiments of knowledge—the ability to read and write—would cause
> the blacks to become dissatisfied, meddlesome in political affairs,
> and ambitious in civil and political rights and privileges. Their am-
> bition and desire for elevation and equality is a natural consequence
> of their suddenly obtained liberty, but so far from its being in-
> creased . . . , we believe that education would be a powerful agent
> for its control and regulation within proper bounds. . . . The farther
> the negroes advanced in education, the more fully would they under-
> stand and appreciate the difference of caste and social position exist-
> ing between themselves and the whites, and the more firmly would
> they become impressed with the necessity of laboring earnestly.[12]

Because most white North Carolinians probably supported the education of blacks as a means of instructing them as to their proper role
in southern society, many objected to blacks being taught by northerners
who presumably did not understand the peculiar nature of the black race
and the special qualities of southern life. They called upon their native
white fellow citizens to take up the task of the freedmen's education. The
Raleigh *Sentinel* clearly presented this view in several articles. While
always insisting that whites supported and aided black education, the
editors explained that whites opposed northern teachers "because of their

almost universal disposition to mingle, upon terms of social equality, with the blacks—to visit them as equals, to eat and drink with them as equals,—the 'school marms' kissing and fondling their pupils, &c." More important, these northerners taught blacks a philosophy "intensely hostile to the peace and harmony of the races." The editors maintained that "where colored children are taught . . . as a daily exercise, to sing, 'Hang Jeff Davis on a sour apple tree,' and such other songs and teachings, nothing but a full crop of evil to both black and white can be looked for." Thus they claimed it was necessary for southern whites to educate blacks.[13]

To discourage northern educators from coming to or remaining in North Carolina, whites often refused to board them or to associate with them.[14] Ashley, the assistant superintendent of education for the Southern District, complained "that Northern teachers are most thoroughly hated. The violent calumnies are published and circulated concerning them. They are pointed at and insulted as they pass along the streets." He noted that one white man had "attempted to set a savage dog upon one of our lady teachers" and claimed that he himself received warnings "almost every day . . . to look to . . . [his] personal safety."[15] A few whites also protested the presence of northern educators by refusing to lease or to sell land or buildings for educational purposes to blacks or to their teachers.[16] The sheriff of Cumberland County went further; he prevented two schoolteachers from leaving the steamer that had brought them from Washington.[17]

At least two northern teachers were able to win whites over once they convinced these citizens that they were no threat to the southern order. Yardley Warner, sent to North Carolina as a teacher by the Friends' Freedmen's Aid Association, told whites that the Quakers believed that "one of our first requirements [is] to teach the Freedmen to be law-abiding. . . . Next to this, we teach them to be . . . industrious."[18] Ashley also realized how white North Carolinians felt and attempted to ease tensions. He tried to avoid sending or boarding black and white teachers together, because "such a course . . . brings your white teachers . . . in such sharp contact with the prejudices of the Southern people that their (the teachers['])) situation is made almost intolerable." He noted also that this interracial situation caused southern whites to believe that the teachers were "endeavoring to bring about a condition of *social equality*." But contrary to popular belief, Ashley claimed, this was not the case. Indeed, it was the teacher's "business," he explained, "not only to teach of knowledge of letters, but to instruct them [blacks] in the duties which now devolve upon them in their new relations—to make clear to their understanding the principles by which they must be guided in all their intercourse with their fellowmen—to inculcate obedience to law and respect for the rights and property of others, and reverence for those in authority; enforcing honesty, industry and economy." After following this policy, Ashley found that "hostility" toward black education had "given place to sullen acquiescence."[19]

Although whites divided on the question of whether to educate blacks at all, they were unanimous in their oppositon to integrated education. One planter noted that while he was "willing that the colored population should be educated, . . . white and black children should be taught in separate schools," for "nothing should be done that looked towards the social equality of Negroes and whites." The Raleigh *Sentinel* also spoke out against integrated education. While it bemoaned the fact that there were no "public or charity schools" for whites in Raleigh, and while it granted that the schools operated by northern missionaries would admit white students, it argued that "none of our whites are so poor that they are willing to consent" to send their children to schools "where the colored children are taught."[20]

Fisk Brewer, a northern teacher sent by the American Missionary Association to Raleigh, discovered that the *Sentinel* was correct. He tried to teach both whites and blacks, but public opinion was so opposed to the experiment that eventually all the whites withdrew. As Brewer pointed out, most of the white students who left "go without any schooling at all rather than bear up against the ridicule that meets them for going to a freedman's school." Brewer also tried to establish a class for poor "white young men to prepare [them] for college." This too failed, he maintained, "when they found that I was so much engaged with 'niggers.'"[21]

A majority in the North Carolina General Assembly shared the feelings held by most of their constituents. While many newspapers throughout the state called for the public education of white children, the legislature in March 1866 abolished the common school system established before the war. Several representatives argued that there was no money left in the Literary Fund, which along with local taxes had previously supported public schools, and that the people were too poor to be taxed. Five newspapers, however, pointed out that the legislature had appropriated $7,000 for the University of North Carolina as well as thousands of dollars more for artificial limbs for Confederate soldiers. Lack of funds, they argued, was not the real reason for the abandonment of the public school system.[22] Instead, as Union County State Senator D. A. Covington contended, the true reason for the General Assembly's actions was the fear that "the Freedmen's Bureau might force colored children into them [the schools], to which our people would never consent."[23] Governor Worth also conceded: "I fear we shall have a freedmen's Bureau and Military rule over us, if we make discrimination in education in Common Schools. I mean if we educate white children at public expence,—we will be required to educate negroes in like manner. . . . I think the Com. School system had better be discontinued . . . and thus avoid this question as to educating negroes."[24] Charles Phillips, a professor at the University of North Carolina and the brother of a prominent Whig, agreed that "our common school fund has been swept away . . . and our legislators fear to lay a tax for the support of the schools—lest agitation disturb us and claim that as negroes pay this tax they must also go to school."[25]

The next session of the General Assembly, meeting from November 1866 through March 1867, overcame the fears of its predecessor. It authorized "incorporated towns and cities to establish systems of public schools" for white children. These schools were to be supported by city funds and by a poll tax of not more than two dollars to be paid by all white adult males.[26] While no provision was made for the education of black children, at least blacks were not taxed to support these schools.

Although the General Assembly was unwilling to create a public school system that would educate both blacks and whites, even on a segregated basis, it was willing by narrow majorities to allow blacks to establish their own private educational agencies. In March 1866 the legislature incorporated "a college for the education of teachers and ministers of the gospel of the colored race." This Presbyterian college was to be established in the eastern part of the state and called the Freedmen's College of North Carolina. Despite the fact that this college would be segregated and would cost the public nothing, the Senate passed the incorporation act 18 to 10, after first rejecting it. In the House, it passed 44 to 34.[27] The 1866–67 session of the Assembly incorporated "The Colored Education Association, of North Carolina," formed by the 1866 North Carolina freedmen's convention to establish schools and encourage education among blacks. It also approved incorporation of "the Trustees of the 'Lowell Colored School Society'" in Washington County.[28]

With or without the approval of native whites, schools for blacks were established throughout North Carolina. Four northern missionary societies supported these schools: The American Freedmen Union Commission, the National Freedmen's Relief Association, the American Missionary Association, and the Friends' Freedmen's Aid Association. The Freedmen's Bureau had few funds to assist these educational efforts. While it often provided school buildings and accommodations for the teachers if they lived in the school buildings, it could not reimburse teachers for rent if the instructors lived anywhere other than in the schoolhouses. The Bureau also was not permitted to pay salaries, to provide books, or to improve school facilities.[29] However, it did help to find sites for schools and to organize them, and F. A. Fiske, a white northerner, served under the auspices of the Freedmen's Bureau as the superintendent of education in North Carolina. Through him, the Bureau dispersed the funds received from the various northern benevolent organizations. Fiske also coordinated the assignment of teachers, the curriculum taught, and the school schedules.[30]

One of the major problems that arose out of this voluntaristic situation was a lack of funds. Despite the fact that the freedmen often raised money either to build or lease a school and to pay for most if not all of the educational expenses, except a teacher's salary, they were often unable to obtain teachers.[31] By October 1866 the problem was particularly acute as the benevolent societies, "for want of sufficient funds" as contributions from the North diminished, were forced to withdraw many of the teachers they had already sent. Writing to the secretary of the New York American Freedmen Union Commission, Fiske pleaded for at least the retention of those teachers already in the state. He bemoaned the fact that because of the cutbacks "in many places, where the Freedmen have been struggling to get buildings in readiness and have made such other preparations as their limited means permitted, they can [now] have no schools."[32]

Requests for teachers were so great that an obviously frustrated Ashley wrote to the Reverend George Whipple, secretary of the American Missionary Association, in February 1867: "Cannot some way be devised whereby these freedmen . . . who are helping themselves so extensively can be supplied with teachers?"[33]

But blacks did not passively wait for northerners or the federal government to provide them with an education. Because of their strong desire to educate themselves and their children, they actively supported many schools. They also shared the cost of others with the missionary societies. For example, in the North Carolina superintendent of education's monthly school report for December 1866, of the ninety-five schools about which details were given fifteen were "sustained by freedmen," and another twenty-six were "sustained in part by freedmen." Also, twenty-two of the school buildings were owned by freedmen. The same pattern is seen in the only other extant detailed school reports, those for January and March 1867.

Many blacks also served as teachers in their own or in missionary-sponsored schools. In December 1866, for example, 584 instructors were reported to be teaching in day, night, and sabbath schools for blacks in North Carolina. Of these, 359 were black, but only twenty-seven taught in day or night schools; the remainder worked only in the sabbath schools. Black educators taught in all parts of the state. According to the official Freedmen's Bureau list for December 1866, for example, seventeen black instructors taught in Beaufort, Fayetteville, Goldsboro, Hillsboro, Lumberton, Milton, New Berne, Raleigh, Snow Hill, Statesville, and Warrenton. Obviously they taught elsewhere also, but at least 432 black teachers were not included in the detailed report that discussed the number of schools city by city, because this report dealt only with missionary-sponsored schools and also omitted sabbath schools. Other sources show that blacks also taught in Charlotte, Smithville, Waughton, and Wilmington.[34]

The few detailed reports available indicate that schools with black instructors were well attended and well taught. For example, the Raleigh *Sentinel* reported in June 1866 that several freedmen's schools had been established recently in Raleigh by "competent" native black teachers. It added that "the schools are thronged." A northern white teacher in New Berne claimed that blacks there preferred to attend the private schools taught by blacks rather than those sponsored by the Freedmen's Bureau

Table 7. Schools in North Carolina sponsored by missionary associations

Date	Number of schools	Number of teachers	Number of pupils
December 1865	—	.—	c. 8,500
January 1866	100	132	10,459
May 1866	136	158	10,971
June 1866	119	135	9,084
October 1866	80	75	3,763
November 1866	94	96	5,732
December 1866	118	122	9,673
January 1867	130	134	9,961
February 1867	145	152	11,714
March 1867	156	173	13,039

and missionary associations that were taught primarily by whites. Because this is the only extant comment on this subject, there is no way to discover how widespread such an attitude was. But it should be remembered that the 1865 freedmen's convention debated a resolution urging blacks to employ black teachers whenever possible. Although this resolution was tabled, it does indicate that some delegates preferred black teachers.[35]

Considering white hostility and black poverty, the large number of schools for freedmen established in North Carolina during Presidential Reconstruction is indeed impressive, as the statistics in table 7, drawn from the available sources,[36] show. From these figures, it is clear that a large number of schools were started soon after the Civil War. However, the summer recess and the economic difficulties experienced by the missionary societies caused a sharp decline during the summer and early fall of 1866. Thereafter, new schools began monthly and blacks attended them in increasingly large numbers. These figures are low because they do not include schools not sponsored by the missionary societies. For example, the superintendent of education's report for the month of December 1866 did not include eighty-three sabbath schools, with approximately 6,943 pupils and 462 teachers, 332 of whom were black. Also not listed in the superintendent's figures were twenty-three day and night schools with approximately 812 students and twenty-four teachers, ten of whom were black. The January 1867 figures do not include twenty-nine sabbath schools with 1,150 students and fifty-seven teachers, forty-seven of whom were black; and twenty day and night schools with approximately 852 students and twenty-one teachers, eighteen of whom were black.[37]

If one compares the March 1867 figures just for missionary-sponsored schools with the school attendance figures in the 1870 census, the progress made during Presidential Reconstruction is astounding. While 13,039 black children in North Carolina attended these missionary-sponsored schools in 1867, only 11,419 out of a possible school age population of 135,845 were going to school in 1870. Considering the other schools attended, over 10 percent of school-age blacks were attending school by the close of Presidential Reconstruction.

Schools for freedmen were fairly evenly dispersed throughout North Carolina. The records are the most complete for the Southern District, an area where a large portion of the state's black population resided. The sources indicate many successes in that section. As early as May 1865, 1,500 blacks attended school there. By the fall, however, after the summer recess, the number dropped; in September there was only one school, taught by a black man, in the district.[38] The number increased continually after that, however, and according to various reports, considerable educational achievements were made.[39]

A variety of groups operated these Southern District schools. Individuals or local churches ran a few, but northern missionary groups, led by the American Missionary Association, operated most of them. In Wilmington, besides the A.M.A. schools, the Presbyterian church, the National Freedmen's Relief Association, and the Episcopal church each operated a school. Four of the town's black churches—the African Episcopal, the Zion Methodist Episcopal, the Baptist, and the Presbyterian— each sponsored a sabbath school.[40]

Most of the schools in this area, though, were concentrated in a few major towns and cities. There were no schools in Bladen, Columbus, Duplin, Richmond, Robeson, or Sampson counties. Even in Wilmington and Fayetteville, Fiske estimated in January 1867 that "not more than about fifty per cent of those who should enjoy the benefits of Freedmen's schools are in actual attendance" because of the lack of facilities and teachers. Nor did the situation improve. In the summer of 1867 Fiske's complaint was still accurate.[41]

The quality of these schools in the Southern District was mixed, but a majority of them compiled good records. In January 1866 Ashley

Table 8. Compilation of Freedmen's Bureau reports of schools
in the Southern District

Date and district	Number of schools	Number of teachers		Number of pupils	
		White	Black	Adults	Children
October 1865					
Wilmington	4	9	4	145 [a]	734[b]
Fayetteville	3	0	8	0	198
November 1865					
Wilmington[c]	6	8	3	187	771
Fayetteville	1	0	2	15	25
December 1865[d]					
Wilmington	7	9	2	185	648
Fayetteville	1	0	2	15	60
January 1866					
Wilmington	7	10	3	304	904
Fayetteville	2	2	0	0	245
February 1866[e]					
Wilmington	12	10	7	289	977
Fayetteville	3	2	0	39	263
April 1866 Day Schools					
Wilmington	9	13	5	119	980
Fayetteville	2	2	0	24	181
Lumberton	1	0	2	34	46
April 1866 Night Schools					
Wilmington	4	13	1	227	44
Fayetteville	1	2	0	90	0
March 1867 [f]	12	12	8	—	1,700[g]
June/July 1867 [h]	6	—	—	—	300[g]

[a]Attending night school.
[b]This figure includes seventy-five students attending school in Smithville; the remainder went to schools in Wilmington.
[c]There was also one school of seventy-five students in Smithville.
[d]Five schools were located in Wilmington; one in Brunswick; one in Smithville; and one in Fayetteville.
[e]In March 1866 the day schools were in Wilmington, Brunswick, Fayetteville, Smithville, and Bethlehem. There were night schools in Wilmington and Brunswick.
[f]There were seven schools in Wilmington; two in Fayetteville; one in Middle Sound, New Hanover County; one in Long Creek, New Hanover County; and one in Smithville.
[g]These figures are totals; there are no breakdowns of adults and children.
[h]These figures include schools in Wilmington and Fayetteville only.

reported that the general progress of schools in Wilmington and Fayetteville was very impressive. In March 1867 he maintained that "for the
most part, the schools . . . are supplied with competent teachers and are
in a flourishing condition. The pupils are making rapid improvement. . . . Of the 1700 pupils only 228 are in the Alphabet, 508 are
studying arithmetic and 350 are writing." The *Wilmington Herald* praised
the work of the students in two Wilmington schools. When a Freedmen's
Bureau agent inspected Wilmington and Fayetteville schools during the
summer of 1867, however, his report was not as complimentary. Of the
two free schools in session in Wilmington at that time, he noted, one,
operated by the American Missionary Association, was "excellent." But
the other was "not a good school. . . . The teachers have not the faculty,
of maintaining order . . . , and in only a limited degree that of imparting
instruction." He also turned in a mixed report for the two schools in
Fayetteville open that summer. He argued that one, taught by two black
men from Ohio and "assisted" by a black woman from Fayetteville, was
"an excellent school," one of the best in the state: "The attendance is
large and regular and the teaching thorough and complete." The other,
run by the Episcopal church, had a "positively discouraging" record:
"There is no discipline, little study, less teaching and pretty nearly no
progress."[42]

Statistics are sparse for the Eastern District, another area with a
large black population. As of June 1, 1865, sixty-eight teachers taught
in nineteen day schools and eight night schools located in New Berne,
the Trent River Camp, Beaufort, Morehead City, and Clamford Creek,
and operated by three northern missionary groups—the New England
Freedmen's Relief Association, the American Missionary Association,
and the National Freedmen's Relief Association. Freedmen's Bureau records contain no other district-wide figures. But in June 1867 General
Robert Avery reported that "the schools in this Dist. are flourishing well,
the attendance is good, the teachers earnest, and generally successful."[43]

The reports from various towns and counties in the Eastern District
also show that many schools were thriving throughout this period. Several
schools were operating in New Berne, including a high school. James E.
O'Hara, a northern-born black who had lived in the West Indies until
"early manhood" and later became a prominent North Carolina lawyer

and politician, ran the largest tuition school in the city. In January 1866 he had eighty-two students, seventy-six of whom could read, fifty-four of whom could write, fifty-two of whom were studying arithmetic, and fifteen of whom were advanced enough to be learning Spanish.[44]

In September 1865, Captain Underdue of the Thirty-ninth United States Colored Troops operated a successful school in Kinston with 240 students. This school was forced to close in October, however, when Underdue's regiment was mustered out. In December the town had a day school with 327 students and a night school with 110 pupils. But in April 1866 one correspondent complained that while there were enough students for three or four teachers, no schoolrooms were available. Throughout this period schools also operated in Plymouth, Beaufort, Edenton, Elizabeth City, and Bertie County. All reportedly were thriving, with the students eager for knowledge and learning rapidly.[45]

There were also several flourishing schools in the Central District. Raleigh had the largest concentration of schools in this area. As early as July 1865 two schools existed there. One, the Lincoln School, with two hundred students, was taught by a Baptist minister and his two assistants. The other had 170 students and three teachers. By January 1866, 553 black children attended day schools in Raleigh. Several night schools instructed a total of 175 pupils. In September eleven teachers taught in six well-established schools with 830 students. Northern missionary associations supported five of these schools; the other was a private tuition school run by a black teacher. The Quakers had also just opened another school, and an eighth was to be started soon by the Baptists. The American Missionary Association began a school in the fall of 1866. By February 1867 it had eighty-eight students, seventy of whom could spell and read and twenty-five of whom were doing arithmetic. In March the eight schools in Raleigh were "in a very prosperous condition. About one person in every four of the entire colored population attends schools." Seven other schools operated elsewhere in Wake County.[46]

Schools also existed in Orange, Caswell, Alamance, Franklin, Johnston, and Wayne counties. In March 1867 each of four towns in Orange County had a school; these were attended by a total of 345 students. Three of the schools were free, sponsored by the missionary associations, and the other charged tuition. Isaac Porter, the assistant superintendent of the subdistrict of Orange, reported that two of the free schools were "successfully conducted." The teacher of the third free school, however, was "incompitent [sic] from want of education."⁴⁷

The only two schools in Caswell County were located in Milton and near Yanceyville. Both were tuition schools taught by blacks. In Alamance County northern missionaries taught schools in Graham and at Company Shops. Flora Leland, a northerner, started a school in Louisburg, Franklin County, in April 1866. Within a month she had ninety students, twenty-four of whom were "very good readers. The others," she said, were "doing well" and all her pupils were "very orderly & intelligent." By the first of October a hundred students attended this school regularly, with forty more going to the night school. Smithfield, in Johnston County, had well-attended day and night schools. There were two "successful" schools in Goldsboro, one supported by the Friends' Freedmen's Aid Association and the other a tuition school operated by a black man.⁴⁸

Despite these achievements many black children in the Central District received no education. Nash County, an area with about five hundred black children, had no schools, and the same situation existed in Harnett County. There were no teachers in Halifax and Northampton counties, despite the fact that the freedmen were "anxious to educate their children" and would "contribute according to their means." In Orange County six new schools were ready but no teachers were available.⁴⁹

The Western District also boasted many successes in education. In September 1865, black teachers ran two schools in Charlotte, and the Society of Friends planned to open a school there as soon as a building could be found. In October the Quakers started a school in Greensboro that within a month had four hundred students. By October 1866 five schools existed in Guilford County, although they only had a total of 150 students. In Lincolnton in March 1866 there was "a flourishing school of 108 scholars taught by a Quaker Yankee." Two schools were operating in Salisbury in November 1865. By December one of the schools, supported by the Friends' Freedmen's Aid Association, had 222 day and 120 night students. In the fall of 1866 eight schools with 350 students were operating in Forsyth County, five schools with three hundred students in Davidson County, and two schools with 350 students in Randolph County. Union County possessed "several day schools" and "a good many sunday [sic] schools" that were "well-attended." One of the schools in Forsyth County, located in Waughton, was built and supported solely by blacks and taught by a native black North Carolinian. By January of 1867 it had been operating for several months and was "progressing finely" with "the pupils . . . fast improving."[50]

Besides these town and city schools, many whites established schools on their plantations. The various northern benevolent societies aided most of the schools, but the freedmen also contributed to their support and the planters often provided room and board for the teachers.[51] Other planters wanted schools as soon as the northern associations could send teachers.[52] Some of these planters may have been motivated to start schools for their employees out of a sense of moral duty, but Ashley claimed that many were doing so "as a matter of self defence, i.e., the Freedmen insist on coming to the City because by so doing their children can attend schools. Therefore plantation schools are a necessity if the Farmers would retain their hands."[53]

During Presidential Reconstruction, then, many notable achievements were made in the area of black education. Because of the efforts of northern benevolent societies and blacks themselves, many good schools taught thousands of North Carolina freedmen; however, many other blacks were still deprived of an education through lack of funds to pay teachers. North Carolina whites, on the other hand, generally accepted the necessity of black education only reluctantly. While some violently opposed education for the freedmen, most saw it as a useful tool for social control which could also ensure whites a hard-working labor force, and consequently they wanted to control the curriculum and the teachers. But they were reluctant to create a full-scale public school system for this purpose because they feared that northerners would force them to establish integrated schools. As a result, no statewide system of public education existed in North Carolina throughout Presidential Reconstruction. A few public schools for whites existed in some large cities, supported by local poll taxes. But most whites were denied a free public education during this period, and the only free schools for blacks were those supported by the northern missionary societies and the state's freedmen.

The 1870 census demonstrates clearly the unfortunate consequences of these racist attitudes on the part of whites and the lack of resources on the part of blacks. The census shows that about one-third of North

Table 9. Those who could not write in North Carolina in 1870

	10–15 years	15–21 years	21 years and older
White	38,647	31,911	95,839
Black	40,955	44,805	144,846

Carolina's population over the age of ten could not read or write. And blacks were lagging dramatically behind whites. While 25 percent of whites over ten could not write, a staggering 89 percent of the black population was illiterate. However, as table 9 indicates, the figures for those under twenty-one—that is, those who benefited from Reconstruction education—show the progress made from 1865 to 1870. However, the future did not look bright for either race. Only 8 percent of blacks and 24 percent of whites between five and seventeen years of age were attending school in 1870.

8 Conclusion

FROM 1865 TO 1867, under President Johnson's lenient policies, white North Carolinians were relatively free to shape their own destinies. While the military and the Freedmen's Bureau occasionally interfered to prevent legal discrimination and racial abuse and while their presence may have inhibited some excesses by whites, generally civil authorities, not the military, ruled. Those civil authorities, along with most white citizens, quickly set about to establish a pattern of race relations that would maintain black dependence and inferiority. The continual conflict one sees during this important transition period from slavery to freedom resulted, in large part, from black attempts to thwart these plans. In every area—politics, labor, the law, education, and religion—whites and blacks battled over the future status of the races and their place in southern society.

During these years blacks began their long struggle to become truly free. Many had observed successful whites all of their lives. They had learned that economic independence provided security and respect, that education was one way to achieve success, and that justice meant equality before the law and security of person and property. Therefore numerous former slaves and free blacks opposed in a variety of ways their white neighbors' racial attitudes and repressive measures. In 1865 the delegates to the freedmen's state convention adopted a conciliatory tone. They were willing to postpone political rights in order to achieve legal equality and the opportunity for education and economic security. By 1866, however, many were angry. They discovered that many whites would not treat them fairly. Many became convinced that their only hope for true freedom was through the vote, economic independence, and education. Black leaders demanded all these things at their 1866 convention and at other meetings. But while demanding the rights and opportunities that are the birthright of every American, blacks remained peaceful. Their crime rate was relatively low and there were no insurrections.

Despite the freedmen's peaceable deportment and hard work, the majority of white leaders refused to compromise. As the *Christian Century* noted on December 9, 1936: "Slavery was too integral a part of the social life of the South and too vital to the interests of certain classes to be suddenly eliminated by a mere constitutional amendment." It is true that in May 1865 most white North Carolinians felt defeated. They awaited word from President Johnson on their fate. But they also lived in fear of the newly emancipated blacks. They believed that freedom would bring economic disaster, social chaos, and possibly bloodshed through insurrection. The president's lenient policy obviously emboldened them to work quickly to establish new laws curtailing the black citizens' freedom. The evidence indicates that nothing short of a full-scale military occupation with war-crimes trials, land redistribution, and massive disfranchisement would have forced them to alter their course.

The speed with which the majority of white North Carolinians became outspokenly reluctant unionists, increasingly talking about "their rights," is one indication of the validity of this conclusion. Another is their early and oft-repeated proslavery arguments. The beliefs that had created a unique southern civilization had not been altered by the war. Moreover, white North Carolinians even hesitated to carry out Johnson's moderate program. They elected prominent secessionists to national and state offices and rejected those who could take the ironclad oath required by Congress. The state convention only grudgingly repudiated the Confederate debt.

It is also clear that white North Carolinians were well aware of what northerners expected. They knew of the struggle between the president and Congress and were aware that what Johnson would accept, other northerners would not. Nevertheless, the legislature passed a Black Code and other discriminatory laws to keep blacks in an inferior condition and to ensure whites a cheap labor force. It also rejected the Fourteenth Amendment, which would have granted blacks citizenship.

More important for the future were the new devices white planters created to replace slavery. For economic and socio-psychological reasons, they quickly searched for new ways to perpetuate black subserviency and economic dependency. Because their foremost concern was a stable labor force, white landowners were most innovative in this area. Planters joined together to maintain low wages. They wrote contracts that kept blacks in a servile condition and experimented with the "company store"—supplying their employees with goods at high prices, thereby keeping them in debt. They also worked with the General Assembly to obtain favorable labor legislation. Through the apprenticeship of black children and the selling of black adults in debt from court costs, additional cheap labor was secured. Many whites used violence to supplement legislation, and many involved in the legal system, including law enforcement officers, worked with the planters to keep blacks working diligently and behaving docilely.

Blacks developed their own institutions to survive this oppression and poverty. They reunited their families and developed a socially active black community. Political organizations worked for equality and black leaders educated the freedmen. Blacks also left white churches in protest over demeaning, discriminatory policies. Quickly, they established their own churches and began statewide ecclesiastical organizations. Led by their ministers they worked within their new religious bodies to find dignity as God's children. To further their economic ambitions some freedmen tried to organize joint stock companies to buy land. Many others supported a sharecropping system that they believed offered them the best opportunity to accumulate enough money to buy their own land. Some courageously resisted white intimidation, reported abuses, fought apprenticeships, and refused to deport themselves as slaves.

Many sacrificed to gain an education for themselves and their children. With the help of the Freedmen's Bureau and northern benevolent societies they established new schools, including three colleges. But in spite of these efforts, most blacks would find life in the South for the next hundred years to be fraught with ignorance and poverty, discrimination and violence. They were free, but the struggle for equality had just begun.

List of Abbreviations

Amend Rept	*Report and Resolution of the Joint Select Committee of Both Houses of the General Assembly of North Carolina, on the Proposition to Adopt the Congressional Constitutional Amendment* (Raleigh: Wm. E. Pell, 1866)
CHW Papers	Calvin Henderson Wiley Papers, Southern Historical Collection
CI	*Church Intelligencer* (Charlotte)
Conv, 1865	*Journal of the Convention of the State of North Carolina At Its Session of 1865* (Raleigh: Cannon and Holden, 1865)
Conv, 1866	*Journal of the Convention of the State of North Carolina, At Its Adjourned Session of 1866* (Raleigh: Cannon and Holden, 1866)
DES Rpt	Report by Major General D. E. Sickles, October 30, 1866, House Executive Documents, vol. III, Report of the Secretary of War, 39th Congress, 1st Session
DU	Duke University, Manuscript Division, Durham, North Carolina
DUMC	Duke University, Microfilm Collection, Durham, North Carolina
EDC, 1865	*Executive Documents, Constitution of North Carolina with Amendments, and Ordinances and Resolutions Passed by the Convention, Session, 1865* (Raleigh: Cannon and Holden, 1865)
FBP	Bureau of Refugees, Freedmen, and Abandoned Lands, Record Group 105, National Archives
Holden GP	Governor's Papers, William W. Holden, North Carolina Department of Archives and History
Holden LB	William W. Holden, Letter Book of the Provisional

	Governor, 1865, North Carolina Department of Archives and History
H Report, 1865	O. O. Howard, "Report of the Commissioner of the Bureau of Refugees, Freedmen and Abandoned Lands," December 1865, House Executive Document No. 11, 39th Congress, 1st Session
H Report, 1866	Report of the Commissioner of the Bureau of Refugees, Freedmen, and Abandoned Lands, November 1, 1866, House Executive Documents, vol. III, Report of the Secretary of War, 39th Congress, 2nd Session
H Report, 1867	Report of the Commissioner of the Bureau of Refugees, Freedmen and Abandoned Lands, November 1, 1867, House Executive Documents, vol. II, Report of the Secretary of War, 40th Congress, 2d Session
JH, 1865–66	*Journal of the House of Commons of the General Assembly of the State of North Carolina at its Session of 1865–66* (Raleigh: Wm. E. Pell, 1865–66)
JH, 1866	*Journal of the House of Commons at Its Special Session of 1866* (Raleigh: Wm. E. Pell, 1866)
JH, 1866–67	*Journal of the House of Commons of the General Assembly of the State of North Carolina at its Session of 1866–67* (Raleigh: Wm. E. Pell, 1867)
JS, 1865–66	*Journal of the Senate of the General Assembly of the State of North Carolina at its Session of 1865–66* (Raleigh: Wm. E. Pell, 1865)
JS, 1866	*Journal of the Senate at its Special Session of 1866* (Raleigh: Wm. E. Pell, 1866)
JS, 1866–67	*Journal of the Senate of the General Assembly of the State of North Carolina at its Session of 1866–67* (Raleigh: Wm. E. Pell, 1867)
LC	Library of Congress, Manuscript Division, Washington, D.C.
LP	Legislative Papers, North Carolina Department of Archives and History
LRAC	Letters Received by the Assistant Commissioner, FBP
LRAGO	Letters Received by the Office of the Adjutant General

	(Main Series) 1861–1870, Record Group 94, File No. 1370 A, National Archives
LRE	Letters Received by the Superintendent of the Eastern District, FBP
LRFB	Freedmen's Bureau Records, Education Division, Letters Received Relating to Freedman's Savings Bank, 1865–1869, Record Group 105, National Archives
LRS	Letters Received by the Superintendent of the Southern District, FBP
LRW	Letters Received by the Superintendent of the Western District, FBP
LSAC	Letters Sent by the Assistant Commissioner, FBP
LSEd	Letters Sent by the Superintendent of Education, FBP
LSS	Letters Sent by the Superintendent of the Southern District, FBP
LSW	Letters Sent by the Superintendent of the Western District, FBP
NBT	*New Berne Daily Times* (also, at various times during the years 1865–67, called the *Daily North Carolina Times* or *The North Carolina Times*)
NCA	North Carolina Department of Archives and History, Raleigh, North Carolina
NR	Narrative Reports submitted to the Assistant Commissioner, FBP
OC	*Ordinances Passed by the North Carolina State Convention, at the Sessions of 1865–66* (Raleigh: Wm. E. Pell, 1867)
PL,1865	*Public Laws of the State of North Carolina, Passed by the General Assembly at the Session of 1865* (Raleigh: Wm. E. Pell, 1866)
PL,1866	*Public Laws of the State of North Carolina, Passed by the General Assembly at the Session of 1866* (Raleigh: Wm. E. Pell, 1866)
PL,1866–67	*Public Laws of the State of North Carolina, Passed by the General Assembly at the Session of 1866–67* (Raleigh: Wm. E. Pell, 1867)

RCC	Records of the United States Continental Command, Army of Ohio and Department of North Carolina, National Archives
RRH Papers	Ruffin–Roulhac–Hamilton Papers, Southern Historical Collection
RRI	Ration Returns Issued, FBP
Sch Rpts, CD	Superintendent of the Central District, School Reports, FBP
Sch Rpts, SD	Superintendent of the Southern District, School Reports, FBP
SHC	Southern Historical Collection, University of North Carolina, Chapel Hill, North Carolina
SMR	Semi-Monthly Reports on the Conditions of Freedmen, and the Operations of the Freedmen's Bureau Submitted to the Assistant Commissioner, FBP
SR	Statistical Reports Regarding the Condition of the Freedmen, FBP
SWR	Report of Major General D. E. Sickles, October 30, 1866, House Executive Documents, vol. 3, Report of the Secretary of War, 39th Congress, 2d Session
ULRAC	Unentered Letters Received by the Assistant Commissioner, FBP
ULRE	Unentered Letters Received by the Superintendent of the Eastern District, FBP
ULREd	Unentered Letters Received by the Superintendent of Education, FBP
Worth Corr.	J. G. de Roulhac Hamilton (ed.), *The Correspondence of Jonathan Worth* in *Publications of the North Carolina Historical Commission* (2 vols.; Raleigh: Edwards and Broughton, 1909)
Worth GP	Governor's Papers, Jonathan Worth, North Carolina Department of Archives and History
Worth LB	Jonathan Worth, Letter Book, North Carolina Department of Archives and History

Notes

Preface notes

1   Most Reconstruction historians writing in the early twentieth century concurred with
the basic thesis presented by William A. Dunning in his *Reconstruction, Political and
Economic, 1865–1877* (New York: Harper, 1907). A professor at Columbia University, Dunning taught a generation or more of graduate students, many of whom came
from the South. The monographs they and others who shared their beliefs wrote
condemning the Republican Reconstruction program comprise the so-called Dunning
school. Some works that exemplify the Dunning interpretation are Claude J. Bowers,
The Tragic Era (Boston: Literary Guild of America, 1929); John W. Burgess, *Reconstruction and the Constitution, 1866–1876* (New York: Charles Scribner's Sons, 1902);
Walter L. Fleming, *The Sequel of Appomatox* (New Haven: Yale University Press,
1919); George F. Milton, *The Age of Hate; Andrew Johnson and the Radicals* (New
York: Coward–McCann, 1930); James Ford Rhodes, *History of The United States
from the Compromise of 1850* (7 vols.; New York: Macmillan, 1909), vol. 7. For a
good summary of the Dunning interpretation, see Kenneth M. Stampp, *The Era of
Reconstruction 1865–1877* (New York: Knopf, 1965), pp. 4–8.
2   For a good summary of the revisionist interpretation, see Stampp, *Era of Reconstruction*, pp. 8–13. An excellent historiographical article is Bernard A. Weisberger, "The
Dark and Bloody Ground of Reconstruction Historiography," *The Journal of Southern
History* 25 (November 1959): 427–47. In addition to Stampp's *Era of Reconstruction*,
some examples of Reconstruction history in the revisionist tradition are W. R. Brock,
An American Crisis: Congress and Reconstruction 1865–1867 (London: Macmillan,
1963); LaWanda and John H. Cox, *Politics, Principle and Prejudice 1865–1866* (Glen-
coe, Ill.: The Free Press, 1963); John Hope Franklin, *Reconstruction After the Civil
War* (Chicago: University of Chicago Press, 1961); Eric L. McKitrick, *Andrew Johnson
and Reconstruction* (Chicago: University of Chicago Press, 1960); Rembert W. Patrick,
The Reconstruction of the Nation (New York: Oxford University Press, 1967).
3   Joel Williamson, *After Slavery: The Negro in South Carolina During Reconstruction,
1861–1877* (Chapel Hill: University of North Carolina Press, 1965); Peter Kolchin,
*First Freedom: The Responses of Alabama's Blacks to Emancipation and Reconstruc-
tion* (Westport, Conn.: Greenwood Press, 1972); Herbert G. Gutman, *The Black
Family in Slavery and Freedom 1750–1925* (New York: Pantheon Books, 1976);
Edward Magdol, *A Right to Land: Essays on the Freedmen's Community* (Westport,
Conn.: Greenwood Press, 1977); Leon Litwack, *Been in the Storm So Long: The
Aftermath of Slavery* (New York: Random House, 1980).

4   See, e.g., Roger L. Ransom and Richard Sutch, *One Kind of Freedom: The Economic Consequences of Emancipation* (Cambridge: Cambridge University Press, 1977); Dwight B. Billings, Jr., *Planters and the Making of a "New South": Class, Politics, and Development in North Carolina, 1865–1910* (Chapel Hill: University of North Carolina Press, 1979); Stephen J. DeCanio, *Agriculture in the Postbellum South: The Economics of Production and Supply* (Cambridge, Mass.: M.I.T. Press, 1974); Robert Higgs, *Competition and Coercion: Blacks in the American Economy 1865–1914* (Cambridge: Cambridge University Press, 1977); Jay R. Mandle, *The Roots of Black Poverty: The Southern Plantation Economy After the Civil War* (Durham: Duke University Press, 1978); Daniel A. Novak, *The Wheel of Servitude: Black Forced Labor After Slavery* (Lexington: University of Kentucky Press, 1978).

5   Litwack, *Been in the Storm So Long*, p. xi.

6   Otto H. Olsen, "Setting the Record Straight on the Reconstruction South," *Reviews in American History* 3, no. 3 (1975): 333–34; Michael Les Benedict, "Equality and Expediency in the Reconstruction Era: A Review Essay," *Civil War History* 23, no. 4 (1977): 322–35. Some good state studies in the revisionist tradition have already been written. See Thomas Holt, *Black Over White: Negro Political Leadership in South Carolina During Reconstruction* (Urbana: University of Illinois Press, 1977); Kolchin, *First Freedom;* Otto H. Olsen (ed.), *Reconstruction and Redemption in the South* (Baton Rouge: Louisiana State University Press, 1980); Joe M. Richardson, *The Negro in the Reconstruction of Florida* (Tallahassee: Florida State University Press, 1965); Jerrell H. Shofner, *Nor Is It Over Yet: Florida in the Era of Reconstruction 1863–1877* (Gainesville: The University Presses of Florida, 1974); Joe Taylor Gray, *Louisiana Reconstructed, 1863–1877* (Baton Rouge: Louisiana State University Press, 1974); Vernon L. Wharton, *The Negro in Mississippi, 1865–1900* (Chapel Hill: University of North Carolina Press, 1947); Williamson, *After Slavery*.

7   J. G. de Roulhac Hamilton, *Reconstruction in North Carolina* (New York: Columbia University Press, 1914), especially chaps. iii–iv. Hamilton believed that white North Carolinians were willing to treat blacks fairly. He argued that they were sincerely loyal and anxious to gain reentry into the Union. With only a few exceptions, he praised Johnson's policies. He only superficially treated the enactment of the Black Code and concluded that the "code, if it could be so called, was characterized by justice and moderation" (p. 170). Further, Hamilton felt that such legislation was necessary because blacks were either unwilling or unable to work and that, indeed, "the efforts of the freedmen, unless under white direction, for the most part resulted in failure and disaster" (pp. 199–200). Hamilton thus blamed the blacks themselves as well as the Freedmen's Bureau for what he saw as the intolerable conditions under which North Carolinians had to live during Presidential Reconstruction (p. 157).

8   Horace Wilson Raper, "William Woods Holden: A Political Biography" (unpublished Ph.D. dissertation, University of North Carolina, 1951).

9   Otto H. Olsen, *Carpetbagger's Crusade: The Life of Albion Winegar Tourgee* (Balti-

more: The Johns Hopkins University Press, 1965); Olsen, *Reconstruction and Redemption in the South*, pp. 156–201.

10   Billings, *Planters and the Making of a "New South."*

11   W. McKee Evans, *Ballots and Fence Rails: Reconstruction on the Lower Cape Fear* (Chapel Hill: University of North Carolina Press, 1966), quotation from p. 251.

12   Olsen, *Reconstruction and Redemption in the South*, pp. 6–11.

13   Michael Perman, *Reunion without Compromise[:] The South and Reconstruction: 1865–1868* (Cambridge: Cambridge University Press, 1973).

14   See U. S. Census Office, *Agriculture of the United States in 1860; Compiled from the Original Returns of the Eighth Census* (Washington, D.C.: Government Printing Office, 1864), pp. 104–9, 210, 235–36; U. S. Census Office, *Statistics of the United States (Including Mortality, Property, &c.), in 1860: Compiled from the Original Returns and Being the Final Exhibit of the Eighth Census* (Washington, D.C.: Government Printing Office, 1866), p. 309; U. S. Census Office, *Population of the United States in 1860; Compiled from the Original Returns of the Eighth Census* (Washington, D.C.: Government Printing Office, 1864), pp. 358–59; U. S. Census Office, *A Century of Population Growth from the First Census of the United States to the Twelfth, 1790–1900* (Washington, D.C.: Government Printing Office, 1909), pp. 135, 140; Guion Johnson, *Ante-Bellum North Carolina A Social History* (Chapel Hill: University of North Carolina Press, 1937), pp. 468–69, 528–83; Joseph Carlyle Sitterson, *The Secession Movement in North Carolina, James Sprunt Studies in History and Political Science,* vol. 23, no. 2 (Chapel Hill: University of North Carolina Press, 1939), p. 18; John Hope Franklin, *Free Negro in North Carolina* (New York: W. W. Norton, 1971), pp. 17–19. See also map 1.

For additional information on North Carolina before Reconstruction, see also Henry McGilbert Wagstaff, "States' Rights and Political Parties in North Carolina—1776–1861," *Johns Hopkins University Studies in Historical and Political Science,* series 24, nos. 7–8 (Baltimore: Johns Hopkins University Press, July–August 1906); Hugh Talmadge Lefler and Albert Ray Newsome, *North Carolina* (Chapel Hill: University of North Carolina Press, 1954); William K. Boyd, "North Carolina on the Eve of Secession," *Annual Report of the American Historical Association for the Year 1910;* Richard L. Zuber, *Jonathan Worth, A Biography of a Southern Unionist* (Chapel Hill: University of North Carolina Press, 1965) as well as Johnson, *Ante-Bellum North Carolina* and Sitterson, *Secession Movement.*

The counties with populations containing over 50 percent slaves were Anson, Bertie, Caswell, Chowan, Edgecombe, Franklin, Greene, Halifax, Hertford, Jones, Lenoir, Northampton, Perquimans, Pitt, Richmond, and Warren. The three not in the coastal area were in the southern, cotton-producing area.

Chapter 1

1   Quotation from Colonel E. Whittlesey, "Circular No. 1" (dated Raleigh, July 1, 1865), House Ex. Doc. No. 70, 39th Congress, 1st Session, p. 3.

2 Narrative of Hannah Plummer in George P. Rawick (ed.), *The American Slave: A Composite Autobiography, North Carolina Narratives*, Part 2 (Westport, Conn.: Greenwood Press, 1972), 15: 179, 181 (hereinafter referred to as *North Carolina Narratives*).

3 Narrative of Clara Jones, ibid., pp. 32, 33.

4 Zebulon Baird Vance, *The Duties of Defeat* (Raleigh: William B. Smith and Company, 1866), p. 6.

5 Cited in *The Daily Standard* (Raleigh), May 2, 1865, p. 2. From January 1, 1866, to March 16, 1866, the paper was called *The Daily North Carolina Standard*; from March 20, 1866, to December 25, 1866, *The Tri-Weekly Standard*; and from January 1 through the end of 1867, *The Tri-Weekly Standard*.

6 See LP 817 and LP 819; the following newspapers for the period April–September 1865: *Standard, Daily Sentinel* (Raleigh), *NBT, The Western Democrat* (Charlotte); the following manuscripts for the period March–September 1865: Patterson Papers, NCA; William E. Ardrey Diary of the Family and Farm, DUMC; David Schenck Diary, SHC; Z. B. Vance Papers, NCA; LRAC; LRAGO; Sidney Andrews, *The South Since the War* (Boston: Ticknor and Fields, 1866), p. 111; J. R. Davis, "Reconstruction in Cleveland County," *Historical Papers*, series 10 (Durham: Trinity College Historical Society, 1914), p. 14; John Crouch, *Historical Sketches of Wilkes County* (Wilkesboro: John Crouch, 1902), pp. 85–92; Henry Berry Lowry Papers, NCA; Narrative by W. McKee Evans, "Henry Berry Lowry and the Lowry Gang," NCA; James J. Farris, "The Lowrie Gang: An Episode in the History of Robeson County, North Carolina 1864–1874," *Historical Papers*, series 15 (Durham: Trinity College Historical Society, 1925), pp. 57–93; W. McKee Evans, *To Die Game* (Baton Rouge: Louisiana State University Press, 1971). See also Chap. 6 below for a more detailed discussion of lawlessness and crime.

7 *NBT*, August 1, 1865, p. 2.

8 *Standard*, May 2, 1865, p. 2.

9 *The Daily Union Banner* (Salisbury), May 16, 1865, p. 2.

10 See, e.g., John Hedrick to B. S. Hedrick, June 13, 1865, Benjamin Sherwood Hedrick Papers, DU; Whitelaw Reid, *After the War* (New York: Howard & Hulbert, 1880), p. 51.

11 John R. Dennett, *The South As It Is 1865–1866*, edited by Henry W. Christman (New York: Viking, 1965), pp. 121–22.

12 Mrs. Catherine Roulhac to her daughter, May 21, 1865, RRH Papers.

13 S. S. Murkland to Calvin H. Wiley, September 9, 1865, CHW Papers; Dennett, *South As It Is*, p. 142.

14 Convention of The Freedmen of North Carolina, *Official Proceedings* [1865], pp. 13–14. Hereinafter referred to as Convention of Freedmen, 1865.

15 Reid, *After the War*, p. 45n (see also p. 51); Andrews, *South Since the War*, pp. 178–79, 188.

16 See, e.g., William A. Graham to David L. Swain, May 11, 1865, David Lowry Swain Papers, NCA; *Union Banner*, May 16, 1865, p. 2; *NBT*, August 30, 1865, p. 3;

Charles A. Hill to Horace James, August 26, 1865, ULRE; Convention of Freedmen, 1865, pp. 13–14.

17 See, e.g., *NBT*, August 1, 1865, p. 2, August 30, 1865, p. 3, May 24, 1865, p. 3; *Standard*, July 1, 1865, p. 2; FBP from June–September 1865; Reid, *After the War*, pp. 45n, 51–53; Dennett, *South As It Is*, pp. 176–77; Andrews, *South Since the War*, pp. 178–79; William W. Holden to General Ruger, September 23, 1865, p. 75, Holden LB; General A. Ames to Major Clinton A. Cilley, July 27, 1865, RCC, Letters Received.

18 *The Daily Progress* (Raleigh), August 14, 1865, cited in *NBT*, August 16, 1865, p. 3. I do not know how, or if, this person was punished. Any time a news story is cited from a reprinted article, the original paper in which the story appeared is not extant.

19 Reid, *After the War*, p. 51n.

20 James V. Bomford to O. O. Howard, December [1865], LSAC.

21 William A. Graham to David L. Swain, May 11, 1865, Swain Papers.

22 Joe A. Mobley, *James City: A Black Community in North Carolina 1863–1900* (Raleigh: North Carolina Department of Cultural Resources, Division of Archives and History, 1981), pp. 1–5.

23 John C. Barnett to E. Whittlesey, June 29, 1865, LRAC.

24 Schenck Diary, entry of June 7, 1865, p. 43. See also, *Union Banner*, May 16, 1865, p. 2; Daniel M. Barringer to his wife, May 9, 1865, and W. Barringer to D. M. Barringer, May 14, 1865, Daniel M. Barringer Papers, SHC; Mary Jeffreys Bethell Diary, entry of August 7, 1865, SHC; Lossie Myers to her brother Louis, June 30, 1865, de Rossett Family Papers, SHC; David L. Swain to William A. Graham, May 6, 1865, William A. Graham Paper, NCA; Mrs. Catherine Roulhac to her daughter, May 21, 1865, RRH Papers; Schenck Diary, [May 31, 1865,] pp. 41–42, and June 14, 1865, pp. 46, 49; Ann to her brother, June 12, 1865, Battle Family Papers, SHC. Of course, some freedmen stayed with their former masters. See, e.g., Ardrey Diary, entry of May 1865, pp. 2–3; Mary Patterson to Rufus L. Patterson, July 23, 1865, Patterson Papers.

25 See, e.g., John C. Barnett to E. Whittlesey, June 29, 1865, LRAC; Mary Caldwell to her sister Minerva, July 17, 1865, Caldwell Papers; Robert D. Graham to William A. Graham, July 22, 1865, William A. Graham Papers, SHC.

26 See, e.g., Mary Caldwell to her sister Minerva, July 17, 1865, Caldwell Papers; Nattie A. Croobie to Newton Woody, June 23, 1865, Robert and Newton D. Woody Papers, DU.

27 See, e.g., Asa Teal to E. Whittlesey, July 26, 1865, LRAC; E. Whittlesey to Major C. A. Cilley, August 3, 1865, LSAC; D. Carson to Captain M. Adams, August 7, 1865, RCC, Letters Received; "Freedmen's Bureau Cases," *Standard*, August, 1865; Circular by Captain Charles Emery dated August 12, 1865, cited in the *Union Banner*, August 16, 1865, p. 3; Convention of Freedmen, 1865, pp. 13–14.

28 *Standard*, April 24, 1865, p. 2. See also Reid, *After the War*, p. 31, and "Capt. James' Annual Report," *NBT*, September 12, 1865, p. 2.

29 John A. Hedrick to B. S. Hedrick, April 11, 1865, Hedrick Papers.

30 *The National Freedman* (New York), April 1, 1865, p. 77.

31 *NBT*, August 8, 1865, p. 2. The Charlotte *Western Democrat* (June 6, 1865, p. 3) reported that Negroes in Wilmington were also dying in large numbers.

32 *Freedmen's Record* (Boston), June, 1865, pp. 93–94, "Monthly Report" by Fannie Graves and Annie P. Merriam. The *Standard* (June 9, 1865, p. 2) also reported "much suffering" among freedmen in New Berne.

33 See, e.g., Circular No. 5, May 30, 1865, from O. O. Howard to the Assistant Commissioners printed in the *Standard*, August 8, 1865, p. 4 and E. Whittlesey to Asa Teal, July 19, 1865, LSAC.

34 FBP, passim. See also map 2.

35 Report by Major Aquila Wiley, February 14, 1866, SMR.

36 Samuel P. Fowler, Jr., to Horace James, December 12, 1865, ULRE.

37 FBP, passim.

38 E. Whittlesey to O. O. Howard, January 15, 1866, House Ex. Doc. No. 70; *Sentinel*, August 17, 1866, p. 3; E. Whittlesey to Asa Teal, August 4, 1865, LSAC; Samuel P. Fowler, Jr., to Horace James, December 12, 1865, ULRE; *The News* (Fayetteville), May 15, 1866, p. 3; E. G. Holt to David M. Carter, February 17, 1866, David M. Carter Papers, SHC.

39 Cited in *Standard*, September 29, p. 2. It is likely that the number of freedmen in these camps was much higher in April and September. John Hedrick reported on March 31, 1865, that about five hundred blacks, mostly women and children, had just been sent from Wilmington to the Beaufort camps. (John Hedrick to B. S. Hedrick, March 31, 1865, Hedrick Papers.) Two weeks later he wrote that nearly a thousand refugee freedmen were in Beaufort (Ibid., April 11, 1865). But by June 9, 1865, the *Standard* reported that those ex-slaves who had fled to New Berne as the Union troops passed through were returning to the farms in large numbers. (*Standard*, June 9, 1865, p. 2, dated New Berne, May 30, 1865.)

40 A. G. Tennant to Horace James, November 5, 1865, ULRE.

41 For the Salisbury camp, see the *Union Banner*, June 30, 1865, p. 3; Report by Stephen Moore, June 20, 1866, and June 30, 1866, RRI. For Morehead City, see Sanitary Report issued by W. H. Doherty, July 3, 1866, FBP. For Wilmington, see Report of Camps in the Southern District of North Carolina for October 1865 by C. J. Wickersham, RRI. For Greensboro, see Report of Asa Teal, August 1865, RRI. For Charlotte, see reports by Stephen Moore, June 20, 1866, and June 30, 1866, and by John C. Barnett, July 31, 1865, and September 30, 1865, RRI; Report by Francis M. Bache to A. S. Webb, September 18, 1865, LRAGO. For Raleigh, see Report by Francis M. Bache to A. S. Webb, September 7, 1865, ibid.

42 *Union Banner*, June 30, 1865, p. 3.

43 Horace James to Fred Beecher, September 20, 1865, LRAC; H Report, 1865; Mobley, *James City*, pp. 21–32. Mobley's excellent work provides extensive detail on this settlement and its development through 1900.

44 Report from Charles J. Wickersham, September 6, 1865, NR.

45 Elizabeth Norwood Bingham to her brother, June 3, 1865, William Norwood Tillinghast Papers, 1865–67, DU. This report is probably exaggerated, because in the same

letter Mrs. Bingham gives an extended defense of slavery, claiming that blacks will die out unless whites care for them.

46 Report by Alexander Gaslin, December 31, 1865, SR; John H. Holmden to Solon A. Carter, n.d., ULRAC.

47 *Sentinel*, August 10, 1865, p. 4.

48 T. P. Devereux to Jonathan Worth, October 20, 1866, LP 820. See also *Standard*, June 1, 1865, p. 2; *Western Democrat*, June 13, 1865, p. 2; Sally M. Leach to her mother, August 1, 1865, Willie P. Mangum Papers, 1862–68, LC; Elizabeth Norwood Bingham to her brother, June 3, 1865, Tillinghast Papers.

49 *Standard*, August 3, 1866, p. 2.

50 Franklin, *Reconstruction After the Civil War*, pp. 35–36; George Meade to Edwin Stanton, September 20, 1865, LRAGO; SWR, p. 59; *Standard*, July 26, 1865, p. 2.

51 James E. Sefton, *The United States Army and Reconstruction 1865–1877* (Baton Rouge: Louisiana State University Press, 1967), p. 52 and chap. 2.

52 Ruger to George Meade, September 19, 1865, LRAGO; SWR, p. 59.

53 W. H. Jones to Z. B. Vance, June 8, 1865, Vance Papers. See also *Union Banner*, May 16, 1865, p. 2.

54 See, e.g., Tod R. Caldwell to William Holden, forwarded to General Ruger, September 18, 1865, RCC, Letters Received; J. A. Campbell to George L. Granger, April 5, 1866 and James H. Anderson to Captain Bliss, February 19, 1866, RCC, Letters Sent; *Sentinel*, August 20, 1866, p. 3; J. L. Kirkpatrick to unknown correspondent, October 13, 1865, J. L. Kirkpatrick Papers, NCA.

55 Thomas Heath to J. A. Campbell, October 9, 1865, RCC, Letters Received. See also Schenck Diary, pp. 43–45; Mary Caldwell to Minerva, July 17, 1865, Caldwell Papers; Ann Falkner to her brother, June 12, 1865, Battle Family Papers; letter to the editor from "Christianos," *NBT*, September 14, 1866, p. 1.

56 See, e.g., Holden LB and Holden GP, June–August, 1865; Holden to Mayor and Commissioners of the Town of Wilmington, July 15, 1865, Andrew Johnson Papers, LC; *Standard*, September 25, 1865, p. 3, and January 5, 1866, p. 3; *Sentinel*, August 18, 1865, p. 2; December 11, 1865, p. 2; January 5, 1866, p. 3; and June 27, 1866, p. 3.

57 A. M. Waddell to Holden, June 18, 1865, Holden LB, p. 3; Holden to Mayor and Commissioners of the Town of Wilmington, July 15, 1865, Johnson Papers; Mayor and Commissioners of the Town of Wilmington to Holden, August 3, 1865, Holden GP.

58 *Progress*, May 16, 1865, p. 2.

59 Ibid., August 5, 1865, p. 2; *NBT*, December 4, 1865, p. 4. For similar comments about troops in Elizabeth City and Edenton, see letter by "H" in *Sentinel*, September 25, 1865, p. 2.

60 Holden to Mayor and Commissioners of the Town of Wilmington, including a report from the commissioners dated July 12, 1865, and a statement by the captain of police, July 15, 1865, Johnson Papers.

61 Mayor and Commissioners of the Town of Wilmington to Holden, August 3, 1865, Holden GP.

62 *The Wilmington Herald*, June 12, 1865, p. 2. (After August 1865 it was known as *The Daily Wilmington Herald*.)

63 *Standard*, June 23, 1865, p. 2, and June 29, 1865, p. 2. See also A. M. Worrell to Holden, June 18, 1865, Holden LB.

64 Samuel A. Duncan to the Assistant Adjutant General, July 26, 1865, RCC, Letters Received.

65 General Ruger to General Meade, September 19, 1865, LRAGO.

66 *Sentinel*, August 18, 1865, p. 2.

67 Holden to Andrew Johnson, August 10, 1865, Holden GP; General Meade to Edwin Stanton, September 20, 1865, and General Ruger to General Meade, September 19, 1865, LRAGO.

68 *Daily Journal* (Wilmington), February 12, 1866, p. 1.

Chapter 2

1 *Wilmington Herald*, September 27, 1865, p. 1.

2 *NBT*, August 30, 1865, p. 3.

3 Convention of Freedmen, 1865, p. 13. See also report of Horace James in *The Freedmen's Record*, September, 1865, p. 143; *Progress*, July 6, 1865, p. 1.

4 Mass meeting of New Berne blacks, *NBT*, September 8, 1865, p. 2, and *Standard*, September 12, 1865, p. 3.

5 A.M.E. Zion Church, *Minutes of the North Carolina Annual Conference of the A.M.E. Zion Church in America* (Hartford: Case, Lockwood and Company, 1866), p. 16.

6 *Wilmington Herald*, September 27, 1865, p. 1.

7 Dennett, *South As It Is*, p. 176.

8 *NBT*, December 22, 1865, p. 4. Three other prominent black citizens of New Berne supported Hood's statement: George A. Rue, pastor of the A.M.E. Bethel Church; Henry W. Jones, minister of Clinton Chapel; and Richard Tucker, a coffin maker and undertaker. Rue attended the 1865 freedmen's convention along with Hood. Rue and Tucker were delegates to the 1866 convention.

9 See, e.g., *Progress*, July 6, 1865, p. 1; *Wilmington Herald*, September 23, 1865, p. 1; *NBT*, July 6, 1865, p. 2, and July 12, 1865, p. 1; *Standard*, July 6, 1865, p. 2.

10 H Report, 1865, pp. 25, 39. See also reports by Charles J. Wickersham, October 31, 1865; by John C. Barnett, July 31, 1865, and September 1865; and by Asa Teal, August 1865, RRI. Also A. S. Webb to George Meade, September 18, 1865 and Thomas Ruger to Meade, September 19, 1865, LRAGO. Also Reid, *After the War*, p. 34n; Report of Horace James in *The Freedmen's Record*, September 1865, p. 142; E. Whittlesey to John C. Barnett, July 13, 1865, and Whittlesey to Asa Teal, July 19, 1865, LSAC; *Union Banner*, June 30, 1865, p. 3. The reduction in rations issued was due for the most part to the efforts of the Bureau to make contracts for the freedmen and to get them back to work as soon as possible. For a more complete discussion of this effort along with the willingness of blacks to return to work, see below, chap. 5.

11   The quotation from the Concord man is from Dennett, *South As It Is*, pp. 136–37. See also ibid., p. 116; Austin W. Fuller to the Superintendent of the Eastern District, August 14, 1866, ULRE; the following newspapers from April 1865–February 1866: *Western Democrat, Sentinel, The Daily Dispatch* (Wilmington), *Progress, Standard, Journal, The Southerner* (Tarboro); Mrs. C. P. Spencer to Eliza North, March 10, 1866, Mrs. Cornelia Phillips Spencer Papers, NCA; J.T.P.C. Cohoon to Jonathan Worth, January 1, 1866, Worth GP; Andrews, *South Since the War*, pp. 186–87.

12   Ibid., p. 187.

13   See below, chap. 5.

14   Report of Horace James in *The Freedmen's Record*, September 1865, p. 143.

15   *Standard*, May 30, 1865, p. 1. See also Reid, *After the War*, p. 52, and *Journal of Freedom* (Raleigh), October 21, 1865, p. 2.

16   *Sentinel*, September 20, 1865, p. 2.

17   Report of Horace James in *The Freedmen's Record*, September 1865, p. 143; Samuel A. Duncan to C. A. Cilley, July 26, 1865, RCC, Letters Received; Samuel P. Fowler, Jr., to Horace James, December 12, 1865, ULRE; *NBT*, June 29, 1865, p. 3, and July 7, 1865, p. 3; *Progress*, July 6, 1865, p. 1.

18   *Standard*, July 6, 1865, p. 2; *Progress*, July 6, 1865, p. 1.

19   Letter to the editor from "Waiflet," dated Beaufort, July 10, 1865, *NBT*, July 12, 1865, p. 2, and ibid., June 29, 1865, p. 3.

20   Ibid., July 6, 1865, p. 2. See also July 7, 1865, p. 3.

21   Ibid., July 7, 1865, p. 3.

22   See, e.g., *Standard*, July 6, 1865, p. 2; *Progress*, July 6, 1865, p. 1; *NBT*, July 6, 1865, p. 2, and July 12, 1865, p. 2.

23   *NBT*, August 23, 1865, p. 3, and August 31, 1865, p. 3; *Standard*, August 26, 1865, p. 3; *Wilmington Herald*, September 8, 1865, p. 2. The call in the *Herald* appeared as a paid advertisement.

24   *NBT*, August 30, 1865, p. 3. Biographical information on Good and all other blacks subsequently discussed was gathered from the following sources: U.S., *Eighth Census of the United States, 1860: North Carolina*, Population Schedule; U.S., *Ninth Census of the United States, 1870: North Carolina*, Population Schedule; *Branson & Farrar's North Carolina Business Directory for 1866–1867* (Raleigh: Branson & Farrar, 1866); *Branson's North Carolina Business Directory, For 1867–8* (Raleigh: Branson & Jones, 1867); J. S. Tomlinson, *Tar Heel Sketchbook* (Raleigh: Raleigh News Steam Book & Job Print, 1879); John A. Oates, *The Story of Fayetteville and the Upper Cape Fear* (Charlotte: The Dowd Press, 1950); W. H. Quick, *Negro Stars in All Ages of the World* (2d ed.; Richmond: S. B. Adkins & Company, 1898); J. Harvey Anderson, *Biographical Souvenir Volume of the 23rd Quadrennial Session of the General Conference of the A.M.E. Zion Church* (n.p.: [1908]); James H. Harris Papers, NCA; Jerome Dowd, *Sketches of Prominent Living North Carolinians* (Raleigh: Edwards and Broughton, 1888); Frenise A. Logan, *The Negro in North Carolina 1876–1894* (Chapel Hill: University of North Carolina Press, 1965); Franklin, *Free Negro in North Carolina;* Dennett, *South As It Is;* Andrews, *South Since the War;* several North

Carolina newspapers; Freedmen's Savings and Trust Company, Signature Books, New Berne Branch (2 vols.) and Wilmington (1 vol.), NA; R. R. Wright, *The Bishops of the A.M.E. Church* ([Nashville]: A.M.E. Sunday School Union, 1963).

25 *Standard*, September 12, 1865, p. 3, and September 14, 1865, p. 3; *NBT*, August 30, 1865, p. 3, and September 8, 1865, p. 2; *Wilmington Herald*, September 14, 1865, p. 1, September 15, 1865, p. 1, September 23, 1865, p. 1, September 27, 1865, p. 1; *Journal of Freedom*, October 28, 1865, p. 3; *Sentinel*, September 25, 1865, p. 2; Charles A. Hill to Horace James, September 21, 1865, ULRE; F. M. Garrett to E. Whittlesey, September 25, 1865, ULRAC; and H. C. Thompson to B. S. Hedrick, September 21, 1865, Hedrick Papers. The counties that were reported to have held mass meetings were Craven, Wake, New Hanover, Edgecombe, Carteret, Bladen, Orange, Pasquotank, Perquimans, and Chowan.

26 *Standard*, September 14, 1865, p. 3.

27 *Journal of Freedom*, October 28, 1865, p. 3.

28 *Wilmington Herald*, September 23, 1865, p. 1.

29 *NBT*, August 30, 1865, p. 3.

30 Ibid., August 31, 1865, p. 3, August 28, 1865, p. 3; *Wilmington Herald*, September 27, 1865, p. 1, September 29, 1865, p. 2. See also *Sentinel*, September 16, 1865, p. 2, and *Journal*, September 30, 1865, p. 2, for similar negative press reactions.

31 *Journal*, September 30, 1865. This statement appeared as a paid advertisement. It is possible that no Wilmington paper would print Rue's response as an unpaid letter to the editor.

32 H. C. Thompson to B. S. Hedrick, September 21, 1865, Hedrick Papers; *Journal of Freedom*, October 7, 1865, p. 2, October 28, 1865, p. 3; Andrews, *South Since the War*, p. 131; Dennett, *South As It Is*, p. 175; Convention of Freedmen, 1865, p. 17.

33 Andrews, *South Since the War*, pp. 120–21 and Dennett, *South As It Is*, pp. 149–50.

34 Convention of Freedmen, 1865, pp. 2–3, 6; *Standard*, September 30, 1865, p. 3; Andrews, *South Since the War*, p. 121; *Progress*, October 2, 1865, p. 2; Dennett, *South As It Is*, p. 149. Only the 106 delegates listed on the official roll can be identified by name. Therefore they are the only ones analyzed in the subsequent text.

35 Dennett, *South As It Is*, p. 149. According to the official roll of delegates, New Hanover County (Wilmington) sent three delegates; Craven County (New Berne) was represented by sixteen men—the largest single delegation; and Carteret County (Beaufort) sent seven representatives.

36 Andrews (*South Since the War*, p. 121) also suggested this possibility.

37 *Western Democrat*, 1865–66, passim.

38 Andrews, *South Since the War*, p. 124.

39 Thirty-eight cannot be found in the 1870 census; three were native southerners but not native North Carolinians and therefore might not appear in the 1860 North Carolina census even if they had been free before the war. These delegates, therefore, are not included in the figures listed.

40 The 1870 census might be inaccurate regarding literacy. One example of inaccuracy was found. In the census Joseph Green of New Berne was listed as not being able to read or write. In the Signature Book of the Freedmen's Savings and Trust Company, however, he signed his name.

41 The exact breakdown is one cooper, three barbers, one brick mason, one bricklayer, one shoemaker, eleven carpenters, two blacksmiths, one mechanic, and one wagon maker.

42 Andrews, *South Since the War*, p. 131.

43 Dennett, *South As It Is*, pp. 150–51.

44 Andrews, *South Since the War*, pp. 122–23.

45 Dennett, *South As It Is*, p. 149; Convention of Freedmen, 1865, pp. 4–5. See also *Journal of Freedom*, October 7, 1865, p. 1.

46 Convention of Freedmen, 1865, p. 5. See also *Standard*, September 30, 1865, p. 3.

47 Convention of Freedmen, 1865, p. 5; *Journal of Freedom*, October 7, 1865, p. 1.

48 This is especially true for the historians of the Dunning School, particularly Claude Bowers in *The Tragic Era*.

49 Convention of Freedmen, 1865, pp. 6–7. See also *Journal of Freedom*, October 7, 1865, p. 1.

50 Convention of Freedmen, 1865, pp. 12–14. See also *Standard*, October 4, 1865, p.. 3; *Journal of Freedom*, October 7, 1865, p. 2; *Sentinel*, October 4, 1865, p. 4.

51 Convention of Freedmen, 1865, p. 15; Andrews, *South Since the War*, p. 127.

52 Convention of Freedmen, 1865, pp. 15, 16, 22; *Journal of Freedom*, October 7, 1865, pp. 2, 3. See below, chap. 4, for the actions the freedmen took at their 1866 convention after the white legislative bodies had not acted as they had hoped.

54 Andrews, *South Since the War*, pp. 119–20, 130–31.

55 *Union Banner*, October 3, 1865, p. 2; *Sentinel*, October 2 and October 4, 1865, p. 2; *Progress*, October 2 and October 4, 1865, p. 2.

Chapter 3

1 House Ex. Doc. No. 70, 39th Congress, 1st Session, p. 3.

2 See, e.g., William Sumner Jenkins, *Pro-Slavery Thought in the Old South* (Chapel Hill: University of North Carolina Press, 1935); Eric L. McKitrick (ed.), *Slavery Defended: The Views of the Old South* (Englewood Cliffs, N.J.: Prentice-Hall, 1963); Roberta Sue Alexander, "Slavery Arguments in the South, 1820–1830" (unpublished M.A. thesis, University of Chicago, 1966).

3 Quote from *Goldsboro Daily News*, reprinted in *Standard*, September 22, 1865, p. 3. See also the following North Carolina newspapers from 1865–67: *CI, Dispatch, Sentinel, Greensboro Patriot, Carolina Watchman* (Salisbury); the following manuscript and correspondence collections for 1865–66: Spencer Papers, *Worth Corr.*, Tillinghast Papers, Patterson Family Papers, SHC; Dennett, *South As It Is*, p. 119; Andrews, *South Since the War*, p. 181; LP 812 and 820; Report by Clinton A. Cilley, February 29, 1866, SR.

4 Quote from G. F. Granger to Thaddeus Stevens, January 11, 1866, in James A. Padgett (ed.), "Reconstruction Letters from North Carolina, Part I, Letters to Thaddeus Stevens," *North Carolina Historical Review* 18, no. 2 (April 1941): 176 (hereinafter referred to as "Letter to Stevens"). See also Andrews, *South Since the War*, p. 181;

Dennett, *South As It Is*, p. 119; the following North Carolina newspapers from July 1865–September 1866: *Standard, NBT, CI, Western Democrat, Greensboro Patriot, Sentinel;* A. M. McPheeters to R. L. Patterson, June 10, 1865, Patterson Papers; Eliza Bingham to her brother, June 3, 1865, Tillinghast Papers; Roberta Sue Alexander, "North Carolina Faces the Freedmen: Race Relations During Presidential Reconstruction, 1865–1867" (unpublished Ph.D. dissertation, University of Chicago, 1974), passim, but especially chap. 3.

5   J. R. Richardson (ed.), *Compilation of the Messages and Papers of the Presidents, 1789–1897* (10 vols.; New York: Bureau of National Literature and Art, 1897), V, 3508–12. Also in Holden GP, May–June, 1865.

6   See Dennett, *South As It Is*, p. 2; S. S. Jackson to Jonathan Worth, August 9, 1866, *Worth Corr.* 2: 739–41; William S. Mason to Jonathan Worth, August 17, 1866, in Worth LB, pp. 148–49. The ironclad or test oath had to be sworn to by all members of Congress before they would be seated.

7   Quotations are from Reid, *After the War*, pp. 53, 296–97 and Andrews, *South Since the War*, p. 174. For a fuller description of these groups and examples of their rhetoric, see Alexander, "North Carolina," pp. 125–49.

8   *Standard*, August 16, 1865, p. 2. See also Dennett, *South As It Is*, pp. 115, 145.

9   See Alexander, "North Carolina," pp. 151–58, for a complete analysis of these union meetings.

10   See ibid., chap. 4.

11   Dennett, *South As It Is*, p. 156. See also Andrews, *South Since the War*, pp. 132–33, for a similar opinion.

12   For statements which claimed that most of the delegates were staunch unionists, see William Holden to Andrew Johnson, September 23, 1865, Holden LB, p. 74; *Standard*, October 2, 1865, p. 2 (but cf. with ibid., September 25, 1865, p. 2); *Wilmington Herald*, reprinted in *Sentinel*, September 29, 1865, p. 2; *Sentinel*, September 26, 1865, p. 2; Quarterly report Ending December 31, 1865, E. Whittlesey to O. O. Howard, January 15, 1866, House Ex. Doc. No. 70, 39th Congress, 1st Session; Report of Colonel Elias Wright, May 29, 1865, Holden GP. The major sources used to gain information on white politicians, including their wealth and other biographical information used throughout this discussion, were the 1860 census and sources listed under "County Histories and Biographical Reference Works" and other secondary sources listed in the bibliography. Information was also occasionally found in newspapers, especially around the time of an election, and private correspondence. For more complete data on the delegates, see Alexander, "North Carolina," pp. 180–85.

13   *Conv, 1865*, pp. 28, 30, 31; OC, p. 4; Andrews, *South Since the War*, p. 156; *Sentinel*, August 8, 1865, p. 2.

14   *Standard*, October 7, 1865, p. 2. See also OC, pp. 3, 30; S. F. Phillips to William A. Graham, [October 10, 1865,] Graham Papers, SHC; *Standard*, October 6, 1865, p. 2; Edward Conigland to his wife, October 8, 1865, Edward Conigland Papers, SHC; Andrews, *South Since the War*, pp. 143–44; *Conv, 1865*, pp. 23–24, 25, 29.

15   See OC, p. 30; *EDC, 1865*, pp. 5–7; *Conv, 1865*, pp. 15, 38; the following North Caro-

lina newspapers from July–October 1865: *Sentinel, Standard, NBT;* the following man-uscript collections for October 1865: Johnson Papers; Marmaduke Swain Robins Papers, SHC; Patterson Family Papers; *Worth Corr.* 1: 394, 420.

16   See Alexander, "North Carolina," chap. 4, for an extensive analysis of the November election campaign. See also the following North Carolina newspapers for October–November 1865: *Standard, Western Democrat, NBT, Union Banner, Wilmington Herald, Journal, Sentinel, People's Press, Daily Carolina Times* (Charlotte), *Dispatch, Greensboro Patriot, Journal of Freedom;* the following manuscript collections from July–October 1865: Holden GP; Graham Papers, SHC; Johnson Papers; *Worth Corr.* 1: 430–32, 450, 455. For the election results see *JS, 1865–66,* pp. 89–91.

    For information on Holden and Worth see Horace Wilson Raper, "William Woods Holden: A Political Biography" (unpublished Ph.D. dissertation, University of North Carolina, 1951); William W. Holden, *Memoirs of William W. Holden,* vol. 2 of The John Lawson Monographs of the Trinity College Historical Society (Durham: The Seeman Printery, 1911); Richard L. Zuber, *Jonathan Worth: A Biography of a Southern Unionist* (Chapel Hill: University of North Carolina Press, 1965); Lefler and Newsome, *North Carolina;* William K. Boyd, "North Carolina on the Eve of Secession," *Annual Report of the American Historical Association for the Year 1910.* For a discussion of Holden's biased pardoning practices see Jonathan Truman Dorris, "Pardoning North Caro-linians," *North Carolina Historical Review* 23, no. 3 (July 1946), and Alexander, "North Carolina," pp. 164–69.

17   Smith to William A. Graham, November 5, 1865, Graham Papers, NCA. For a complete discussion of the candidates and the congressional races, see Alexander, "North Carolina," pp. 217–40. Hamilton (*Reconstruction,* p. 140) was incorrect when he claimed that only one of the defeated candidates could take the test oath. For a detailed discussion of the ironclad oath, see Harold M. Hyman, *Era of the Oath: Northern Loyalty Tests During the Civil War and Reconstruction* (Philadelphia: University of Pennsylvania Press, 1954). While I disagree with Hyman's emphasis on the political motivation of Con-gress in supporting this oath (see, e.g., p. 83) and his contention that southerners were intransigent on this issue because they believed Johnson would have the oath requirement repealed (p. 86), this is a very valuable study on the whole issue of loyalty tests.

18   *Standard,* "Official Vote," December 28, 1865, p. 3. See also Alexander, "North Carolina," pp. 242–46.

19   *Standard,* December 11, 1865, p. 2.

20   In the House the average age was 42.5 years; in the Senate it was 46.5. There were no significant differences in occupation and wealth between those elected to the convention and those who served in the General Assembly.

21   *Standard,* May 11, 1865, p. 2. See also *Dispatch,* November 16, 1865, p. 2.

22   *JH, 1865–66,* pp. 23–24, 26–28; *JH, 1866,* pp. 136–37; *JS, 1865–66,* pp. 43, 47, 84–86, 149–55; *PL, 1865,* pp. 9–10; *PL, 1866,* p. 140. See also *Standard,* November 21, 1865, p. 2, and December 2, 1865, p. 2; *Sentinel,* December 2, 1865, p. 2.

23   See, e.g., *Sentinel,* January 9, 1866, p. 2, and January 31, 1866, p. 2; *Standard,* October 13, 1865, p. 2.

24 *Sentinel*, December 5, 1865, p. 2.

25 *Standard*, October 13, 1865, p. 2.

26 Ibid.

27 Ibid., January 18, 1866, p. 2, and October 13, 1865, p. 2; *JS, 1865–66*, pp. 25, 47, 60, 108; *JH, 1865–66*, p. 63.

28 *JH, 1866*, p. 34; *Standard*, January 31, 1866, p. 2; *Sentinel*, January 31, 1866, p. 1.

29 The eight proposed acts were bills (1) "to punish persons pursuing horses and other livestock with intent to steal them"; (2) "to punish vagrancy"; (3) "to prevent willful trespasses on lands and stealing any kind of property therefrom"; (4) "to punish seditious language, insurrections and rebellions . . ."; (5) "to secure to agricultural laborers their payment in kind"; (6) "to prevent enticing servants from fulfilling their contracts, or harboring them"; (7) "more effectually to secure the maintenance of bastard children, and the payment of fines and costs on conviction in criminal cases"; (8) "to establish workhouses . . . ."

30 *JH, 1866*, p. 35, and *JS, 1866*, p. 123. Normally such bills would have been referred to the Judiciary Committee.

31 *Standard*, January 31, 1866, pp. 1, 2; *Sentinel*, January 31, 1866, p. 1; *JH, 1866*, pp. 34–35.

32 "Raleigh Correspondent to the Wilmington Journal," *Journal*, January 29, 1866, p. 3.

33 *Standard*, February 3, 1866, p. 1; *Wilmington Herald*, January 30, 1866, p. 2; R. H. Battle to B. S. Hedrick, January 23, 1866, Hedrick Papers.

34 *Standard*, January 31, 1866, p. 3, February 2, 1866, p. 2, February 9, 1866, p. 2.

35 *PL, 1866*, pp. 99–100, 102. Italics mine.

36 *JH, 1866*, p. 18.

37 Ibid., p. 102.

38 *Standard*, January 31, 1866, p. 2; *Sentinel*, January 31, 1866, p. 1.

39 See, e.g., the following newspapers for February–March 1866: *Standard, Sentinel, NBT, Western Democrat, Journal of Freedom, Progress;* J. Holderby and J. W. Burton to William A. Graham, February 1, 1866, Graham Papers, NCA; *Worth Corr.* 1:467; R. H. Battle to B. S. Hedrick, February 6, 1866, Hedrick Papers; T. P. Devereux to Jonathan Worth, October 20, 1866, LP 820.

40 *Western Democrat*, February 28, 1866, p. 1.

41 *Standard*, February 1, 1866, p. 1. See also "Union" in ibid., February 21, 1866, p. 1; *Sentinel*, February 9, 1866, p. 2, March 5, 1866, p. 2; *Progress*, November 14, 1865, p. 2.

42 Quotation from McAden in *Sentinel*, February 28, 1866, p. 1. See also ibid., February 17, 1866, p. 2, and March 8, 1866, p. 1; *Standard*, February 3, 1866, p. 2; *Western Democrat*, February 6, 1866, p. 3; W. N. H. Smith to Henry T. Clark, February 17, 1866, Henry Toole Clark Papers, DU; William Holden to O. O. Howard, September 26, 1865, Holden LB, p. 78.

43 *Standard*, February 2, 1866, p. 2, February 3, 1866, p. 2; *Sentinel*, February 2, 1866, p. 2, February 3, 1866, p. 2.

44 *Standard*, February 9, 1866, p. 2 *Sentinel*, February 9, 1866, p. 2. See also, *Sentinel*,

February 12, 1866, p. 3, February 16, 1866, p. 2; *Dispatch*, February 7, 1866, p. 2, February 15, 1866, p. 2; Dennett, *South As It Is*, pp. 132, 168.

45   *JH, 1866*, p. 148; *PL, 1866*, p. 102; Andrew Johnson to Jonathan Worth, March 6, 1866 and Jonathan Worth to Andrew Johnson, March 4, 1866, in Worth LB, pp. 56, 54; *Worth Corr.* 1:509; *Standard*, March 3, 1866, p. 2, March 20, 1866, p. 2; *Southerner*, March 3, 1866, p. 2.

46   *Standard*, June 1, 1865, p. 2, October 14, 1865, p. 2, October 18, 1865, p. 2.

47   *Sentinel*, August 11, 1865, p. 2, and January 4, 1866, p. 2. See also the following newspapers from July 1865–March 1866: *Sentinel, Western Democrat, Wilmington Herald, NBT, Progress*.

48   Dennett, *South As It Is*, pp. 130–31; Reid, *After the War*, p. 25; LP, "Petitions and Memorials," October 1865. Italics mine. See also Dennett, *South As It Is*, pp. 156–57, 163–64; S. F. Phillips to William A. Graham, December 28, 1865, Graham Papers, SHC.

49   Reid, *After the War*, p. 44; *Standard*, August 29, 1865, p. 2.

50   *PL, 1866*, p. 101.

51   Ibid., p. 100.

52   *Standard*, March 20, 1866, p. 2. See also *JS, 1866*, pp. 176, 240; Thomas H. Blount to David M. Carter, February 25, 1866, Carter Papers.

53   See below, chap. 5.

54   See, e.g., *Western Democrat*, January 30, 1866, p. 3; *Progress*, September 23, 1865, p. 2; Andrews, *South Since the War*, p. 183.

55   See, e.g., T. P. Devereux to Jonathan Worth, October 20, 1866, LP 820; *Western Democrat*, August 7, 1866, p. 3; and above, chap. 1.

56   *PL, 1866*, p. 111. Italics mine.

57   U. S. Congress, *Report of the Joint Committee on Reconstruction,* 39th Congress, 1st session, 1866, pp. 182, 177–78. See also below, chap. 6, for examples of other blacks being sold to pay court costs.

58   *PL, 1866*, p. 123; Report of the Commission, *Standard*, January 31, 1866, p. 1, and *Sentinel*, January 31, 1866, p. 1.

59   *Report of Joint Committee*, p. 182. See also below, chap. 5.

60   T. P. Devereux to Jonathan Worth, October 20, 1866, LP 820. See also above, chap. 1, and below, chap. 5.

61   *PL, 1866*, p. 122; *Standard*, October 14, 1865, p. 2. See also below, chap. 5.

62   *PL, 1866*, pp. 88–92.

63   *Standard*, January 31, 1866, pp. 1–2; *Sentinel*, January 31, 1866, p. 1.

64   *Dispatch*, April 9, 1866, p. 3. See also ibid., October 17, 1866, p. 3.

65   *PL, 1866*, pp. 101–03.

66   Ibid., pp. 100–101. Italics mine.

67   *Standard*, January 31, 1866, pp. 1–2; *Sentinel*, January 31, 1866, p. 1.

68   *Standard*, January 31, 1866, p. 2; *Sentinel*, January 31, 1866, p. 1; *PL, 1866*, p. 121. See also below, chap. 6.

69   William A. Graham to Jonathan Worth, January 26, 1866, *Worth Corr.* 1:482. See also *Standard*, November 28, 1865, p. 2, January 31, 1866, pp. 1–2; *Sentinel*, January 31,

1866, pp. 1–2; *Sentinel*, January 31, 1866, p. 1; *Report of Joint Committee*, p. 177; Petitions of the Grand Juries, Superior Courts of Buncombe and Transylvania Counties, October 1865, LP 804; see also below, chap. 6.

70 *PL, 1866*, pp. 122–24. An amendment to make an intent to steal punishable by death was defeated in the House 73 to 30 (*JH, 1866*, p. 50).

71 See below, chap. 6.

72 *PL, 1866*, p. 103, and North Carolina, *Revised Code of North Carolina, Enacted by the General Assembly at the Session of 1854* (Boston: Little, Brown, 1855), pp. 575, 577; L. L. Clements and Justices of the Peace to Jonathan Worth, August 6, 1866, and Worth to L. L. Clements, August 11, 1866, *Worth Corr.* 2:731, 744.

73 *PL, 1866*, p. 127.

74 *Report of Joint Committee*, p. 182. Whitelaw Reid, the northern journalist touring North Carolina, as early as May 1865 asserted that North Carolina whites wished "indirectly to make them [blacks] slaves again" (Reid, *After the War*, p. 44n).

75 Report for the Western District, February 28, 1866, SMR.

76 Walter L. Fleming (ed.), *Documentary History of Reconstruction* (2 vols.; New York: McGraw-Hill, 1966), 1:284, 286, 279–80.

77 *JH, 1866*, pp. 174–75; *JS, 1866*, pp. 178, 187–88, 242.

78 *Wilmington Herald*, March 6, 1866, p. 2. See also *Journal*, March 4, 1866, p. 3.

79 This conclusion is based on an analysis of the votes on several key issues of the Black Code. See Alexander, "North Carolina," p. 309, and appendixes F and G.

80 Message of Governor Worth to the Convention, *Conv, 1866*, pp. 6, 64–65, 69–70; OC, pp. 39, 59; *Revised Code*, pp. 575–77; L. S. Gash to Jonathan Worth, April 3, 1866, Worth GP; *Worth Corr.* 1:651, 619, 635; Zuber, *Jonathan Worth*, pp. 216–17; Jonathan Robinson to Jonathan Worth, July 13, 1866, LSAC.

81 *PL, 1866*, pp. 76–80 and *Revised Code*, pp. 398–423. Italics mine.

82 *PL, 1866*, p. 31.

83 Rutherford to Foster, July 25, 1866, LSS; Foster to Rutherford, July 26, 1866, LRS; F. A. Seely to Whittlesey, May 18, 1866, LRAC.

84 F. A. Seely to Whittlesey, May 18, 1866, LRAC.

85 George Hawley to Stephen Moore, December 24, 1866, ULRE.

86 Whittlesey to F. A. Seely, May 23, 1866, LSAC.

87 *PL, 1866*, pp. 97–98, 115.

88 Forsyth County, County Court Minute Docket, NCA, July 15, 1865, p. 109 (because of the way this report was phrased, it seems that all cemeteries in the state were segregated); Person County, Minutes, Commissioners of the Town of Roxboro, NCA, March 1, 1866, pp. 29–30; Allan Rutherford to Justin Hodge, May 26, 1866, LSS; Dennett, *South As It Is*, pp. 176–77; NBT, August 30, 1865, p. 3; A. Coats to F. A. Seely, February 23, 1866, ULRE; Pasquotank County, Minutes of the Town of Elizabeth City, NCA, March 22, 1866.

89 *News*, June 12, 1866, p. 2. See also the following newspapers of August 30, 1866–October 1866: *Carolina Watchman, Goldsboro Daily News, Sentinel, North Carolina Argus* (Wadesboro).

90   *Rutherford Star*, October 10, 1866, p. 2. See also *Standard*, September 8–November 1, 1866.

91   *Standard*, September 22, 1866, p. 3, October 2, 1866, p. 2; *Rutherford Star*, June 13, 1866, p. 2, June 27, 1866, p. 2.

92   Reprinted in *Standard*, September 27, 1866, p. 2. See also the following newspapers from June–October 1866: *Journal, Carolina Watchman, Sentinel, NBT, Southerner, The Old North State* (Salisbury), *People's Press, Dispatch, Western Democrat.* The vote was Worth, 34,250; Dockery, 10,759. Dockery carried only eight counties (Gaston, Henderson, Johnston, Mitchell, Montgomery, Polk, Randolph, and Rutherford). He carried many of these by small majorities (Polk by only one vote, Gaston by six votes, Mitchell by thirty-seven votes, and Henderson by fifty-nine votes). ("Official Vote for Governor," *JS, 1866–67*, pp. 76–78.)

93   The nine counties were Ashe, Brunswick, Davidson, Davie, Forsyth, Guilford, Rowan, Stokes, and Wilkes. See also sources in n. 94 below.

94   For the positions of the candidates see the following newspapers of September–November 2, 1866: *Rutherford Star, Carolina Watchman, Dispatch, Journal, North Carolina Argus, People's Press, Southerner, Old North State, NBT, Greensboro Patriot, Progress, Sentinel, Standard;* Worth LB, p. 210; *Worth Corr.* 2:814–15, 818, 824. For election returns see "Election Returns," LP 819 and 826, and the following newspapers from October 23–November 2, 1866: *News, Standard, Sentinel, Dispatch, Progress.*

95   See, e.g., *Journal*, September 6, 1866, p. 2, September 13, 1866, p. 2; *Dispatch*, September 12, 1866, p. 3; *Carolina Watchman*, September 17, 1866, p. 3.

96   *Standard*, November 20, 1866, p. 2; *JH, 1866–67*, p. 9.

97   *Standard*, November 8, 1866, p. 3.

98   *JS, 1866–67*, pp. 25–30.

99   *Sentinel*, October 9, 1866, p. 2. See also the following newspapers of May–November 1866: *Sentinel, Dispatch, Standard, News, Carolina Watchman, North Carolina Argus, Southerner, Greensboro Patriot, Old North State, Progress; Worth Corr.* 2:666–67; Lewis Hanes to B. S. Hedrick, October 5, 1866, Hedrick Papers; Walter W. Lenoir to his brother, July 16, 1866, Lenoir Letters and Papers; John M. Clement to Edward McPherson, January 30, 1867, in James A. Padgett (ed.), "Reconstruction Letters from North Carolina, Part VII, Letters to Edward McPherson," *North Carolina Historical Review* 19, no. 2 (April 1942): 190 (hereinafter referred to as "Letters to McPherson").

100 *Amend Rept*, pp. 3–16; *JH, 1866–67*, pp. 80–81, 182–85, 190, 217, 426; *JS, 1866–67*, pp. 91–105, 138, 143; the following newspapers of June–December 1866: *Standard, NBT, Western Democrat, People's Press, Henderson Pioneer, Rutherford Star.*

101 *JH, 1866–67*, pp. 30–34, 36–37.

102 *PL, 1866–67*, pp. 10–11, 93.

103 Ibid., pp. 204–6, 47–49, 17.

104 *JH, 1866–67*, p. 34.

105 "Report of Joint Select Committee on a Penitentiary," LP 818. See also the report

printed in *Sentinel*, December 15, 1866, p. 2. See also ibid., November 24, 1866, p. 2; *Union Banner*, November 25, 1866, p. 4.

106   *PL, 1866–67*, pp. 197–98; Petition, February 1867, LP 825.

107   *PL, 1866–67*, p. 3.

Chapter 4

1   *Newbern Journal of Commerce*, reprinted in *Dispatch*, November 21, 1866, p. 1. See also chap. 3 for a discussion of the provision in the Black Code providing for the registration of marriages for the freedmen.

2   Edgecombe County, Marriage Bond Abstracts, NCA; Duplin County, Marriage Bond Abstracts, NCA. For numbers in other counties, see other county marriage bond abstracts in NCA under county records. For most counties the records are either incomplete or they do not specify whether the couple applying for a marriage license was black or white. All these numbers of people are in addition to those who registered under the provisions of the Black Code.

3   See Gutman, *Black Family*, for an excellent analysis of slave families. The following county cohabitation records, all located in NCA under country records, were used for all the figures in this chapter: Bertie, Beaufort, Catawba, Chowan, Currituck, Duplin, Edgecombe, Forsyth, Franklin, Gates, Granville (microfilm more complete than mss. collection), Halifax, Hyde, Iredell, Johnston, Lincoln, Nash, New Hanover, Orange, Pasquotank, Perquimans, Person, Pitt, Richmond, Robeson, Stokes, Wake, Warren, and Washington. In addition to these records, the following census material was used to compile statistical data for the charts included in this chapter: *Population of the United States in 1860; Compiled from the Original Returns; Agriculture of the United States in 1860;* 1860 Census, Population Schedule; 1860 Census, Slave Schedule. For a discussion of marriage records in states where freedmen's marriages were supervised by the Freedmen's Bureau, see Elaine C. Everly, "Marriage Registers of Freedmen," *Prologue*, Fall 1972, pp. 150–54.

4   See table 1. Gates and Surry counties are not included in this or any subsequent chart because only a few of the records exist today (six recordings of marriages in Gates and nine in Surry). Therefore, no remotely reliable figures can be derived. For one of the four counties where the percentage recording marriages was less than 30 percent (Halifax County), the records are also obviously incomplete.

5   See table 1.

6   Gutman, *Black Family*, passim. Gutman uses some of the North Carolina cohabitation records. The figures in our tables sometimes differ for two reasons. Gutman used records covering only 1866; I used documents for 1866 and 1867. Moreover, the North Carolina Archives added records from more counties after Gutman had completed his research. I am greatly indebted to Professor Gutman for sharing his findings with me and for providing me with suggestions as to how to analyze this material.

7   See table 2.

8   See, e.g., Samuel Jordan Wheeler Diary, vol. 1 (Dr. Thomas O'Dwyer's Diary [1825],

January 24–26, 1825, pp. 4–6, and also pp. 1, 3, 7, 11, 18, 21, 27, 41, 43, SHC; Bertie County, Slave Papers 1744–1815, NCA; Charles B. Dew, "Black Ironworkers and the Slave Insurrection Panic of 1856," *Journal of Southern History* 41, no. 3 (August 1975): 328–29; C. Peter Ripley, "The Black Family in Transition: Louisiana, 1860–1865," ibid., pp. 369–80; Gutman, *Black Family*, pp. 131, 136–37, 139, 140–43.

9   *North Carolina Narratives* 14:360.

10 The six counties are Beaufort, Edgecombe, Forsyth, Granville, Hyde, and Surry.

11 Beaufort County, Cohabitation Record.

12 J. A. Rosenkrans to Horace James, December 4, 1865, LRE. See also J. A. Rosenkrans to Simon Bryant, March 24, 1866, LSAS, and FBP, passim.

13 J. R. Edie to unknown correspondent, October 1866, LSW.

14 FBP, passim. See especially LSW.

15 FBP, passim, and *North Carolina Narratives* 14:221.

16 Gutman, *Black Family*, pp. 230–56.

17 *North Carolina Narratives* 15:301.

18 Ibid. 14:96 and sources in n. 3 above.

19 Ibid.: 360.

20 See e.g., ibid.: 447 and 15:31–33, 310.

21 Ibid. 14:373–74. See also pp. 360, 368–69.

22 Franklin, *Free Negro in North Carolina*, pp. 174–82.

23 For a discussion of religious developments throughout the entire Reconstruction period, see John Luther Bell, Jr., "Protestant Churches and the Negro in North Carolina During Reconstruction" (unpublished M.A. thesis, University of North Carolina, 1961).

24 See CI, October 5, 1865, p. 146, May 3, 1866, p. 61; *Proceedings of the Thirty-fifth Annual Session of the Baptist State Convention of North Carolina, Held with the Church at Forestville, November 1–4, 1865* (Raleigh: Biblical Recorder Book and Job Printing Office, 1866), p. 16; *Minutes and Proceedings of the Fifty-first Anniversary of the Pee Dee Baptist Association, Held with Forks of Little River Church, (Montgomery County,) October 19, 20, 21, 1866* (Wadesboro: Argus Office, 1867), pp. 6–7; *North Carolina Presbyterian* (Fayetteville), May 16, 1866, p. 2, August 8, 1866, p. 1, August 22, 1866, p. 2; *Minutes of the Fifty-third Session of the Synod of North Carolina, Held in Charlotte, on the 10th, 11th, 12th and 13th of October, 1866* (Fayetteville: North Carolina Presbyterian Office, 1867), pp. 17–20; *Episcopal Methodist* (Raleigh), July 17, 1867, p. 2.

25 See *Dispatch*, November 6, 1865, p. 2, November 22, 1866, p. 2; *North Carolina Presbyterian*, November 7, 1866, April 24, 1867; Bell, "Protestant Churches," pp. 2, 6, 13–16, 32–36.

26 *Journal of the Forty-Ninth Annual Council of the Protestant Episcopal Church in the State of North Carolina, Held in Christ's Church, Raleigh. September 13–15, 1865* (Raleigh: J. C. Gorman's Book and Job Printing Office, 1865), pp. 36–38; *Journal of the Fiftieth Annual Convention of the Protestant Episcopal Church in the State of North Carolina, Held in Christ's Church, Newbern, May 30–June 4th, 1866* (Fayetteville: n.p., 1866), pp. 16–19, 22–23; *Standard*, September 18, 1865, p. 3; *Journal*, June 7, 1866,

p. 2. See also *CI*, October–December 1865, February 22 and May 3, 1866, and February 28, 1867. For the views of Atkinson and his role in the state, see *Journal of the Fiftieth Convention*, pp. 17–19; *Journal of the Forty-ninth Annual Council*, pp. 22–24; reprint of a letter from Atkinson in *CI*, May 3, 1866, p. 61.

27 Quarterly Report of the Executive Committee of the Protestant Episcopal Freedmen's Commission, May 24, 1866, in *CI*, July 26, 1866, pp. 110–11; "letter to the editor," in ibid., February 28, 1867, p. 26; Bell, "Protestant Churches," pp. 123–24.

28 Ibid., pp. 107–11. While this concept was accepted at the 1866 annual meeting, it was not until 1870 that the first black minister and the first black church were admitted into the Diocese of North Carolina.

29 Ibid., pp. 106–7, 117.

30 *Minutes of the Twenty-second Annual Session of the Eastern Baptist Association, Held with the Church at Moore's Creek, October 3–4, 1865* (Raleigh: Biblical Recorder Book and Job Printing Office, 1866), p. 5; *Minutes of Sixth Annual Session of the Central Baptist Association, Held with the Church at Franklinton, Franklin County, N. C., October 5th–7th, 1865* (Raleigh: Biblical Recorder Book and Job Printing Establishment, 1865), p. 13; *Minutes of Pee Dee Association*, p. 7.

31 *Journal*, July 10, 1866, p. 3; Bell, "Protestant Churches," pp. 54–55, 58; George S. Hawley to F. A. Seely, April 30, 1866, ULRE; S. J. Wheeler, "Letter from Murfreesboro," *The Biblical Recorder* (Raleigh), January 16, 1867, p. 2.

32 "To the Speakers and Members of the Legislature of North Carolina," LP.

33 Report of the Building Committee on the memorial of sundry white citizens and colored Freedmen, [December 1866 or January 1867,] LP.

34 *Minutes of the Central Association*, p. 13; *Minutes of Pee Dee Association*, pp. 15–16; *Minutes of Eastern Association*, pp. 16–17.

35 See, e.g., *Biblical Recorder*, April 5, 1866, p. 2; *Dispatch*, May 18, 1866, p. 2; *Minutes of Pee Dee Association*, pp. 15–17.

36 *The Biblical Recorder*, June 5, 1867; Bell, "Protestant Churches," pp. 68–69; Davis, "Reconstruction in Cleveland County," p. 18.

37 *Journal of the Thirtieth Session of the North Carolina Annual Conference of the Methodist Episcopal Church South, Fayetteville, November 7–12, 1866* (Raleigh: Branson & Farrar, 1866), pp. 6–7, 18–19.

38 See, e.g., George S. Hawley to F. A. Seely, April 30, 1866, ULRE, for other cases.

39 Reverend L. S. Burkhead, "History of the Difficulties of the Pastorate of the Front Street Methodist Church, Wilmington, North Carolina, For the Year 1865," *Annual Publication of Historical Papers* (Durham: Historical Society of Trinity College, 1908–9), Series 8, pp. 42, 44, 49–50, 54, 56, 63, 70, 73–74.

40 *Wilmington Herald*, June 20, 1865, p. 2; *Dispatch*, October 13, 1865, p. 3.

41 *Wilmington Herald*, January 24, 1866, p. 1; *Dispatch*, January 24, 1866, p. 3.

42 Burkhead, "History," pp. 74–80; *Carolina Watchman*, May 7, 1866, p. 2.

43 *Journal of Thirtieth Annual Conference*, p. 13; *Minutes of the North Carolina Annual Conference of the A.M.E. Zion Church in America, 1865* (Hartford: Case, Lockwood & Co., 1866), p. 8; Bell, "Protestant Churches," p. 92.

44 Petition by blacks of the Wesley Chapel African Methodist Episcopal Church of Raleigh, April 23, 1865, RCC, Letters Received. Spelling as in original petition.
45 *Minutes of the A.M.E. Zion Church*, pp. 16, 11, 15.
46 George S. Hawley to F. A. Seely, April 30, 1866, ULRE; *Southerner*, December 20, 1866, p. 3; *Western Democrat*, October 2, 1866, p. 2.
47 *Minutes of the A.M.E. Zion Church*, p. 11.
48 Ibid., pp. 8–13, 18.
49 See, e.g., the following newspapers from October 1865–December 1866: *NBT, Progress, Sentinel, Wilmington Herald, Dispatch, Standard;* A. Rutherford to J. C. Robinson, August 25, 1866, LRS.
50 *NBT*, July 6, 1865, p. 2.
51 *Journal of Freedom*, passim. This quotation was at the head of each edition of the paper. Brooks had served four years in the United States army during the Civil War. He went to North Carolina as a correspondent from the *New York Times* and became one of the editors of the Raleigh *Progress* before starting the *Journal of Freedom*. (*Journal of Freedom*, October 14, 1865, p. 3.)
52 Convention of Freedmen, 1865, pp. 17–18; *Journal of Freedom*, October 7, 1865, p. 2.
53 *Wilmington Herald*, November 13, 1865, p. 3. See Olsen, *Carpetbagger's Crusade*, p. 51, and Hamilton, *Reconstruction*, pp. 179, 357, for further information on Sinclair.
54 *Standard*, January 2, 1866, p. 3, June 19, 1866, p. 2; *Sentinel*, January 3, 1866, p. 2; *Progress*, January 6, 1866, p. 1; Samuel P. Fowler, Jr., to Horace James, December 12, 1865, ULRE; Worth LB, pp. 216, 279, 304–5, 343.
55 See, e.g., the following newspapers for January 1866 and January 1867: *Wilmington Herald, Progress, NBT, Journal, Western Democrat, Standard;* Report of Dexter E. Clapp, January 14, 1866, SMR.
56 See the following newspapers of July 1866: *Dispatch, Southerner, Sentinel, Standard.*
57 *Sentinel*, July 3, 1866, p. 2. See also *Dispatch*, July 5, 1866, p. 3; *Southerner*, July 7, 1866, p. 3.
58 *Dispatch*, February 23, 1867, p. 3; *Wilmington Herald*, January 2, 1866, p. 1; *Journal*, January 2, 1866, p. 1, January 3, 1867, p. 3.
59 *Standard*, June 19, 1866, p. 2.
60 *Wilmington Herald*, January 18, 1866, p. 1. The text of this speech was not reported.
61 *Wilmington Herald*, October 31, 1865, p. 1, November 1, 1865, p. 1, November 2, 1865, p. 1. See also *Dispatch*, November 1, 1865, p. 1.
62 *Standard*, March 5, 1866, p. 3.
63 *NBT*, June 15, 1866, p. 3, and *Standard*, June 5, 1866, p. 2.
64 S. W. Laidler to Thaddeus Stevens, May 7, 1866, "Letters to Stevens," pp. 184–86.
65 *NBT*, August 17, 1866, p. 1.
66 *Standard*, July 10, 1866, p. 2, July 17, 1866, p. 2, August 11, 1866, p. 3. This notice was signed by the officers of the league.
67 Extant records report meetings for Craven, Wake, Rowan, Forsyth, Greene, Stokes, and Union counties. No proceedings were reported for the Stokes County and Union

County meetings. The fact that they took place was noted in the *Sentinel*, October 1, 1866, p. 3, and by F. S. Wiatt to J. R. Edie, October 8, 1866, LRW.

68 *People's Press*, reprinted in *Carolina Watchman*, October 8, 1866, p. 4.

69 *Sentinel*, September 12, 1866, p. 3. The *Sentinel* did not report any of the specific stands the candidates took.

70 *Standard*, August 2, 1866, p. 2.

71 *NBT*, September 14, 1866, p. 1.

72 *Union Banner*, reprinted in *Carolina Watchman*, August 13, 1866, p. 4.

73 Ibid.

74 *Minutes of the Freedmen's Convention, Held in the City of Raleigh, on the 2nd, 3rd, 4th and 5th of October, 1866* (Raleigh: Standard Book and Job Office, 1866), pp. 6–7, 20, 31.

75 See map 4 and compare with map 3.

76 The forty-eight assumed to have been slaves were those native North Carolinians who were found in the 1870 census but not in the 1860 census, which listed only free persons. Not counted were the forty delegates who could not be located in either census and the five representatives who were born in other southern states.

 Biographical information on the delegates was obtained from the 1860 and 1870 censuses; Harris Papers; Dowd, *Sketches of Prominent Living North Carolinians;* Wright, *Bishops of the A.M.E. Church;* Franklin, *Free Negro in North Carolina;* Logan, *The Negro in North Carolina;* Quick, *Negro Stars;* Oates, *Story of Fayetteville;* Tomlinson, *Tar Heel Sketch-Book; Business Directory for 1867–8; Biographical Directory;* Freedmen's Savings and Trust Company, Signature Books, New Berne, November 20, 1872; Mrs. D. M. Barringer to her son, October 10, 1865, Barringer Papers; *NBT*, December 22, 1865, p. 4; Manly Wade Wellman, *The County of Warren North Carolina* (Chapel Hill: University of North Carolina Press, 1959); Lizzie Wilsen Montgomery, *Sketches of Old Warrenton* (Raleigh: Edward & Broughton Printing Company, 1924); James Absalom Padgett, "From Slavery to Prominence in North Carolina," *Journal of Negro History* 22 (October 1937): 433–87; [Fayetteville *Observer,*] "Death of a Prominent Colored Man," *North Carolina Journal of Law* 2, no. 1 (January 1905): 23–24.

77 The breakdown is five blacksmiths, one coffin maker and undertaker, ten carpenters, one brick mason, one barber, one wagon maker, one cabinetmaker, and one house-painter.

78 The occupations of thirty-nine of the delegates cannot be found.

79 *Sentinel*, October 1, 1866, p. 3. See also ibid., October 4, 1866, p. 3, and *Standard*, October 6, 1866, p. 2.

80 *Minutes of Freedmen's Convention, 1866*, pp. 3, 4, 7. See chap. 2 for additional information on Harris. I could not determine if Brown was a practicing physician or if "Doctor" was a church title or stood for something else.

81 Ibid., p. 13; *Sentinel*, October 4, 1866, p. 3; *Standard*, October 6, 1866, p. 2; *Western Democrat*, October 9, 1866, p. 2.

82 *Minutes of Freedmennnn's Convention, 1866*, p. 10.

83 Ibid., pp. 15–16.

84 John Randolph, Jr., Secretary, North Carolina Equal Rights League, "To the Colored Citizens of North Carolina to Assemble in Convention in Raleigh," dated September 30, 1866, and read into ibid., p. 20.

85 Ibid., pp. 12, 32, 14–15.

86 *Western Democrat*, October 9, 1866, p. 2; *Sentinel*, October 6, 1866, p. 2. See also ibid., October 12, 1866, p. 2. Compare with *Standard*, October 9, 1866, p. 2.

87 *Minutes of Freedmen's Convention, 1866*, pp. 16–22.

88 Ibid., pp. 24–25.

89 Ibid., pp. 29, 32, 26–27, 28–30.

90 *Sentinel*, January 9, 1867, p. 2. The *Sentinel* did not report the proceedings of these meetings.

91 *Standard*, January 17, 1867, p. 2, January 19, 1867, p. 2, January 31, 1867, p. 2. See also ibid., January 8, 1867, p. 2, and January 26, 1867, p. 3.

92 U. S. Congress, House, Committee on Freedmen's Affairs, 39th Congress, "The memoriel [sic] of Isaac Alston, John Crosin, Sampson Brean, Darcus Mitchell, John Chuk, Jack Alston, Sam Daniel and others whoese [sic] names are signed freed men and women of Warren County," January 26, 1867, NA, Legislative Division.

93 *Western Democrat*, May 7, 1867, p. 2; *Standard*, February 28, 1867, p. 2, March 26, 1867, p. 2, March 12, 1867, p. 3; Thomas W. Conway to Salmon P. Chase, April 23, 1867, "Letters to Chase," pp. 234–35; John C. MacRae to his brother, March 17, 1867, Hugh MacRae Papers, DU.

94 *Western Democrat*, May 7, 1867, p. 2.

95 *Standard*, February 28, 1867, p. 3.

Chapter 5

1 Quotations from Kenneth Rayner to Dr. William Elder, September 20, 1865, printed in *Standard*, November 1, 1865, p. 1, and *Western Democrat*, November 14, 1865, p. 3. For a discussion of the Black Code, see above, chap. 3. For statements of similar views, see the following newspapers for the period of June 1865–February 1867: *Sentinel, Western Democrat, Progress, NBT, People's Press, Wilmington Herald, Union Banner, Journal, Dispatch, Goldsboro Daily News, North Carolina Presbyterian;* the following manuscript collections for the period of June 1865–February 1867: Tillinghast Papers, Pettigrew Family Papers, SHC, Walter Clark Mss, NCA, de Rosset Family Papers, Mangum Papers, Hedrick Papers, Patterson Papers, Kirkpatrick Papers, Wiley Papers, NCA, MacRae Papers, Battle Family Papers, Graham Papers, NCA, Patterson Family Papers, Ardrey Diary; Worth GP, May 1866; *Worth Corr.* 1:570; T. P. Devereux to Jonathan Worth, October 20, 1866, LP 820; William Holden to George C. Meade,

September 12, 1865, LRAGO; John Brevard Alexander, *Reminiscences of the Past Sixty Years* (Charlotte: Ray Printing Company, 1908), p. 9, and above, chaps. 1 and 3.

2 Quotations from William A. Graham to David L. Swain, October 16, 1865, Swain Papers, and *Sentinel*, August 21, 1866, p. 2. See also the following newspapers for the period of June 1865–February 1867: *Sentinel, Western Democrat, NBT, Journal, Dispatch, Southerner, Progress, The News;* J. L. Kirkpatrick to unknown correspondent, October 13, 1865, Kirkpatrick Papers; E. J. Thompson to B. S. Hedrick, September 24, 1865, Hedrick Papers.

3 *North Carolina Narratives* 14:450.

4 Schenck Diary, [entry of May 31, 1865,] p. 42. See also ibid., entry of June 24, 1865, pp. 49–50; *Tri-Weekly Bulletin* (Charlotte), May 30, 1865, p. 2; Mary Patterson to her mother, December 6, 1865, Patterson Family Papers; Mary B. to William Pettigrew, July 27, 1865, Pettigrew Family Papers; Ardrey Diary, entry of May 1865, p. 3; William H. to Kemp Battle, December 4, 1865, Battle Family Papers. See also n. 1 above and compare with sources here and in n. 5 below.

5 *Sentinel*, June 19, 1866, p. 2; Charles to Caroline Pettigrew, June 26, 1866, Pettigrew Family Papers. See also the following newspapers for January 1866–January 1867: *Sentinel, NBT, Standard, Southerner, The News, Journal, Wilmington Herald, Dispatch, Western Democrat, Greensboro Patriot;* Pettigrew Family Papers, January–June 1866; Worth GP, April 21, 1866; Schenck Diary, entries of March 13 and June 18, 1866.

6 *Dispatch*, December 23, 1865, p. 3. Many Freedmen's Bureau agents made similar comments. See sources in n. 18 below.

7 See, e.g., *Dispatch*, December 23, 1865, p. 3; *Sentinel*, January 5, 1866, p. 2, January 19, 1866, p. 4; *Journal*, January 1, 1867, p. 2; Walter W. Lenoir to Thomas Isaac Lenoir, July 16, 1866, Lenoir Papers; Charles to Caroline Pettigrew, March 6, 1866, Pettigrew Family Papers.

8 Quotations from Andrews, *South Since the War*, October 16, 1865, pp. 179–80; *NBT*, May 18, 1866, p. 2; *Sentinel*, May 25, 1866, p. 3. See also the following newspapers for the period of July 1865–November 1866: *Dispatch, Standard, Journal, NBT, Western Democrat, The News, Sentinel, People's Press, Union Banner; Worth Corr.* 1:451, 453; H. B. Williams to the Secretary of War, October 5, 1865, LRAC; M. S. Sherwood to B. S. Hedrick, March 31, 1866, Hedrick Papers; Holden LB, p. 79; Andrews, *South Since the War*, p. 190. Occasionally whites did applaud the activities of the Freedmen's Bureau in attempting to see that blacks worked well. The Agricultural Association of New Hanover County praised Major Charles Wickersham's fairness to both whites and blacks and complimented him on his efforts to stop "negro stealing and negro vagrancy" (*Journal*, April 28, 1866, p. 2). The *Sentinel* admitted that Bureau officers were "doing their utmost to advise and encourage" the freedmen to work (September 16, 1865, p. 2; see also September 28, 1865, p. 2, and January 6, 1866, p. 2).

9 *Standard*, May 2, 1865, p. 2; *Western Democrat*, October 31, 1865, p. 2, December

26, 1865, p. 1; *North Carolina Argus*, October 21, 1865, p. 3; *Sentinel*, November 9, 1865, p. 3; *Journal*, October 13, 1865, p. 1, December 14, 1865, p. 2; *The News*, November 17, 1865, p. 3; *NBT*, December 12, 1865, p. 1. See map 2 on the Freedmen's Bureau districts to locate where the agents discussed in this chapter were operating.

10   A. W. McKillip to Stephen Moore, November 12, 1866, ULRE; Census of Trent River Settlement by Stephen Moore, February 2, 1867, and Sanitary Report by W. W. Doherty, June 11, 1866, June 12, 1866, July 3, 1866, LRAC. See also chap. 1 above.

11   Circular No. 4, printed in *Standard*, December 1, 1865, p. 4, and Whittlesey to Charles Wickersham, March 23, 1866, LSAC.

12   See, e.g., Circular by Major Charles Wickersham, December 11, 1865, in *Western Democrat*, December 26, 1865, p. 1; *Progress*, September 27, 1865, p. 1; *Dispatch*, February 21, 1866, p. 3; NBT, March 7, 1866, p. 8; H. C. Lawrence to the Assistant Commissioner, January 15, 1866, LRAC; Endorsements and Memoranda by the Assistant Commissioner, December 5, 1865, FBP.

13   See, e.g., Circular by Major Charles Wickersham, December 11, 1865, in *Western Democrat*, December 26, 1865, p. 1; "Address to the Freedmen," by Major Mann in *The News*, November 17, 1865, p. 3; Circular by Captain John C. Barnett, October 1, 1865, in *Sentinel*, November 9, 1865, p. 3; ibid., January 6, 1866, p. 2; *Dispatch*, November 21, 1865, p. 2; *NBT*, November 24, 1865, p. 2; Report by John C. Barnett, October 29, 1865, NR; Report by Jaspard Packard, November 30, 1865, SMR; DES Rpt, p. 61.

14   General Meade to Edwin Stanton, September 20, 1865, LRAGO; Horace James to Whittlesey, September 29, 1865 and July 20, 1865, and J. T. Seely to Whittlesey, August 18, 1865, LRAC; H Report, 1865, p. 25. See also S. S. Ashley to the Secretary of the American Missionary Association, October 5, 1865, American Missionary Association Archives (Selections), Ashley Letters, 1851–78, SHC (hereinafter cited as Ashley Letters).

15   Wickersham to Whittlesey, October 11, 1865, LRAC.

16   FBP, passim. See especially Whittlesey to James S. Fullerton, August 7, 1865, and to John C. Barnett, August 14, 1865, LSAC; C. A. Cilley to Whittlesey, December 5, 1865, LRAC; *Standard*, July 1, 1865.

17   Only two agents were not optimistic. See F. M. Garrett to E. Whittlesey, September 25, 1865, ULRAC; Francis Bache to A. S. Webb, September 8, 1865, LRAGO. There were also reports from North Carolina whites to Freedmen's Bureau agents complaining that blacks were not fulfilling their Freedmen's Bureau-approved contracts. See E. Whittlesey to Dr. Gorrell, August 19, 1865, LSAC; R. M. Garrett to E. Whittlesey, [December 1865,] LRAC; I. A. Rosekrans to Horace James, December 4, 1865, LRE.

18   E. Whittlesey to O. O. Howard, House Ex. Doc. 70, 39th Congress, 1st Session, p. 390; Report of the Assistant Commissioner, December 31, 1865, SMR; DES Rpt, p. 735. For the detailed reports by the agents in the field see FBP, September 1865–November 1867. Complaints that freedmen did not work were very few. See C. W. Dodge to F. A. Seely, April 20, 1866, ULRE; J. V. Bomford to O. O. Howard, April 23, 1867, LRAC. See also letter from Major Lawrence in *Sentinel*, January 19, 1866, p. 4.

19   *North Carolina Narratives* 14:97. See also ibid. 15:368–69 and Thurston James to H. Wilson, January 10, 1866, LRAC. See also chap. 1 above.

20 Whittlesey to O. O. Howard, January 15, 1866, House Ex. Doc. No. 70, p. 241; Dennett, *South As It Is*, September 12, 1865, pp. 124–25; E. A. Harris to C. A. Cilley, December 28, 1865, NR; Report of Operations in the Western District, December 31, 1865, SR. See also FBP, July–December 1865, passim; the *Banner* and the *Wilmington Herald* for September 1865; Dennett, *South As It Is*, pp. 124–25. Most of these sources note that the employers eventually acceded to the Bureau's orders and paid their laborers a fair wage.

21 C. A. Cilley to Fred Beecher, December 30, 1865, LRAC. For similar comments and conclusions, see C. W. Mills to E. Whittlesey, September 18, 1865, LRAC; Francis Baches to A. S. Webb, September 19, 1865, LRAGO; Report by Dexter E. Clapp, December 13, 1865, SMR; Report by Dexter Clapp, October 10, 1865 and Report by John C. Barnett, October 29, 1865, NR; Nicholas Yeager to Charles Wickersham, November 20, 1865, LRS.

22 George Hawley to F. A. Seely, April 30, 1866, ULRE. See also Hawley's letters of March 1, 1866, and February 25, 1867, ibid.; Austin W. Fuller to F. A. Seely, May 30, 1866, ibid.; William B. Bowe to E. Whittlesey, ULRAC; Report of A. G. Brady, May 14, 1866, SMR; H. C. Vogell to Assistant Commissioner, July 1, 1867, LRAC.

23 See FBP, passim; *Union Banner*, September 1865; H Report, 1867, p. 667.

24 Petition to superintendent of the Eastern District, February 10, 1866, ULRE (spelling as in original); *NBT*, August 1, 1865, p. 2. For other examples of freedmen's complaints, see FBP, passim; Dennett, *South As It Is*, pp. 109–10, 113–15.

25 *Wilmington Herald*, August 10, 1865, p. 2 (also reprinted in *NBT*, August 14, 1865, p. 2); Dennett, *South As It Is*, pp. 124–25.

26 Thomas Ruger to General J. W. Ames, August 14, 1865, Holden GP. See also J. C. Williams to Major Oliver, [August 30, 1865,] ibid.

27 *NBT*, November 24, 1865, p. 2. See also the following newspapers for the period of June 1865–November 1866: *Wilmington Herald, Sentinel, Journal, Standard, Dispatch, Western Democrat*; Andrews, *South Since the War*, p. 177.

28 See, e.g., *Standard*, September 23, 1865, p. 3; *New York Journal of Commerce*, reprinted in *Journal*, September 29, 1865, p. 2; Hamilton, *Ruffin Papers*, p. 40; William S. Pettigrew to Messrs. John Williams and Son, December 26, 1865, Pettigrew Family Papers. For more details, see Alexander, "North Carolina," pp. 458–60.

29 See, e.g., Dennett, *South As It Is*, pp. 169, 171; Petition, October 1865, LP 804; *Standard*, December 20, 1865, p. 3; "S.F.," in ibid., June 22, 1865, p. 3; Kenneth Rayner in ibid., November 1, 1865, p. 1; *Sentinel*, January 23, 1866, p. 2, August 21, 1865, p. 2; *Old North State*, April 26, 1866, p. 2; Hamilton, *Ruffin Papers*, p. 45.

30 See, e.g., E. Whittlesey to D. D. Gurley, July 18, 1865, LSAC; *Journal of Freedom*, October 21, 1865, p. 2; *Western Democrat*, February 26, 1867, p. 1; *Carolina Times*, reprinted in *Standard*, February 21, 1867, p. 2.

31 FBP, Files of the Assistant Commissioner. See also other contracts in this file. This contract was written on a printed form used by the Freedmen's Bureau. Similar contracts were privately written. See Ledger Book, John M. and Ruth Hodges Collection, NCA; several contracts for 1866 and 1867, Archibald Hunter Arrington Papers, SHC; con-

tract dated January 1, 1866, Carter Papers; one contract for 1866 and two contracts dated January 4, 1867, Peter Evans Smith Papers, SHC; contract dated October 26, 1865, Pettigrew Family Papers.

32   FBP, files of the Assistant Commissioner; Alexander McMillan Letters, DU. See also contract for 1866, H. T. Clark Papers; contracts dated May 1866 and November 1866, Pettigrew Family Papers for similar contracts.

33   FBP, files of the Assistant Commissioner. Similar provisions are found in contracts for the years 1866 and 1867, Arrington Papers; contract dated January 1, 1866, Carter Papers; contracts dated January 1866 and January 4, 1867, P. E. Smith Papers; contract dated October 26, 1865, Pettigrew Family Papers; contract for the year 1866, H. T. Clark Papers.

34   FBP, files of the Assistant Commissioner; contract dated January 1, 1866, Carter Papers; contracts dated January 4, 1867, P. E. Smith Papers; contract dated October 26, 1865, Pettigrew Family Papers.

35   FBP, files of the Assistant Commissioner; Ledger Book, contract dated December 4, 1865, Hodges Collection; several contracts for the years 1866 and 1867, Arrington Papers; contracts dated October 26, 1865, and November 1866, Pettigrew Family Papers; contract dated January 1, 1866, Carter Papers; contract for the year 1866, P. E. Smith Papers; H. T. Clark Papers; contract dated January 11, 1866, McMillan Letters.

36   FBP, files of the Assistant Commissioner; contract dated January 1, 1866, Carter Papers; contract dated January 11, 1866, McMillan Letters; contracts of October 26, 1865, and November 1866, Pettigrew Family Papers.

37   Report of I. A. Rosekrans, December 4, 1865, NR. See also report by Horace James, , 1865, SMR.

38   J. G. Hart to Horace James, November 30, 1865, ULRE. See also Report by Jaspard Packard, November 15, 1865, and Report of F. A. Seely, January 14, 1866, SMR; *Sentinel*, November 9, 1865, p. 3, printing the "Circular to Freedmen" issued by Captain John C. Barnett, assistant superintendent at Charlotte, October 1, 1865.

39   These figures were compiled from FBP, passim; LRAGO; the following manuscript collections: Hedrick Papers, Cameron Family Papers (SHC), de Rouset Family Papers, Schenck Diary, Ardrey Diary; the following newspapers for the period of January 1866– January 1867: *Dispatch, Journal, Sentinel, Southerner, Greensboro Patriot, Western Democrat, Standard;* Andrews, *South Since the War*, pp. 189–90; Dennett, *South As It Is*, pp. 108–9.

40   Andrews, *South Since the War*, pp. 189–90. It is impossible to determine the cost of living in North Carolina during this period. Andrews's statement is the only source that gives any clue. However, in the resolution passed by blacks in Rowan County, they assumed it cost 50¢ per day to board oneself. (They asked for 50¢ per day with board or $1 per day without.) While "board" is a vague term, I assume this means food and shelter. Also it is not known whether they felt it cost 50¢ per day to board one person or an entire family. Nonetheless, even if one assumes 50¢ per day for board for an entire family, this shred of evidence indicates that Andrews was correct; the freedmen's wages were below the subsistence level. At 50¢ per day, it cost about $15 a month just for food and shelter. (See also elsewhere in this chapter for prices charged some freedmen for clothing and other needs.) This evidence is very sketchy but it is the only evidence available.

41 Mrs. E. J. Warren to E. J. Warren, October 14, 1865, Warren Papers; *The News*, August 14, 1866, p. 2.

42 *Journal*, April 26, 1866, p. 4. Also printed in *Western Democrat*, May 1, 1866, p. 2 and *Greensboro Patriot*, May 4, 1866, p. 1.

43 Caldwell to John Sherman, January 18, 1867, in James A. Padgett (ed.), "Reconstruction Letters from North Carolina, Part II, Letters to John Sherman," *North Carolina Historical Review* 18, no. 3 (July 1941): 290–91 (hereinafter referred to as "Letters to Sherman"); Report by F. A. Seely, January 14, 1866, SMR; F. S. Wiatt to J. R. Edie, February 2, 1867, and W. MacFarland to J. R. Edie, January 31, 1867, LRW; *Western Democrat*, April 17, 1866, p. 2, December 25, 1866, p. 3; *Dispatch*, January 27, 1867, p. 2, and February 2, 1867, p. 3; *Sentinel*, December 17, 1866, p. 2, and January 28, 1867, p. 3; *Standard*, January 29, 1866, p. 3; William Ruffin to Samuel Ashe, February 7, 1867, Samuel A'Court Ashe Papers, NCA.

44 The actual numbers were 100,000 blacks versus 20,000 whites. Sen. Ex. Doc. No. 2, 39th Congress, 1st Session, p. 29; *Freedmen's Record* 4 (July 1868): 108–9.

45 Sen. Ex. Doc. No. 2, 39th Congress, 1st Session, p. 29; *Freedmen's Record* 4 (July 1868): 108–9; *Dispatch*, December 6, 1866, p. 2; *Worth Corr.* 1:520; Report by J. F. Conner, November 25, 1866, SMR; *Wilmington Herald*, June 9, 1865, p. 3; *NBT*, August 3, 1865, p. 2. All daily wages seem quite high. Either the figures in the documents are wrong or wages were high when paid on a daily basis because the work was unsteady and difficult to get.

46 *Dispatch*, December 6, 1866, p. 2; *NBT*, September 2, 1865, p. 3 (the results of the strike were not found); *Wilmington Herald*, September 29, 1865, p. 1 (see also *Journal*, September 29, 1865, p. 3).

47 Report of Major Horton, April 28, 1866, SMR; *Dispatch*, November 11, 1865, p. 2; *Journal*, January 1, 1867, p. 2, reporting the meeting held December 29, 1866. See also Thomas Ruffin to Paul Cameron, November 12, 1865, Cameron Family Papers, and Dennett, *South As It Is*, p. 108.

48 Johnson, *Ante-bellum North Carolina*, p. 70.

49 Charles to Caroline Pettigrew, April 1, 1866, Pettigrew Family Papers, citing white girls doing housework for $5 per month.

50 Logan, *Negro in North Carolina*, pp. 76–78.

51 Dennett, *South As It Is*, p. 108. See also Reports by Charles Wickersham, November 28, 1865; by Jasper Packard, December 15, 1865, and December 30, 1865; by A. Rutherford, October 27, 1866; by C. A. Cilley, December 30, 1865, and January 30, 1866, SMR. Also Asa Teal to E. Whittlesey, October 19, 1865, LRAC; E. R. Bell to S. Moore, June 13, 1866, LRW; Reports by Thomas Hay, June 25, 1867, and by J. F. Conners, January 25, 1867, NR; *Journal*, January 4, 1867, p. 3, and January 16, 1867, p. 3.

52 *Union Banner*, November 4, 1865, p. 2; *Sentinel*, March 15, 1866, p. 2; *Journal*, October 11, 1866, p. 2, December 16, 1866, p. 2.

53 H Report, 1865, p. 25.

54 Hawley to Stephen Moore, December 24, 1866, ULRE.

55   Report by J. F. Conners, December 25, 1866, NR. In his report of January 25, 1867, however, he noted that the freedmen still preferred to work for shares.

56   Ibid., report dated January 25, 1867. See also chap. 6 for a more detailed discussion of such thievery.

57   Report by John R. Edie, May 31, 1866, SMR; George Hawley to Stephen Moore, December 24, 1866, ULRE.

58   *Dispatch*, January 16, 1866, p. 2; A. Coats to F. A. Seely, February 1, 1866, ULRE; *Journal*, January 1, 1867, p. 2, and October 11, 1866, p. 2.

59   Jacob F. Blum to Stephen Moore, October 9, 1866, LSAC; Jacob Chur to Moore, October 9, 1866, ULRE.

60   Report by James printed in *Freedmen's Record*, September 1865, p. 143; DES Rpt, p. 61. See also Dennett, *South As It Is*, p. 122.

61   Edmund Woag to D. L. Lambert, January 20, 1866, LRFB. The Freedmen's Savings and Trust Company was established "under the auspices of the Freedman's Savings and Trust Company of New York by an act of Congress," with branches opened in New Berne and Wilmington during 1865 and 1866. Its purpose was to give freedmen a safe place to deposit their savings "and to pay a liberal interest on time deposits." In 1866 the interest rate was 5 percent a year on deposits of six months or more. (See *NBT*, October 25, 1865, p. 2; *Wilmington Herald*, January 2, 1866, p. 1, February 2, 1866, p. 1; *Dispatch*, January 1, 1866, p. 3.) In August 1866 the New Berne branch had $3,920 on deposit. However, the Wilmington branch had only $170. (Statement for the months of July and August 1866, LRFB.) The cashier at New Berne explained that the freedmen in the countryside manifested a "want of confidence . . . in the bank." However, he believed that "if someone visit[ed] the plantations, he could secure some considerable amts, especially near the end of the year." He gave no reason for this distrust. (A. A. Ellsworth to J. W. Alvord, March 12, 1867, LRFB.) For a detailed account of the Freedmen's Savings Bank, see Carl R. Osthaus, *Freedmen, Philanthropy, and Fraud: A History of the Freedmen's Savings Bank* (Urbana: University of Illinois Press, 1976).

62   Reid, *After the War*, p. 31.

63   "From Committee of Freedmen" to E. Whittlesey, August 7, 1865, LRAC; Whittlesey to O. O. Howard, quarterly report ending September 30, 1865, H. Ex. Doc. No. 70, 39th Congress, 1st Session, p. 391. It is not known whether this venture succeeded or failed.

64   Samuel P. Fowler, Jr., to F. A. Seely, December 21, 1865, ULRE.

65   Hope Bain to the Assistant Commissioner, April 3, 1866, LRAC. The minister concluded his letter with the following request: "Do not bring me into trouble by making this public." It is obvious that he was no radical out to exploit a cause; he was merely a concerned person.

66   Account Book, vol. 4, Arrington Papers.

67   *North Carolina Narratives* 15:428.

68   *Standard*, January 17, 1867, p. 2.

69   Rebecca Scott, "The Battle Over the Child: Child Apprenticeship and the Freedmen's Bureau in North Carolina," *Prologue* 10, no. 2: 102.

70 E. Whittlesey to Charles Emery, July 13, 1865; Whittlesey to Asa Teal, July 28, 1865; Whittlesey to C. A. Cilley, November 16, 1865; Whittlesey to S. F. Patterson, February 27, 1866, LSAC.

71 E. Whittlesey to O. O. Howard, January 15, 1866, H. Ex. Doc. No. 70, 39th Congress, 1st Session, pp. 242–43.

72 Scott, "Battle Over the Child," p. 111.

73 County Court Minutes, NCA, passim; County Apprentice Records, NCA, passim; Indentures for Apprentices, NCA, passim; petition to superintendent of the Eastern District, February 10, 1866, ULRE; William Beadle to Fred Beecher, February 12, 1866, and William Beadle to E. Whittlesey, March 10, 1866, LRAC.

74 *PL, 1866*, p. 100; *JH, 1866–67*, p. 36.

75 E. Whittlesey to George S. Hawley, May 23, 1866, LSAC; General Robinson to J. Worth, October 30, 1866, Worth GP; *JH, 1866–67*, pp. 36–37, and above, chap. 3.

76 A. Rutherford to A. Coats, September 11, 1866, and September 13, 1866, LSS. See also similar charges and conclusions in A. Rutherford to J. C. Robinson, November 1, 1866, ibid. For other similar cases in the Southern District, see report by Allan Rutherford, September 12, 1866, SMR; A. Rutherford to W. F. Cox, April 19, 1867, LSS; *Dispatch*, January 31, 1867, p. 3.

77 J. C. Robinson to J. Worth, October 30, 1866, and Daniel Russell to Worth, October 23, 1866, Worth GP; Endorsement on letter of Sylvia Ann Saunders, December 29, 1865, and on letter of Jenny Russell, January 11, 1866, Endorsements and Memoranda of the Assistant Commissioner; A. Rutherford to A. Coats, September 13, 1866, LSS; *Worth Corr.* 2:832–33; Worth LB, pp. 236–37; *Sentinel*, January 30, 1867, p. 2. In January 1867 the Supreme Court of North Carolina ordered Russell to release the children because the parents had not been duly notified (*Sentinel*, January 30, 1867, p. 2).

78 John R. Edie to W. F. Henderson, August 8, 1866, and August 11, 1866, and passim, LSW; J. C. Robinson to A. G. Brady, July 2, 1866, and J. V. Bomford to J. Worth, December 14, 1866, LSAC; H. D. Norton to M. Cogswell, March 18, 1866, LRAC; Worth LB, pp. 307–8; George S. Hawley to S. Moore, August 25, 1866, ULRE.

79 Johnson, *Ante-bellum North Carolina*, p. 707.

80 County Court Minutes, passim.

81 County Court Minutes, Jones County; William A. Matthis, Clerk, Sampson County Court, to Allan Rutherford, May 16, 1866, LRS. See also Sampson County Court Minutes.

82 County Court Minutes, passim; County Apprentice Records, passim; Indentures for Apprentices, passim; Scott, "Battle Over the Child," pp. 104–5.

83 See above, chap. 4.

84 Petition dated February 10, 1866, ULRE; Group of Freedmen's petition, April 4, 1866, LRAC.

85 See, e.g., H. D. Norton to M. Cogswell, March 18, 1867, ibid., John R. Edie to W. F. Henderson, August 8, 1866, and August 11, 1866, LSW; Allan Rutherford to W. F. Cox, April 19, 1867, and Rutherford to A. Coats, September 11, 1866, and

September 13, 1866, LSS; A. Coats to Allan Rutherford, September 11, 1866, and September 13, 1866, LRS; Letters by Sylvia Ann Saunders, December 29, 1865, and Jenny Russell, January 11, 1866, Endorsements and Memoranda by the Assistant Commissioner.

86 See, e.g., Allan Rutherford to A. Coats, September 13, 1866, Allan Rutherford to W. F. Cox, April 19, 1867, LSS; J. C. Robinson to J. Worth, October 30, 1866, LSAC (also in Worth GP).

87 61 *N.C. Reports*, pp. 90–94. See also, *Sentinel*, January 30, 1867, p. 2; Minutes, Carteret County Court, Sampson County Court, and Rutherford County Court, February–November 1867; H Report, 1867, p. 667.

88 *Standard*, January 12, 1866, p. 2.

89 Allan Rutherford to David Cowan, January 23, 1867, LSS; Proceedings of the House of Representatives, February 12, 1867, reported in *Sentinel*, February 28, 1867. For other cases of abuse, see County Court Minutes, Edgecombe County, February Term, 1866, p. 194.

90 *Sentinel*, April 11, 1866, p. 2, August 18, 1866, p. 2; *Carolina Watchman*, July 2, 1866, p. 2.

91 Quotation from *Dispatch*, April 25, 1866, p. 2. See also the following newspapers for the period of April–October 1866: *Journal, Standard, NBT, Southerner, Dispatch, Western Democrat*; S. F. Patterson to R. L. Patterson, May 20, 1866, Patterson Family Papers.

92 *Journal*, June 7, 1866, p. 4. See also the following newspapers for the period of April 1866–March 1867: *Journal, NBT, Southerner, Dispatch, The News, Western Democrat*.

93 *Sentinel*, August 18, 1866, p. 2; *Journal*, August 23, 1866, p. 4; *NBT*, August 26, 1866, p. 2; *Dispatch*, August 7, 1866, p. 3; *The News*, August 14, 1866, p. 2; *Journal*, August 9, 1866, p. 3. See also *Sentinel*, August 30, 1866, p. 2; *Dispatch*, August 7, 1866, p. 3; Dennett, *South As It Is*, p. 141; W. A. Graham to W. A. Graham, Jr., August 23, 1866, Graham Papers, NCA.

94 *Standard*, June 23, 1866, p. 2; *Western Democrat*, September 11, 1866, p. 3; S. H. Walkup to Jonathan Worth, March 26, 1867, Worth GP; L. S. Gash to the Assistant Commissioner, May 5, 1866, LRAC; Landy Wood to Jonathan Worth, March 26, 1867, Worth GP; petition dated November 1866, LP 818. See also H. M. Waugh to C. A. Cilley, May 22, 1866, LRW; W. F. Henderson to O. O. Howard, June 11, 1866, LRAC; A. C. Bryan to E. Whittlesey, May 25, 1866, ULRAC.

95 *Standard*, June 23, 1866, p. 2.

96 H. D. Norton to the Superintendent of the Western District, September 30, 1866, Semi-monthly Report to the Superintendent of the Western District, FBP. See also *NBT*, August 26, 1866, p. 2.

97 *JS, 1866–67*, pp. 27, 34, 42, 62–63; Worth "To the Chairman of the Warden Court," December 18, 1866, Worth LB, p. 283; J. V. Bomford to O. O. Howard, March 9, 1867, Worth GP; responses of individual chairmen to Worth, December 1866 through February 1867, ibid., passim.

98 See chairmen's reports of the following counties in Worth GP, December 1866–Feb-

ruary 1867: Jones, Columbus, Transylvania, Perquimans, Macon, Northampton, Buncombe, Lenoir, Halifax, Alleghany, Lincoln, Beaufort, Granville, Guilford, Union, and Rowan.

99 DES Rpt., p. 66.

100 Edward B. Northup to A. Rutherford, October 1, 1866, George McComber to A. Rutherford, October 1, 1866, H. H. Foster to A. Rutherford, October 1, 1866, LRS; report of the number of rations issued in western North Carolina, November 1, 1866, through September 20, 1867, RRI; *Sentinel*, October 19, 1866, p. 3; *Standard*, September 3, 1866, p. 3.

101 See reports from Allan Rutherford, from A. G. Brady, from William H. Wiegel, from John R. Edie, RRI, passim.

102 See George McComber to Allan Rutherford, October 1, 1866, and Edward B. Northup to A. Rutherford, October 1, 1866, LRS; George S. Hawley to Stephen Moore, February 25, 1867, and March 29, 1867, and C. W. Dodge to F. A. Seely, April 16, 1866, ULRE; A. Rutherford to C. A. Cilley, August 23, 1866, LRAC; Minutes, New Hanover County Court, March Term, 1866, March 14, 1866, p. 115; Surry County Warden's Court Minutes, 1865–67, passim.

103 Edwin Patrick to General Sickles, [June] 1867, LRAC.

104 George S. Hawley to Stephen Moore, March 29, 1867, ULRE.

105 See the minutes of the following county courts for the period 1865–67: Johnston, Wake, Perquimans, Montgomery, and Guilford; *Greensboro Patriot*, May 25, 1866, p. 1; Petition from citizens of Chowan County, June 6, 1866, LRAC; H. H. Foster to Allan Rutherford, October 1, 1866, LRS.

106 F. A. Fiske to Mr. G. Warren, October 11, 1866, LSEd.

107 Report by J. V. Bomford, RRI, 1867, passim; J. V. Bomford to O. O. Howard, March 9, 1867, Worth GP.

Chapter 6

1 W. N. H. Smith and Jesse J. Yeates to Governor Holden, July 17, 1865, Holden GP.

2 Hyde County Court Minutes, August Term, 1865, p. 34; W. W. Holden "to the Mayor and Commissioners of the Town of Wilmington," July 15, 1865, Holden LB, p. 19.

3 Ruger to D. D. Ferebee, December 13, 1865, RCC, Letters Sent; T. H. Ruger to Jonathan Worth, January 13, 1866, Worth LB, p. 34, and chap. 1 above. See also R. W. Best to T. H. Ruger, December 13, 1865, RCC, Letters Received. For similar accounts about the organizations of police and militia and the fear of insurrection, see Holden and Worth GP and LB; the county court minutes of 1865 for the following counties: Wake, Rutherford, Pasquotank, Edgecombe, Johnston, Sampson; Minutes of the City Commissioners of Morganton, September, 1865, p. 13, NCA; *Dispatch*, December 11, 1865, p. 3; *Wilmington Herald*, December 15, 1865, p. 1; Jonathan C. Robinson to Jonathan Worth, July 25, 1866, RCC, Letters Sent; T. H. Ruger to Worth, April 4, 1866, ibid.

4 *NBT*, December 12, 1865, p. 4. Also reprinted in *Sentinel*, December 16, 1865, p. 3.

See also *Wilmington Herald*, January 3, 1866, p. 2; Donald MacRae to his wife Julia, September 4, 1865, MacRae Papers; J. G. Hart to Horace James, November 30, 1865, ULRE; and chaps. 1 and 3 above. For similar general fears of an insurrection by blacks, see *Wilmington Herald*, November 27, 1865, p. 2; George D. Pool to W. W. Holden, December 16, 1865, Holden GP; *Western Democrat*, August 1, 1865, p. 3.

5 J. G. Hart to Horace James, November 30, 1865, ULRE. See also *Standard*, November 30, 1865, p. 3, and Andrews, *South Since the War*, p. 179.

6 See, e.g., *Sentinel*, January 6, 1866, p. 2, August 11, 1866, p. 2, August 15, 1866, p. 2; *The News*, May 8, 1866, p. 3. Also Abner S. Williams to Jonathan Worth, September 8, 1866; C. W. Dodge to Stephen Moore, January 15, 1867; Jonathan Worth to J. W. Bomford, January 3, 1867, LRAC.

7 Allan Rutherford to A. H. Van Bokkelen, May 26, 1866, LSS; C. A. Cilley to J. W. W. Stickney, June 11, 1866, LSAC; William H. Wiegel to C. A. Cilley, June 11, 1866, LRAC; Isaac A. Rosekrans to Joe Banks, January 31, 1866, Letters Sent by the Assistant Superintendent at New Berne; Jonathan Bizzell et al. to E. Whittlesey, January 18, 1866, ULRE; William Beadle to J. M. Stallings, February 12, 1866, LSS; Endorsement by E. Whittlesey on letter from Samuel Gilmore, December 27, 1865, Endorsements and Memoranda by the Assistant Commissioner. Only one case was found where a county court granted a license to a black man to carry a gun (Rowan County Court Minutes, August Term, 1865).

8 *Western Democrat*, June 6, 1865, p. 3. See also Worth GP, January 1866; *NBT*, January 10, 1866, p. 4; *Western Democrat*, September 18, 1866, p. 3; J.T.S. to William Gaston Lewis, December 20, 1865, William Gaston Lewis Papers, SHC; *Worth Corr.* 1: 482, 2:746; H. C. Thompson to B. S. Hedrick, June 14, 1865, Hedrick Papers; B. F. Moore to Thomas Ruffin, September 22, 1865, Hamilton, *Ruffin Papers*, p. 31; M. J. Foust to M. S. Robins, December 26, 1865, Robins Papers; William K. Ruffin to Samuel A'Court Ashe, February 7, 1867, Ashe Papers.

9 Quotation from *Sentinel*, September 19, 1866, p. 3. See also ibid., January 15, 1866, p. 3, May 8, 1866, p. 2; William A. Graham to Jonathan Worth, January 26, 1866, *Worth Corr.* 1:482.

10 See, e.g., T. H. Ruger to Jonathan Worth, January 15, 1866, Worth GP; M. J. Foust to M. S. Robins, December 26, 1865, Robins Papers; B. F. Moore to Thomas Ruffin, September 22, 1865, Hamilton, *Ruffin Papers*, p. 31. Also *Sentinel*, December 12, 1865, p. 2, March 22, 1866, p. 3, and *Standard*, January 10, 1866, p. 3.

11 See *Standard*, September 26, 1865, p. 3, and January 20, 1866, p. 3; *Western Democrat*, October 17, 1865, p. 3.

12 Report of Outrages by T. H. Ruger to T. S. Brown, January 9, 1866, Letters Received by the Office of the Adjutant General (Main Series) 1861–70, "Report of racial violence in the South and of consequent action taken by military authorities, April, 1865–January, 1866," NA, Microcopy 619, Roll 505, File No. 770P1866.

13 Ibid.

14 H Report, 1866, p. 735.

15 See, e.g., Report of Outrages by the Superintendent of the Eastern District, March

1866–March 1867, FBP; Reports of outrages by various assistant superintendents, June 1866–March 1867, FBP; Semi-monthly reports of outrages by whites against blacks by the Superintendent of the Southern District, June 15–October 13, 1866, and January–May 1867, LRAC; various assistant superintendents to the superintendent of the Western District, March–September 1866, ibid.

16 Printed circular by Jonathan Worth to the "Clerk of the Superior Court" for all counties, August 17, 1867, Worth GP, and the various clerks to Worth, 1867, passim, ibid. The reason for the survey was to gather necessary information for a board, formed by General Sickles, "to report on the expediency, &c., of providing a suitable temporary place of confinement for prisoners undergoing sentence for felony."

17 Johnson, *Ante-bellum North Carolina*, pp. 667, 670.

18 W. E. Vanyhave to Jonathan Worth, August 28, 1867, Worth GP.

19 Reprinted in *Carolina Watchman*, November 5, 1866, p. 3. See also the following newspapers for the period of May 1865–November 1866: *Sentinel, NBT, Journal, Western Democrat, People's Press, Standard;* Daniel L. Goodloe to B. S. Hedrick, September 29, 1865, Hedrick Papers; J. M. Clement to Edward McPherson, April 13, 1867, "Letters to McPherson," p. 195. See also Jesse Parker Bogue, Jr., "Violence and Oppression in North Carolina During Reconstruction, 1865–1873" (unpublished Ph.D. dissertation, University of Maryland, 1973), which details a great deal of violence in North Carolina during the era.

20 G. F. Granger to Thaddeus Stevens, January 11, 1866, "Letters to Stevens," p. 176. See also the following newspapers for the period of July 1865–January 1867: *Standard, Sentinel, Western Democrat, Journal, People's Press, Dispatch, NBT.* Also R. L. Patterson to Governor Holden, June 8, 1865, Holden GP; Holden to Johnson, December 6, 1865, Johnson Papers; E. J. Thompson to B. S. Hedrick, March 17, 1866, Hedrick Papers; F. A. Seely to E. Whittlesey, May 14, 1866, LSE; Report by C. A. Cilley, March 14, 1866, and Report by Dexter Clapp, November 14, 1865, SMR.

21 For examples of newspaper reports of thefts by blacks, see the following papers for June 1865–January 1867: *Standard, Sentinel, Western Democrat, NBT, Progress, Southerner, Wilmington Herald, Dispatch, Journal, Greensboro Patriot, The News.* Some Freedmen's Bureau agents also reported that theft by blacks was prevalent. LRW, December 1865–August 1866; George Hawley to Stephen Moore, September 25, 1866, ULRE; F. A. Seely to Edward Slade, May 9, 1866, LSE; Report by Jasper Packard, December 15, 1865, SMR.

22 *Southerner*, August 18, 1866, p. 2; *Dispatch*, January 13, 1867, p. 2, and February 14, 1867, p. 3; *NBT*, September 18, 1866, p. 2; *Standard*, September 23, 1865, p. 3, and January 15, 1866, p. 3, and February 16, 1866, p. 3, and August 9, 1866, p. 2; *The News*, January 15, 1867, p. 2, and February 12, 1867; *Western Democrat*, July 18, 1865, p. 2; *Wilmington Herald*, July 10, 1865, p. 1; *Journal*, December 28, 1865, p. 1, and December 15, 1866, p. 3. There are, of course, many more cases in the court records. It is also important to note that in three cases where blacks were accused of either rape or attempted rape, white mobs broke into the jails and murdered the accused but yet unconvicted blacks. (*Dispatch*, January 13, 1867, p. 2, and February 14, 1867, p. 3; *The News*, Feb-

ruary 12, 1867; Robert Avery to Jacob F. Chur, May 4, 1867, RCC, Letters Received; J. W. Claus to N. A. Miles, May 11, 1867, ibid., Letters Sent.)

23 George Glavis to E. Whittlesey, March 21, 1866, LRAC. See also the following records for August 1865–February 1867: RCC, Letters Sent; LRAC; ULRE; ULREd; LSS; SMR; Endorsements and Memoranda by the Assistant Commissioner; *Standard, Dispatch, NBT*. It should be pointed out that when whites were the victims of robbers, they too were often beaten.

24 Hugo Hillebrandt to A. Coats, May 31, 1866, ULRE. See also William F. Cox to Stephen Moore, November 10, 1866, ibid.

25 George Glavis to E. Whittlesey, March 21, 1866, LRAC. See also the following records for the period of August 1865–February 1867: ULRE; LRAC; SMR; RCC, Letters Sent.

26 H. H. Foster to Allan Rutherford, June 4, 1866, LRS and Rutherford to Foster, June 4, 1866, LSS.

27 William Beadle to Fred Beecher, February 12, 1866, LSS; E. Whittlesey to T. H. Ruger, February 20, 1866, and Whittlesey to James Anderson, May 14, 1866, LSAC; Allan Rutherford to A. H. Van Bokkelen, June 30, 1866, LRAC. See also T. H. Ruger to A. Ames, August 14, 1865, RCC, Letters Sent.

28 Besides the Regulators two other gangs plagued North Carolina. One was the Lowry gang. For information on it, see W. McKee Evans, *To Die Game: The Story of the Lowry Band, Indian Guerrillas of Reconstruction* (Baton Rouge: Louisiana State University Press, 1971); Lowry Papers, NCA; R. McNair to Jonathan Worth, December 6, 1866, Worth GP; Anonymous reports of cases of outrages upon Union men and Freedmen in North Carolina, June 1866, LRAC. The other gang was referred to as the "Red Strings" or the "Black Strings." It is unclear whether this was a gang or whether it was just a political organization of southern Unionists. The latter was probably the case, although the group was sometimes charged with crimes of retaliation and defense against former Confederates. See *Wadesboro Argus*, October 18, 1866, p. 2; Report of Major F. E. Walcott, August 16, 1866, Worth GP; Report of William S. Mason, August 17, 1866, ibid.; J. Claus to the Commanding Officer at Salisbury, March 25, 1867, Records of the United States Continental Command, Second Military District: North Carolina and South Carolina, Letters Sent, NA, Record Group 393.

29 Allan Rutherford to Jacob F. Chur, February 12, 1867, LRAC (also in Worth LB, p. 378); Allan Rutherford to Jacob F. Chur, February 27, 1867, ibid.; *Journal*, February 9, 1867, p. 2; J. V. Bomford to Jonathan Worth, February 18, 1867, LSAC; Jacob F. Chur to Allan Rutherford, February 20, 1867, ibid.; *Journal*, February 9, 1867, p. 2, and February 17, 1867, p. 3. For other accounts of Regulator activities against blacks and of the civil authorities' reluctance or inability to act, see Sidney A. Busbee to F. A. Fiske, April 8, 1867, and H. D. Norton to M. Cogswell, April 19, 1867, LRAC; DES Rpt, p. 63; E. Whittlesey to J. A. Campbell, January 8, 1866, LSAC; the following newspapers for the period of November 1866–February 1867: *Standard, Dispatch, Progress, Journal, Sentinel*. See also Bogue, "Violence and Oppression," pp. 83–103.

30 "Cases of Outrages," June 1866, Misc. LRAC; Hugo Hillebrandt to A. Coats, May 31, 1866, ULRE and Hugo Hillebrandt to C. A. Cilley, June 29, 1866, LRAC; T. H.

Ruger to A. Ames, August 14, 1865, RCC, Letters Sent. See also Holden LB, pp. 39–40; Holden GP, June 1865; H. H. Foster to Allan Rutherford, June 4, 1866, LRS.

31 Dennett, *South As It Is*, pp. 110–11.

32 Edward B. Northup to Allan Rutherford, August 10, 1866, Worth LB, p. 169; Dennett, *South As It Is*, p. 140; Andrews, *South Since the War*, p. 118; William H. Coleman to Calvin Wiley, October 2, 1865, Wiley Papers, NCA; T. H. Ruger to George D. Ruggles, October 4, 1865, RCC, Letters Sent; Edwin W. Fuller to Jones Fuller, September 14, 1865, Fuller-Thomas Papers; *Standard*, September 25, 1865, p. 3; Charles Phillips to K. P. Battle, December 17, 1866, Battle Family Papers. For reports of other similar incidents, see *Wilmington Herald*, December 5, 1865, p. 1; *Sentinel*, August 21, 1866, p. 3; *Standard*, March 21, 1867, p. 2; *Union Banner*, September, 1865, passim; the following Freedmen's Bureau records for July 1865–March 1867: SMR; LRAC; ULRE; ULRAC; LSAC; NR; LSEd; LRW; LSW; SR; Holden LB, pp. 26–27, 58; Worth GP, June 29, 1866; LRAGO, September 7, 1865.

33 Petition of several citizens of Montgomery County to Jonathan Worth [November 1866,] Worth LB, pp. 280–81.

34 *NBT*, June 24, 1865, p. 3; William B. Bowe to E. Whittlesey, January 27, 1866, ULRAC; Thomas Heath to J. A. Campbell, September 22, 1865, RCC, Letters Received; *Wilmington Herald*, September 23, 1865, Supplement. For other cases of blacks being murdered by whites, see T. H. Ruger to George D. Ruggles, February 15, 1866, RCC, Letters Sent; the following Freedmen's Bureau records for January 1866–February 1867: LSAC; Endorsements and Memoranda by the Assistant Commissioner; LRAC; LSW; LSE; ULRE; the following newspapers from September 1865–January 1867: *Dispatch, Standard, Sentinel, Journal;* Jones County Court Minutes, September Term, 1866; Forsyth County Court, Minute Docket, July 14, 1865, p. 109.

35 T. H. Ruger to W. W. Holden, August 1, 1865, Holden LB, p. 27. See also ibid., August 8, 1865, pp. 34–35.

36 Hugo Hillebrandt to Stephen Moore, August 10, 1866, LRE.

37 Broadside entitled "Vindication of the Freedman's [sic] Bureau! By the Freedmen in a Public Meeting," Broadsides, North Carolina, May 1866, The Flowers Collection, DU, Rare Book Room.

38 *NBT*, December 11, 1865, p. 1.

39 *Newbern Commercial*, reprinted in *Sentinel*, October 22, 1866, p. 2, and *Dispatch*, October 23, 1866, p. 1. The stories in the *Sentinel* and the *Dispatch* are identical except that the former said that the trouble was in Greensboro and the latter wrote that it was in Goldsboro. Inasmuch as the original story in the *Commercial* is not extant, it is impossible to determine which reprinted article contained the typographical error. For reports of other incidents, see *Standard*, November 4, 1865, p. 3, and Asa Teal to Stephen Moore, June 22, 1866, LRW; *Sentinel*, June 7, 1866, p. 2, June 10, 1866, p. 2; *Journal*, June 7, 1866, p. 2; *NBT*, June 5, 1866, p. 1.

40 Reprinted in *People's Press*, September 30, 1865, p. 1, and *Standard*, September 29, 1865, p. 3.

41 Dennett, *South As It Is*, p. 140; Andrews, *South Since the War*, p. 118. See also

William Coleman to Calvin Wiley, October 2, 1865, Wiley Papers, NCA. There are no existing records of the trial, if one was held.

42 Reprinted in *Western Democrat*, February 19, 1867, p. 2. A similar account appeared in the *Sentinel*, February 12, 1867, p. 2.

43 *Dispatch*, February 13, 1867, p. 3.

44 *Wilmington Herald*, July 10, 1865, pp. 1, 2.

45 Ibid., August 3, 1865, p. 1, and August 4, 1865, p. 1, and August 5, 1865, p. 1; *NBT*, August 16, 1865, p. 3; *Standard*, December 29, 1865, p. 3; *Dispatch*, December 28, 1865, p. 3; *Sentinel*, March 30, 1866, p. 3.

46 33 *NC Repts*, 555.

47 *Revised Code*, 1854, Chapter 52, pp. 361–62, 367; Chapter 31, pp. 154–55; Chapter 62, pp. 365–66; Chapter 31, pp. 147–85 passim, and especially p. 159.

48 See George G. Meade to Edwin Stanton, September 20, 1865, LRAGO; George G. Meade to W. W. Holden, September 22, 1865, Holden LB, p. 73; Circular of February 16, 1866, by Colonel Whittlesey, printed in *NBT*, March 7, 1866, p. 8; E. Whittlesey to Ralph P. Buxton, February 16, 1866, LSAC; *Sentinel*, August 23, 1865, p. 2. For a detailed analysis of the biases and ineffectiveness of the military, see Bogue, "Violence and Oppression," pp. 28–49 and passim. Kenneth Edson St. Clair ("The Administration of Justice in North Carolina During Reconstruction, 1865–1876" [unpublished Ph.D. dissertation, Ohio State University, 1939]), on the other hand, argues that throughout Presidential Reconstruction North Carolina "remained under military control." However, even he admits that there were relatively few trials of civilians by the military between 1865 and 1868 (see especially pp. 2, 30, 68–69, 93).

49 *Sentinel*, August 23, 1865, p. 2; *JH, 1866*, pp. 19–24; clipping in a letter from C. W. Dodge to F. A. Seely, March 5, 1866, ULRAC. See also Chap. 3 of this book for details on the debate over the admission of black testimony in North Carolina's courts.

50 Order of July 13, 1866, H Report, 1866, p. 734; *Standard*, July 26, 1866, p. 3.

51 H Report, 1866, p. 735. See also DES Rpt, p. 65.

52 Reports by John R. Edie, September 30, 1866, and by Stephen Moore, September 13, 1866, SMR; H. H. Foster to Allan Rutherford, October 30, 1866, LRS; George S. Hawley to A. Coats, May 21, 1866, ULRE. See also George S. Hawley to Stephen Moore, March 20 1867, ibid. Also W. F. Henderson to J. R. Edie, March 4, 1867; F. S. Wiatt to J. R. Edie, December 3, 1866, and February 2, 1867; F. S. Wiatt to Stephen Moore, July 4, 1866, and July 9, 1866, LRW.

53 See, e.g., *Standard*, April 19, 1866, p. 3, and May 10, 1866, p. 2; *Western Democrat*, January 29, 1867, p. 3; *NBT*, May 6, 1866, p. 7; *Dispatch*, May 2, 1866, p. 2; *Old North State*, May 25, 1866, p. 3; *Sentinel*, July 23, 1866, p. 3.

54 Petition to Worth, October 27, 1866, Worth LB, p. 239; Jonathan Worth to M. E. Manly et al., November 2, 1866, ibid., p. 240. See also David A. Barnes to Worth, Craven County Superior Court Minutes Docket, Fall Term, 1866, pp. 250–51.

55 See above chaps. 2 and 4.

56 Charles Wolff to Jacob Chur, June 10, 1867, LRAC.

57 Allan Rutherford to A. Coats, September 15, 1866, LRAC.

58   George Hawley to Stephen Moore, September 25, 1866, ULRE; E. J. Warren to Jennie Warren, October 28, 1866, Warren Papers; *Western Democrat*, October 16, 1866, p. 3.

59   *Union Banner*, September 8, 1865, p. 3.

60   *NBT*, July through October 1865, passim.

61   *Wilmington Herald*, September 18, 1865, p. 1.

62   See *Dispatch* and *Wilmington Herald*, September 1865 through January 1866, passim, and especially *Dispatch*, May 8, 1866, p. 3, and May 9, 1866, p. 3.

63   *Wilmington Herald*, November 2, 1865, p. 1; *Dispatch*, November 15, 1865, p. 3, and November 28, 1865, p. 3; Allan Rutherford to A. H. Van Bokkelen, May 18, 1866, LSS.

64   *Wilmington Herald* and *Dispatch*, passim; Letter from Allan Rutherford, May 18, 1866, Endorsements and Memoranda by the Assistant Commissioner.

65   A. W. Shaffer to C. A. Cilley, June 13, 1866, LRAC.

66   For additional examples of the lack of discrimination in the courts of North Carolina, see also the records of Cabarrus, Jones, Sampson, Wake, and New Hanover county courts and the Mecklenberg Superior Court. All of the above and subsequent information on the courts is derived from the court minutes and minute dockets, NCA, unless otherwise noted.

67   *Western Democrat*, November 6, 1866, p. 3.

68   H Report, 1867, p. 667.

69   There were three versus seven convicted in the county court; five versus sixteen in the superior court. W. P. Harris to Jonathan Worth, August 22, 1867, Worth GP, and minutes of the county and superior courts. Population as of 1870. (L. L. Polk, *Handbook of North Carolina* [Raleigh: n.p., 1879], p. 258.)

70   L. F. Koonce to Jonathan Worth, September 7, 1867, Worth GP; Jones County Superior Court Minutes. Population as of 1870. (Polk, *Handbook*, p. 262.)

71   Court minutes of Forsyth County, Sampson County, Rowan County and Superior, and Montgomery Superior courts. Also Jonathan Blackburn to Jonathan Worth, August 20, 1867; W. R. Clark to Jonathan Worth, [July 1867]; J. B. Ballard to Jonathan Worth, September 9, 1867; William R. Webb to Jonathan Worth, September 2, 1867, Worth GP. Also Polk, *Handbook*, pp. 257–66.

72   E. Whittlesey to O. O. Howard, March 23, 1866, LSAC.

73   Richard Dillon to Andrew Coats, May 21, 1866, LRAC; George Hawley to Stephen Moore, December 24, 1866, ULRE; Asa Teal to Stephen Moore, June 23, 1866, and June 25, 1866, LRW; Stephen Moore to Asa Teal, June 26, 1866, LSW; Justin Hodge to Allan Rutherford, December 10, 1866, LRAC; Allan Rutherford to C. A. Cilley, July 3, 1866, and July 5, 1866, LSS; C. A. Cilley to Allan Rutherford, July 5, 1866, LSAC. For additional examples of favoritism to whites, see the following FBP from May 1866–July 1867: LSS; LRAC; LSAC; Holden LB, pp. 6, 20, 22; Worth LB, p. 169; Jonathan Worth to E. J. Warren, August 22, 1866, Warren Papers; *Wilmington Herald*, February 14, 1866, p. 1; *NBT*, July 24, 1866, p. 1; *Wilmington Herald*, September 23, 1865, Supplement, September 29, 1865, p. 1, and October 11, 1865, p. 1; *Dispatch*, February 27, 1867, p. 2.

74 C. W. Dodge to Stephen Moore, September 20, 1866, ULRE.

75 *Revised Code*, Chapter 34, Sections 26 and 27, p. 207.

76 *Western Democrat*, September 4, 1866, p. 3, and November 6, 1866, p. 3; *Standard*, March 20, 1866, p. 3, and April 14, 1866, p. 2, and August 28, 1866, p. 2; *Sentinel*, March 19, 1866, p. 3, and August 25, 1866, p. 3; Daniel G. Fowler to E. Whittlesey, April 4, 1866, LRAC; George S. Hawley to A. Coats, May 21, 1866, ULRE; various court minute dockets; clerks of the superior courts of the various counties to Jonathan Worth, 1867, Worth GP, passim. Blacks and whites received corporal punishment in at least Alamance, Bertie, Cabarrus, Forsyth, Henderson, Hyde, Johnston, Lincoln, Mecklenburg, Montgomery, New Hanover, Pasquotank, Person, Polk, Rowan, Sampson, and Wake counties.

77 *Standard*, April 14, 1866, p. 2; *Western Democrat*, reprinted in *Sentinel*, November 14, 1865, p. 2; *Sentinel*, December 20, 1866, p. 2; *NBT*, reprinted in *Sentinel*, September 14, 1865, p. 2.

78 Johnson, *Ante-bellum North Carolina*, pp. 661–73.

79 C. W. Miles to E. Whittlesey, September 18, 1865; Allan Rutherford to F. A. Seely, February 4, 1867; John R. Edie to Jacob Chur, February 1867; Stephen Moore to Jacob Chur, February 18, 1867; M. Cogswell to Chur, February 19, 1867, LRAC. Also E. Whittlesey to O. O. Howard, April 4, 1866, LSAC; and various court records.

80 *PL, 1866*, p. 121.

81 Johnson, *Ante-bellum North Carolina*, pp. 648–49, 649n, 600.

82 *Revised Code*, Chapter 59, pp. 334–35; S. F. Phillips to Jonathan Worth, February 6, 1867, Worth GP.

83 See, e.g., superior court records for Mecklenburg and Rowan counties.

84 Sampson County Court Minutes, February Term, 1866.

85 The eleven counties were Alamance, Craven, Davidson, Forsyth, Hyde, Iredell, Johnston, New Hanover, Rowan, Sampson, and Wake.

86 Quotation from Allan Rutherford to R. T. Frank, April 23, 1867, LSS. See also New Hanover County Court Minutes, passim; Charles J. Wickersham to E. Whittlesey, December 28, 1865; Allan Rutherford to Jacob F. Chur, September 24, 1866; Allan Rutherford to S. R. Bunting, June 30, 1866, LSS. Also E. Whittlesey to Charles Wickersham, December 25, 1865, LSAC. Also miscellaneous papers regarding court cases in the files of the assistant commissioner; *NBT*, December 27, 1865, p. 1; *Sentinel*, January 3, 1866,. p. 1; *Journal*, December 27, 1865, p. 1.

87 H. C. Lawrence to Charles Wickersham, January 10, 1866, LRS; Charles Wickersham to E. Whittlesey, January 22, 1866, and January 25, 1866, LRAC. The results of this trial are unknown.

88 *Wilmington Herald*, January 24, 1866, p. 2; *Sentinel*, January 27, 1866, p. 2.

89 W. H. Doherty to Stephen Moore, September 19, 1866, ULRE; W. F. Henderson to John R. Edie, May 4, 1867, LRW; Forsyth County Court Minute Docket, Apprenticeship Cases, June Term, 1866, pp. 159, 164–65, and September Term, 1866, pp. 197–98, 219; Jonathan Blackburn to Jonathan Worth, August 20, 1867, Worth GP; Rowan County Court Minutes, August 1866–November 1866, passim.

90 Wake County Court Minutes, August Term, 1866, pp. 102–103, and November Term, 1866, pp. 186, 201, 205, 217–23, 233; Hyde County Court Minutes, Fall Term, 1867, p. 122; *Statesville American* cited in *Western Democrat*, October 30, 1866, p. 1; *Dispatch*, October 26, 1866, p. 1; Alamance County Court Minutes, December Term, 1866, p. 196; Johnston County Court Minutes, November Term, pp. 173–75, 181, and August Term, 1866, p. 119; Indenture for Apprentice, August 28, 1866, November 29, 1866, November 30, 1866.

91 Pete Daniel, *The Shadow of Slavery: Peonage in the South 1901–1969* (Urbana: University of Illinois Press, 1972), p. 29.

92 Wake County Court Minutes, August Term, 1866, pp. 141–42, and November Term, 1866, pp. 201, 204, 217, 219; and 1865–67 passim. Also Wake County Court, State Docket, 1865–67, passim.

93 *People's Press*, November 16, 1866, p. 2 and December 7, 1866, p. 2. Also Superior Court Minute Docket, Rowan County, November Term 1866.

94 Report by Dexter E. Clapp, October 10, 1865, NR; Robert Vance to Zebulon Vance, July 12, 1865, Vance Papers. For other examples see Stephen Moore to William Cox, January 5, 1867, LSE; Allan Rutherford to H. H. Foster, October 31, 1866, LSS; William Beaty to Lieutenant McAlpens, May 20, 1867, LRAC; Report of Hannibal D. Norton, August 27, 1866, SMR; J. V. Bomford to Jonathan Worth, December 14, 1866, LSAC. Also *NBT*, August 30, 1865, p. 3; September 19, 1865, p. 3; August 9, 1866, p. 1; *Journal*, June 14, 1866, p. 4.

Chapter 7

1 *Freedmen's Record*, July 1866, p. 133. See also S. S. Ashley to S. Hunt, November 2, 1865, Ashley Letters; Amos McCollough and Samuel Highsmith to O. O. Howard, May 6, 1866, and H. C. Vogell to N. A. Miles, July 1, 1867, LRAC; *Freedmen's Record*, August 1865, p. 133, and September 1865, p. 144; G. William Walker to F. A. Fiske, May 21, 1866, ULREd; S. S. Ashley to Allan Rutherford, November 20, 1866, Superintendent of the Southern District, Department of Education, Letters Sent, FBP; *NBT*, August 1, 1865, p. 2.

2 See, e.g., Amos G. Tennent to Horace James, October 28, 1865, ULRE; *Standard*, January 15, 1867, p. 2; *NBT*, September 12, 1866, p. 1; McAvery to Mrs. R. L. Patterson, February 21, 1866, Patterson Family Papers. Also Charles Wolff to Fiske, September 25, 1866; William N. Thompson to Fiske, October 20, 1866; J. T. Phillips to Fiske, November 8, 1866; George Newcomb to F. A. Fiske, October 2, 1865; J. F. Conners to Fisk P. Brewer, September 14, 1866, ULREd. Also J. F. Conners to M. Cogswell, March 30, 1867, Sch Rpts, CD; S. S. Ashley to Reverend George Whipple, February 26, 1867, Ashley Letters.

3 Group of Freedmen to F. A. Fiske, July 11, 1866, ULREd; "To the Commander of the United States forces at Morgantown, N.C.," April 27, 1867, ULRAC.

4 See above, chaps. 2 and 4. See also *Standard*, July 3, 1866, p. 2; Fisk Brewer to O. O. Howard, April 3, 1867, American Missionary Association Archives (Selections), Brewer Letters, SHC.

5 *Sentinel*, August 8, 1865, p. 4; T. P. Devereux to Jonathan Worth, October 20, 1866, LP 820; *Standard*, July 11, 1865, p. 3; *Wilmington Herald*, January 13, 1866, p. 1.

6 *Charlotte Times*, reprinted in *Standard*, November 6, 1866, p. 2. See also George Newcomb to F. A. Fiske, Ooctober 2, 1865, ULREd; Report by J. F. Conners to M. Cogswell, March 30, 1867, Sch Rpts, CD; S. S. Ashley to Reverend P. E. Smith, January 7, 1867, and S. S. Ashley to S. Hunt, November 2, 1865, Ashley Letters; F. S. Wiatt to John R. Edie, October 8, 1866, LRW; Lyman Abbott to Calvin Wiley, April 16, 1866, Wiley Papers, SHC; Calvin Wiley to Jonathan Worth, January 13, 1866, Worth GP; Caroline Pettigrew to her sister, Louise, March 10, 1867, Pettigrew Family Papers; Mary Denke to Ella Jones, January 28, 1866, Jones Family Papers, SHC.

7 The Reverend W. L. Miller to F. A. Fiske, November 9, 1866, ULREd. See also Dennett, *South As It Is*, p. 109; Letter from "Spectator" of Beaufort in *Standard*, March 3, 1866, p. 2; McAvery to Mrs. R. L. Patterson, February 21, 1866, Patterson Family Papers.

8 Charles Wickersham to Fred Beecher, [September 1865], NR; Report by Major Henry Camp, May 1, 1866, Monthly Reports to the Superintendent of the Eastern District, FBP; Report by W. C. Miles, October 14, 1865, SMR. See also J. F. Conners to M. Cogswell, March 30, 1867, Sch Rpts, CD.

9 Thomas Barton to Allan Rutherford, January 10, 1867, LRS. For additional information on this incident, see F. A. Fiske to Thomas Barton, April 3, 1867, LSEd. For other examples of white violence directed against black education, see the following FBP collections for July 1865–May 1866: LSS; ULRE; ULREd; LRAC; LSAC; NR; H Report, 1867, p. 668; *Standard*, February 26, 1867, p. 2; *Freedmen's Record*, September 1865, pp. 142–43.

10 McLean to Ashley, February 20, 1866, American Missionary Association Archives, Amistad Research Center, Fisk University.

11 See, e.g., *Dispatch*, December 6, 1866, p. 2; *Sentinel*, October 23, 1866, p. 2; *Wilmington Herald*, June 15, 1865, p. 2, and February 23, 1866, p. 2; *Journal*, December 5, 1866, p. 2; Prospectus of the *Carolina Times* in Dennett, *South As It Is*, p. 133.

12 *The News*, September 11, 1866, p. 2. See also *Journal*, November 22, 1866, p. 2; Goldsboro *News*, reprinted in *Standard*, October 16, 1866, p. 2; *Progress*, August 19, 1865, p. 2; Charles Phillips to J. B. Killebrew, March 12, 1866, Spencer Papers.

13 *Sentinel*, October 23, 1866, p. 2; June 9, 1866, p. 2; June 14, 1866, p. 3; June 19, 1866, p. 2. See also the following newspapers for the period of July 1865–January 1867: *Journal, Standard, Dispatch, Greensboro Patriot, Sentinel; Worth Corr.* 2:874–75; H Report, 1865, p. 13.

14 See, e.g., correspondent for the *Philadelphia Inquirer* in NBT, August 1, 1865, p. 2; S. S. Ashley to the Reverend P. E. Smith, January 21, 1867, and S. S.. Ashley to S. Hunt, May 8, 1866, Ashley Letters; Mrs. E. J. Warren to her daughter Julie, March 11, 1866, Warren Papers; Mary Bowers to F. A. Fiske, October 10, 1866, and William N. Thompson to F. A. Fiske, October 20, 1866, and William Willey to F. A. Fiske, November 10, 1865, ULREd; Charles to Caroline Pettigrew, April 6, 1866, Pettigrew Family Papers; A. Coats to F. A. Seely, February 23, 1866, ULRE; *Journal*, January 11, 1866, p. 2.

15 S. S. Ashley to S. Hunt, April 10, 1866, Ashley Letters.

16 See, e.g., Clem S. Camper to F. A. Fiske, November 11, 1865; William Elliott to F. A. Fiske, April 14, 1866; William N. Thompson to F. A. Fiske, October 20, 1866, ULREd.

17 *Standard*, September 6, 1865, p. 1.

18 Yardley Warner to Calvin Wiley, July 27, 1865, Wiley Papers, NCA.

19 S. S. Ashley to S. Hunt, January 22, 1866, and S. S. Ashley to N. A. McLean, February 7, 1866, Ashley Letters; S. S. Ashley to Allan Rutherford, November 20, 1866, Sch Rpts, SD. See also J. F. Allison to M. Cogswell, March 27, 1867, Sch Rpts, CD; Flora A. Leland to F. A. Fiske, May 2, 1866, ULREd; F. A. Fiske to G. Warren, October 11, 1866, LSEd.

20 Dennett, *South As It Is*, pp. 132–33; *Sentinel*, January 19, 1867, p. 3. See also *Journal*, January 30, 1867, p. 2.

21 Fisk Brewer to George Whipple, February 6, 1867, and November 8, 1866, Brewer Letters. See also ibid., November 8, 1866, December 2, 1866, and January 5, 1867.

22 *JS, 1866*, p. 71; *JH, 1866*, pp. 92, 232–33; *PL, 1866*, pp. 87–88, 138; *NBT*, March 15, 1866, p. 4; *Western Democrat*, March 6, 1866, p. 3; *People's Press*, March 17, 1866, p. 3; *Greensboro Patriot*, March 2, 1866, p. 1, and March 9, 1866, p. 1; *Dispatch*, January 4, 1867, p. 3. For additional details see Alexander, "North Carolina," pp. 316–19.

23 *Standard*, March 1, 1866, p. 2; *Sentinel*, March 1, 1866, p. 2.

24 Jonathan Worth to W. A. Graham, January 12, 1866, Graham Papers. See also *Worth Corr.* 1:465.

25 Charles Phillips to J. B. Killebrew, March 12, 1866, Spencer Papers. See also N. A. McLean to S. S. Ashley, February 20, 1866, American Missionary Association Archives.

26 *PL, 1866–67*, pp. 17–21. White insistence on segregated schools supported by taxes laid upon whites and blacks separately continued in North Carolina during Radical Reconstruction and beyond. (See Olsen, *Carpetbagger's Crusade*.)

27 *PL, 1866*, pp. 18–20; *JS, 1866*, pp. 134, 140, 181, 235–36; *JH, 1866*, pp. 240–41; *Standard*, March 5, 1866, p. 2.

28 *Private Laws of the State of North Carolina, Passed by the General Assembly at the Sessions of 1866–'67* (Raleigh: Wm. E. Pell, 1867), pp. 254–55, 294–95.

29 F. A. Fiske to Miss H. E. Stevenson, October 13, 1866, LSEd.

30 See, e.g., F. A. Fiske to Henry Stricker, July 6, 1866, ibid.; ibid., 1866, passim; E. Whittlesey to Charles Emery, July 22, 1865, LSAC.

31 See n. 2 above and F. A. Fiske to the Reverend Samuel Hurst, October 13, 1866, LSEd; ULREd for the period of October 1865–December 1866; S. S. Ashley to the Reverend George Whipple, February 26, 1867, and S. S. Ashley to S. Hunt, January 22, 1866 and November 23, 1865, Ashley Letters.

32 F. A. Fiske to Miss H. E. Stevenson, October 13, 1866, LSEd. See also F. A. Fiske to Jonathan M. Foote, October 9, 1866, ibid.; J. F. Conners to Fisk Brewer, September 14, 1866, ULREd.

33 S. S. Ashley to George Whipple, February 26, 1867, Ashley Letters.

34 State Superintendent's Monthly School Reports for December 1866, FBP. See also reports of January 1867 and March 1867. These reports generally did not include sabbath schools.

35 *Sentinel*, June 14, 1866, p. 3; Benjamin W. Pond to F. A. Fiske, October 12, 1865, ULREd; and chap. 2 above.

36 *Journal*, April 3, 1866, p. 4; Jonathan C. Robinson to General O. H. Hart, July 10, 1866, RCC, Letters Sent; F. A. Fiske to Jacob F. Chur, April 11, 1867, LSEd; H Report, 1866, p. 735; H Report, 1867, p. 668; J. V. Bomford to O. O. Howard, February 20, 1867, LSAC; State Superintendent's Monthly School Reports for December 1866, January 1867, and March 1867, FBP.

37 State Superintendent's Monthly School Reports for December 1866 and January 1867, FBP. The same pattern can be seen in the March 1867 report.

38 J. R. Hawley to J. A. Campbell, RCC, Letters Received; Charles Wickersham to Fred Beecher, September 1865, NR.

39 Sch Rpts, SD, October 1865–April 1866; Ashley, "Report of Schools for Freedmen . . . ," December 31, 1865, Ashley Letters; Ashley, "Superintendent's Monthly Report . . . ," January 1866, ibid.; Charles Wickersham to the Assistant Commissioner, October 31, 1865, RRI; Allan Rutherford to Jacob Chur, March 25, 1867, LSS; S. S. Ashley to Allan Rutherford, March 25, 1867, LRS; Report by Allan Rutherford, March 31, 1867, SMR; Robert Avery to the Assistant Commissioner, June 27, 1867, and July 6, 1867, LRAC.

40 These four schools were not included in table 8. See "Tabular Statement of Schools . . . ," by S. S. Ashley, November 1865, Ashley Letters; *Dispatch*, March 14, 1866, p. 3; *Wilmington Herald*, September 9, 1865, p. 1; Robert Avery to the Assistant Commissioner, June 27, 1867, and July 6, 1867, LRAC.

41 Allan Rutherford to Jacob Chur, March 25, 1867, LSS; S. S. Ashley to Allan Rutherford, March 25, 1867, and H. H. Foster to Rutherford, October 30, 1866, LRS; S. S. Ashley to S. Hunt, November 2, 1865, Ashley Letters; F. A. Fiske to O. O. Howard, January 30, 1867, LSEd; Robert Avery to the Assistant Commissioner, June 27, 1867 and July 6, 1867, LRAC.

42 "Superintendent's Monthly Report . . . ," January 1866, Ashley Letters; S. S. Ashley to Allan Rutherford, March 25, 1867, LRS; *Wilmington Herald*, September 9, 1865, p. 1, and January 13, 1866, p. 1; Robert Avery to the Assistant Commissioner, June 27, 1867, and July 6, 1867, LRAC.

43 *NBT*, August 1, 1865, p. 2; Robert Avery to the Assistant Commissioner, June 19, 1867, LRAC.

44 Benjamin W. Pond to F. A. Fiske, October 12, 1865, ULREd; letter to the editor from James O'Hara in *NBT*, January 16, 1866, p. 1. For information on O'Hara, see Logan, *Negro in North Carolina*, pp. 32n, 33–34; Padgett, "Slavery to Prominence," p. 484; *North Carolina Journal of Law* 2, no. 1: 23; James Harris Papers.

45 ULREd for the period of September 1865–April 1866; Samuel P. Fowler, Jr., to F. A. Seely, December 30, 1865, and George Hawley to Stephen Moore, August 25, 1866, ULRE; Charles to Caroline Pettigrew, April 6, 1866, Pettigrew Family Papers; Henry Camp to the Assistant Commissioner, May 1866, LRAC.

46 *Standard*, July 11, 1865, p. 3, and January 26, 1866, p. 3; Fisk Brewer to George Whipple,

September 18, 1866, and Monthly School Reports by Fisk Brewer, December 1866 and February 1867, Brewer Letters; T. McAlpine to M. Cogswell, March 30, 1867, Sch Rpts, CD.

47 Isaac Porter to M. Cogswell, March 30, 1867, ibid. See also Mary Bowers to F. A. Fiske, October 10, 1866, and Isaac Porter to F. A. Fiske, October 1, 1866, ULREd.

48 *Sentinel*, March 28, 1866, p. 2; *Journal*, April 5, 1866, p. 1. Also Charles Wolff to F. A. Fiske, December 14, 1866; Flora A. Leland to Fiske, May 2, 1866, and May 12, 1866; Jonathan H. Hay to Fiske, October 1, 1866; J. F. Conners to Fisk Brewer, September 14, 1866, ULREd. Also Charles Wolff to M. Cogswell, March 29, 1867, and Hannibal D. Norton to Cogswell, March 30, 1867, Sch Rpts, CD.

49 J. F. Allison to M. Cogswell, March 27, 1867; T. McAlpine to M. Cogswell, March 30, 1867; Jonathan M. Foote to M. Cogswell, March 30, 1867; Isaac Porter to M. Cogswell, March 30, 1867, Sch Rpts, CD.

50 Dennett, *South As It Is*, p. 134; Report by John C. Barnett, October 29, 1865, NR; Report by W. C. Mills, October 14, 1865, by Jaspard Packard, November 15, 1865, SMR; F. A. Fiske to unknown correspondent, October 1866, LSEd; Schenck Diary, March 13, 1866, p. 60; *Standard*, December 15, 1865, p. 2, and January 15, 1867, p. 2; F. S. Wiatt to John R. Edie, October 8, 1866, LRW.

51 See, e.g., Fisk Brewer to George Whipple, February 6, 1867, Brewer Letters; S. S. Ashley to S. Hunt, March 7, 1866, Ashley Letters; Letter from C. F. Thompson in *Freedmen's Record*, July 1866, p. 134; S. S. Ashley to F. A. Fiske, November 7, 1867, ULREd; E. Whittlesey, "Quarterly Report Ending December 31, 1865," House Ex. Doc. No. 70, 39th Congress, 1st Session.

52 See, e.g., Elias Bryan to F. A. Fiske, February 16, 1866, and Huthie F. Stove to F. A. Fiske, April 4, 1866, ULREd; Jonathan M. Foote to M. Cogswell, March 30, 1867, Superintendent of the Western District, School Reports, FBP; T. McAlpine to M. Cogswell, March 30, 1867, Sch Rpts, CD; S. S. Ashley to S. Hunt, January 25, 1866, Ashley Letters.

53 S. S. Ashley to F. A. Fiske, May 5, 1866, ULREd. See also S. S. Ashley to S. Hunt, March 11, 1867, Ashley Letters.

Bibliography

Contemporary Sources

NEWSPAPERS

The Biblical Recorder (Raleigh), February 1866–67. North Carolina newspapers often underwent numerous changes in their titles, although the papers typically were continuations without change in the volume numbering. In this bibliography I shall list the exact title of the first issue consulted.

Carolina Watchman (Salisbury), January 1866–December 1866.

The Church Intelligencer (Charlotte), 1865–67.

Daily Carolina Times (Charlotte), 1865–67.

The Daily Dispatch (Wilmington), October 9, 1865–March 1867.

The Daily Journal (Wilmington), September 28, 1865–March 1867.

The Daily Progress (Raleigh), April–December 1865.

Daily Sentinel (Raleigh), August 1865–67.

The Daily Standard (Raleigh), April 1865–March 16, 1866.

The Daily Union Banner (Salisbury), May 15, 1865–August 20, 1866.

The Episcopal Methodist (Raleigh), February–December 1867.

Freedmen's Record (Boston), 1865–67.

The Greensboro Patriot, 1865–67.

Goldsboro Daily News, 1865–66.

The Henderson Pioneer (Hendersonville), May 30–December 18, 1866.

Journal of Freedom (Raleigh), September 30–October 28, 1865.

The National Freedman (New York), 1865–67.

Newbern Weekly Journal of Commerce, 1866–67.

The News (Fayetteville), 1865–67.

North Carolina Argus (Wadesboro), 1865–66.

North Carolina Daily Times (New Berne), 1865–66.

North Carolina Presbyterian (Fayetteville), April 1866–67.

The Old North State (Salisbury), April 1866–March 1867.

The People's Press (Salem), May 27, 1865–December 14, 1866.

The Rutherford Star (Rutherfordton), May 2, 1866–March 30, 1867.

The Southerner (Tarboro), January 1866–March 1867.

TriWeekly Bulletin (Charlotte), May 30, 1865, and June 8, 1865.

The Tri-Weekly Standard (Raleigh), March 20, 1866–67.

The Weekly Progress (Raleigh), January 1866–March 1867.
The Western Democrat (Charlotte), 1865–67.
The Wilmington Herald, 1865–66.
Wilmington Journal, 1866–67.

MANUSCRIPT MATERIAL, OTHER THAN GOVERNMENT RECORDS

Duke University. Manuscript Division. The following collections were consulted: Henry Toole Clark Papers; John Marshall Clement Papers; Fuller-Thomas Papers; William Woods Holden Papers; Thomas Lenoir Letters and Papers; Alexander McMillan Letters; Hugh MacRae Papers; Isaiah Respess Letters and Papers; William Norwood Tillinghast Papers; Van Noppen Papers including Biographical Sketches by Charles Leonard Van Noppen; Robert and Newton D. Woody Papers.
———. Microfilm Collection. William E. Ardrey Diary of the Family and Farm.
———. Rare Book Room. "Vindication of the Freedmen's Bureau! By the Freedmen in a Public Meeting." Wilmington: n.p., May 1866.
———. William R. Perkins Library, Benjamin Sherwood Hedrick Papers.
Fisk University. Amistad Research Center. American Missionary Association Archives.
Library of Congress. Manuscript Division. The following papers were consulted: Andrew Johnson; James Morrison MacKay; Willie P. Mangum Family.
North Carolina Department of Archives and History. Archives. The following collections were consulted: Samuel A'Court Ashe Papers; John H. Bryan Collection; Walter Clark Manuscripts; Fries Papers; Fulford Papers; Thomas M. Gorman Papers; William A. Graham Papers; James E. Green Diary; James Henry Harris Papers; John M. and Ruth Hodges Collection; William W. Holden Papers; J. L. Kirkpatrick Papers; Henry Berry Lowry Papers; Patterson Papers; Cornelia Phillips Spencer Papers; David Lowry Swain Papers; Calvin H. Wiley Papers; Z. B. Vance Papers.
University of North Carolina. North Carolina Collection. Jones, I. W. "An Address to the People of Rowan County." N.p.: n.p., [1865].
———. Southern Historical Collection. The following collections were consulted: American Missionary Association Archives (Selections), Ashley Letters 1851–78 and Brewer Letters; Archibald Hunter Arrington Papers; Alphonso Calhoun Avery Papers; Daniel M. Barringer Papers; Battle Family Papers; Mary Jeffreys Bethell Diary; Tod R. Caldwell Papers; Cameron Family Papers; David M. Carter Papers; Edward Conigland Papers; de Rosset Family Papers; Donnell Papers; James Clarence Harper Diary; Edmond Walter Jones Papers; Jones Family Papers; Lenoir Family Papers; William Gaston Lewis Papers; Hanson F. Murphy Letters; Patterson Family Papers; Pettigrew Family Papers; James G. Ramsay Papers; Marmaduke Swain Robins Papers; Ruffin-Roulhac-Hamilton Papers; David Schenck Books, vol. 5: Diary of David Schenck; Thomas Settle Papers, no. 2; Peter Evans Smith Papers; Cornelia Phillips Spencer Papers; Albion W. Tourgee Papers; Edward Jenner Warren Papers; J. T. Wheat Papers; Calvin Henderson Wiley Papers; Willis R. Williams Papers; William Henry Wills Papers.

MANUSCRIPT GOVERNMENT RECORDS

Duke University. Manuscript Collection. Minutes of City Commissioners, Morganton, 1865–80.

Library of Congress. Manuscript Division. Petitions of Pardon.

National Archives. Attorney General's Papers. Letters Received, North Carolina, 1824–70.

———. Freedmen's Bureau Papers.

———. Freedmen's Bureau Records. Education Division. Letters Received Relating to Freedmen's Savings Bank, 1865–69.

———. Office of the Adjutant General. The following collections were consulted: Amnesty Papers, North Carolina; Letters Received (Main Series), 1861–70, "Inspection reports of Major General George G. Meade and other officers relating to conditions in Virginia, North Carolina, and South Carolina, September 1865," "Papers relating to the surrender of General Joseph E. Johnston's Army to General W. T. Sherman at Greensboro, North Carolina, April–May, 1865," "Reports of racial violence in the South and of consequent actions taken by military authorities, April 1865–January 1866"; Records of the Continental Command, Army of Ohio and Department of North Carolina; Records of the United States Continental Command, Second Military District: North Carolina and South Carolina.

North Carolina Department of Archives and History. Archives. The following county records were consulted:

—Alamance County: County Court, Minute Docket, State Docket; Marriage Bond Abstracts; Superior Court, Minute Docket.

—Ashe County: Marriage Bond Abstracts.

—Beaufort County: Cohabitation Record (Marriage Record), 1851–68.

—Bertie County: Common School Record; Marriage Certificate Abstracts; Negro Cohabitation Records, 1866.

—Brunswick County: Apprentice Records; Marriage Bond Abstracts.

—Buncombe County: Reports of Superintendent of Public Instruction.

—Burke County: County Court Minutes, August 1865 (Marriage Certificates, 1865–67); Election Returns; Marriage Bond Abstracts.

—Carteret County: County Court Minutes; Superior Court Minute Docket; Minutes of the Wardens of the Poor.

—Catawba County: County Court Minutes; Minutes of the Common Schools; Register of Deeds, Freedmen's Marriage Record, 1866.

—Chowan County: Election Returns; Record of Marriage 1851–67.

—Cleveland County: Minutes of the Wardens of the Poor.

—Craven County: Election Returns; Minutes of the Wardens of the Poor; Superior Court Minutes.

—Cumberland County: County Court Minutes; Superior Court, Minute Docket.

—Currituck County: Negro Cohabitation Certificates, 1866.

—Davidson County: Election Returns.

—Duplin County: Marriage Certificates, 1866–68; Marriage of Freed People, 1866.

—Edgecombe County: County Court, Minutes and State Trial Docket; Criminal Action Papers; Marriage Bond Abstracts; Minutes of the Wardens of the Poor; Negro Cohabitation Certificates, 1866.

—Forsyth County: Acknowledgement of Cohabitation as Man and Wife, 1820–66; County Court, Minute Docket.

—Franklin County: Negro Cohabitation Certificates, 1866.

—Gates County: Indentures for Apprentices; Miscellaneous Records, 1780–1912.

—Granville County: Marriage of Freed People.

—Guilford County: Warden's Court Minutes.

—Halifax County: Miscellaneous Records 1761–1910 ("Cohabitation Certificates, 1866").

—Henderson County: Superior Court, Minute Docket.

—Hyde County: Cohabitation Records, 1866; County Court Minutes and State Docket; Civil and Criminal Papers; Superior Court, Minutes.

—Iredell County: Marriage and Cohabitation Certificates, 1851–67.

—Johnston County: Cohabitation Records, 1866; County Court, Minutes; Indentures for Apprentices.

—Jones County: County Court, Minutes; Superior Court, State Docket.

—Lincoln County: Record of Freedmen's Marriages, 1866.

—Mecklenburg County: Marriage Record (colored), 1850–67; Superior Court, Minute Book.

—Montgomery County: Minutes of the Wardens of the Poor.

—Nash County: Marriages of Colored People and Division of Slaves, 1862–66.

—New Hanover County: Apprenticeship Records; County Court, Minutes; Election Returns; Minutes of the Court of Pleas and Quarter Sessions; Minutes of the Wardens of the Poor; Negro Cohabitation and Marriage Certificates, 1866–67; Record of Cohabitation.

—Orange County: County Court, Minutes; Negro Cohabitation Certificates, 1866, 1868; Superior Court, Minutes; Proceedings of the Wardens of the Poor.

—Pasquotank County: Account Book, Cohabitation of Negroes, 1856–67; County Court, Minutes and Prosecution Docket; Indentures for Apprentices.

—Perquimans County: Records of Marriages of Freedmen, 1866–67.

—Person County: Record of Cohabitations.

—Pitt County: Cohabitation Record, 1866.

—Richmond County: Cohabitation Certificates, 1866–68.

—Robeson County: Register of Deeds, Record of Marriage and Cohabitation, 1850–66.

—Rowan County: County Court, Minutes and State Docket; Superior Court, Minute Docket.

—Rutherford County: County Court, Minutes and State Docket; Superior Court, Minute Docket and State Docket.

—Sampson County: County Court, Minute Docket.

—Stokes County: Cohabitation and Marriage Records, 1866–72.

—Surry County: Miscellaneous Records 1779–1922 (Negro Cohabitation Certificates, 1866).

—Wake County: County Court, Minutes and State Criminal Docket; Superior Court, Minutes and State Criminal Docket; Record of Cohabitation, 1866.

—Warren County: Register of Deeds, Cohabitation Record, 1866.

—Washington County: Freedmen's Marriage Records, 1866–72.

—Wilkes County: County Court, Minutes; Superior Court, State Docket.

The following additional collections were consulted: Compiled Election Returns; Legislative Papers; Minutes of the Commissioners of the Town of Roxboro; Minutes of the Town of Elizabeth City; Jonathan Worth's Governor's Paper and Letter Book; William W. Holden's Governor's Papers, 1865, Letter Book, 1865, Pardon Book, 1865–67, and Record Book, 1865.

U.S. Congress. House. Committee on Freedmen's Affairs, Post War Record, 39th Congress.

———. House. Judiciary Committee Report entitled "Civil and Legal Rights, Particularly Those of Freedmen," 39th Congress.

U.S., Eighth Census of the United States, 1860: North Carolina.

U.S., Eighth Census of the United States, 1860: Slave Inhabitants, North Carolina.

U.S., Ninth Census of the United States, 1870: North Carolina.

PRINTED GOVERNMENT RECORDS

North Carolina. Executive Documents. Convention Session 1865. *Constitution of North Carolina with Amendments and Ordinances and Resolutions Passed by the Convention Session, 1865.* Raleigh: Cannon & Holden, 1865.

———. *Journal of the Convention of the People of North Carolina, held on the 20th Day of May, A.D., 1861.* Raleigh: Jno. W. Syme, 1862.

———. *Journal of the Convention of the State of North Carolina, at its Adjourned Session of 1866.* Raleigh: Cannon & Holden, 1866.

———. *Journal of the Convention of the State of North Carolina, at its Session of 1865.* Raleigh: Cannon & Holden, 1865.

———. *Journal of the House of Commons at its Special Session of 1866.* Raleigh: Wm. E. Pell, 1866.

———. *Journal of the House of Commons of the General Assembly of the State of North Carolina at its Session of 1865–'66.* Raleigh: Wm. E. Pell, 1865–'66.

———. *Journal of the House of Commons of the General Assembly of the State of North Carolina at its Session of 1866–'67.* Raleigh: Wm. E. Pell, 1867.

———. *Journal of the Senate at its Special Session of 1866.* Raleigh: Wm. E. Pell, 1866.

———. *Journal of the Senate of the General Assembly of the State of North Carolina at its Session of 1865–'66.* Raleigh: Wm. E. Pell, 1865.

———. *Journal of the Senate of the General Assembly of the State of North Carolina at its Session of 1866–'67.* Raleigh: Wm. E. Pell, 1867.

———. *Ordinances Passsed by the North Carolina State Convention, at the Sessions of 1865–'66.* Raleigh: Wm. E. Pell, 1867.

———. *Private Laws of the State of North Carolina, Passed by the General Assembly at the Session of 1866.* Raleigh: Wm. E. Pell, 1866.

————. *Private Laws of the State of North Carolina, Passed by the General Assembly at the Sessions of 1866–'67.* Raleigh: Wm. E. Pell, 1867.

————. *Public Laws of the State of North Carolina, Passed by the General Assembly at the Session of 1865.* Raleigh: Wm. E. Pell, 1866.

————. *Public Laws of the State of North Carolina, Passed by the General Assembly at the Session of 1866.* Raleigh: Wm. E. Pell, 1866.

————. *Public Laws of the State of North Carolina, Passed by the General Assembly at the Sessions of 1866–'67.* Raleigh: Wm. E. Pell, 1867.

————. *Report and Resolution of the Joint Select Committee of Both Houses of the General Assembly of North Carolina, on the Proposition to Adopt the Congressional Constitutional Amendment, Presented by James M. Leach, of Davidson, Chairman, on the 6th of December, and Adopted by Both Houses on the 13th of December, 1866.* Raleigh: Wm. E. Pell, 1866.

————. *Revised Code of North Carolina, Enacted by the General Assembly at the Session of 1854.* Boston: Little, Brown, 1855.

U.S. Census Office. *Agriculture of the United States in 1860; Compiled from the Original Returns of the Eighth Census.* Washington, D.C.: Government Printing Office, 1864.

————. *A Century of Population Growth from the First Census of the United States to the Twelfth, 1790–1900.* Washington, D.C.: Government Printing Office, 1909.

————. *A Compendium of the Ninth Census (June 1, 1870).* Washington, D.C.: Government Printing Office, 1872.

————. *Population of the United States in 1860; Compiled from the Original Returns of the Eighth Census.* Washington, D.C.: Government Printing Office, 1864.

————. *Statistics of the United States, (Including Mortality, Property, &c), in 1860; Compiled from the Original Returns and Being the Final Exhibit of the Eighth Census.* Washington, D.C.: Government Printing Office, 1866.

U.S. Congress. House. *Additional List of Pardons.* H. Rept. 32, 1st Sess., 40th Cong., 1867.

————. House. *Freedmen's Bureau.* H. Rept. 11, 1st Sess., 39th Cong., 1866.

————. House. H. Rept. 99, 1st Sess., 39th Cong., 1865–66.

————. House. *Pardons by the President.* H. Rept. 31, 2d Sess., 39th Cong., 1866–67.

————. House. *Report of the Commissioner of the Bureau of Refugees, Freedmen and Abandoned Lands,* by O. O. Howard, November 1, 1866, 2d Sess., 39th Cong., 1866–67. *Report of the Secretary of War,* vol. 3.

————. House. *Report of the Commissioners of the Bureau of Refugees, Freedmen and Abandoned Lands,* by O. O. Howard, November 1, 1867, 2d Sess., 40th Cong., 1867–68. *Report of the Secretary of War,* vol. 2.

————. House. *Report of Major General D. E. Sickles.* 2d Sess., 39th Cong., 1866–67. *Report of the Secretary of War,* vol. 3.

————. Joint Committee on Reconstruction. *Report of the Joint Committee on Reconstruction.* 1st Sess., 39th Cong., 1866.

————. Joint Select Committee to Investigate the Charges for Murder of Union Soldiers in South Carolina. *Murder of Union Soldiers.* H. Rept. 23, 2d Sess., 39th Cong., 1866–67.

U.S. Congress. Senate. *Report of the Condition of Affairs in the Late Insurrectionary States.* S. Rept. 41, 2d Sess., 42nd Cong., 1871–72.

TRAVELER'S ACCOUNTS, COLLECTED WRITINGS, DIARIES, AND MEMOIRS

Andrews, Sidney. *The South Since the War: As Shown by Fourteen Weeks of Travel and Observation in Georgia and the Carolinas.* Boston: Ticknor & Fields, 1866.

Dennett, John Richard. *The South As It Is 1865–1866.* Edited with an introduction by Henry M. Christman. New York: Viking, 1965.

Hamilton, J. G. de Roulhac (ed.). *The Papers of Thomas Ruffin.* 4 vols. Raleigh: Edwards & Broughton Printing Co., 1920.

Holden, W. W. *Memoirs of W. W. Holden.* The John Lawson Monographs of the Trinity College Historical Society, vol. 2. Durham: The Seeman Printery, 1911.

Johnston, Frontes W. (ed.). *Zebulon B. Vance Letters.* Raleigh: State Department of Archives and History, 1963.

Padgett, James A. (ed.). "Reconstruction Letters from North Carolina, Part I, Letters to Thaddeus Stevens." *North Carolina Historical Review* 18, no. 2 (April 1941): 171–95.

———. "Reconstruction Letters from North Carolina, Part II, Letters to John Sherman." *North Carolina Historical Review* 18, no. 3 (July 1941): 278–300.

———. "Reconstruction Letters from North Carolina, Part VII, Letters to Edward McPherson." *North Carolina Historical Review* 19, no. 2 (April 1942): 187–208.

———. "Reconstruction Letters from North Carolina, Part IX, Letters to Benjamin Franklin Butler." *North Carolina Historical Review* 19, no. 4 (October 1942): 381–404.

———. "Reconstruction Letters from North Carolina, Part XI, Letters from Salmon Portland Chase, Part XII, Other Letters: Letters to Lyman Trumbull; A Letter to Thaddeus Stevens; Three Letters to Edward McPherson; and A Letter to Benjamin Franklin Wade." *North Carolina Historical Review* 21, no. 3 (July 1944): 232–47.

Rawick, George P. (ed.). *The American Slave: A Composite Autobiography. North Carolina Narratives.* Vols. 14, 15. Westport, Conn.: Greenwood Press, 1972.

Reid, Whitlaw. *After the War: A Tour of the Southern States, 1865–1866.* New York: Howard & Hulbert, 1880.

Richardson, J. D. (ed.). *Compilation of the Messages and Papers of the Presidents, 1789–1897.* 10 vols. New York: Bureau of National Literature and Art, 1897.

"Selections from the Correspondence of Bedford Brown, Volume II, 1859–1868." *Annual Publication of Historical Papers Published by the Historical Society of Trinity College,* series 7, 1907, pp. 16–31.

Shanks, Henry Thomas (ed.). *The Papers of Willie Person Mangum,* vol. 5. Raleigh: State Department of Archives and History, 1956.

Worth, Jonathan. *The Correspondence of Jonathan Worth.* Edited by J. G. de Roulhac Hamilton. 2 vols. Raleigh: Edwards & Broughton, 1909.

OTHER CONTEMPORARY PUBLICATIONS

Branson & Farrar's North Carolina Business Directory for 1866–'67. Raleigh: Branson & Farrar, 1866.

Branson's North Carolina Business Directory, For 1867–8. Raleigh: Branson & Jones, 1867.

Convention of the Freedmen of North Carolina. *Official Proceedings.* N.p.: 1865.

Journal of the 30th Session of the North Carolina Annual Conference of the Methodist Episcopal Church South, Fayetteville, November 7–12, 1866. Raleigh: Branson & Farrar, 1866.

Journal of the 49th Annual Council of the Protestant Episcopal Church in the State of North Carolina, Held in Christ's Church, Raleigh, September 13–15, 1865. Raleigh: J. C. Gorman's Book and Job Printing Office, 1865.

Journal of the 50th Annual Convention of the Protestant Episcopal Church in the State of North Carolina, Held in Christ Church, Newbern, May 30–June 4, 1866, 1st Session. Fayetteville: n.p., 1866.

Minutes and Proceedings of the 51st Anniversary of the Pee Dee Baptist Association, Held in Forks of Little River Church (Montgomery County), October 19, 20, 21, 1866. Wadesboro: Argus Office, 1867.

Minutes of the Freedmen's Convention, Held in the City of Raleigh, on the 2nd, 3rd, 4th and 5th of October, 1866. Raleigh: Standard Book and Job Office, 1866.

Minutes of the North Carolina Annual Conference of the A.M.E. Zion Church in America, 1865. Hartford: Case, Lockwood & Co., 1866.

Minutes of the 6th Annual Session of the Central Baptist Association, Held in the Church at Franklinton, Franklin County, N.C., October 5th–7th, 1865. Raleigh: Biblical Recorder Book & Job Printing Establishment, 1865.

Minutes of the 22nd Annual Session of the Eastern Baptist Association, Held in the Church at Moore's Creek, October, 3–4, 1865. Raleigh: Biblical Recorder Book & Job Printing Office, 1866.

Minutes of the 53rd Session of the Synod of North Carolina, Held in Charlotte, on the 10th, 11th, 12th and 13th of October, 1866. Fayetteville: Presbyterian Office, 1867.

Proceedings of the 35th Annual Session of the Baptist State Convention of North Carolina, Held in the Church at Forestville, November 1–4, 1865. Raleigh: Biblical Recorder Book & Job Printing Office, 1866.

Tourgee, Albion W. *A Fool's Errand.* Edited by John Hope Franklin. Cambridge, Mass.: Harvard University Press, 1961.

Vance, Zebulon Baird. *The Duties of Defeat.* An address delivered before the two literary societies of the University of North Carolina, June 7, 1866. Raleigh: Wm. B. Smith & Co., 1866.

Secondary Sources

COUNTY HISTORIES AND BIOGRAPHICAL REFERENCE WORKS

Alexander, J. B. *The History of Mecklenburg County from 1740 to 1900*. Charlotte: Observer Printing House, 1902.

Alexander, John Brevard. *Reminiscences of the Past Sixty Years*. Charlotte: Ray Printing Company, 1908.

Allen, W. C. *The Annals of Haywood County, North Carolina*. N.p.: 1935.

Anderson, Rev. J. Harvey. *Biographical Souvenir Volume of the 23rd Quadrennial Session of the General Conference of the A.M.E. Zion Church [1908]*. N.p.: n.p., n.d.

Arnett, Ethel Stephens. *Greensboro, North Carolina, the County Seat of Guilford*. Chapel Hill: The University of North Carolina Press, 1955.

Arthur, John Preston. *Western North Carolina History*. Raleigh: Edwards & Broughton, 1914.

Ashe, Samuel A., Weeks, Stephen B., and Van Noppen, Charles L. (eds.). *Biographical History of North Carolina from Colonial Times to the Present*. 8 vols. Greensboro: Charles L. Van Noppen, 1905.

Biographical Directory of the American Congress, 1774–1949. Washington, D.C.: Government Printing Office, 1950.

Blackwelder, Ruth. *The Age of Orange. Political and Intellectual Leadership in North Carolina, 1752–1861*. Charlotte: William Loftin, 1961.

Bloodworth, Mattie. *History of Pender County, North Carolina*. Richmond: The Dietz Printing Co., 1947.

Blythe, LeGette, and Brockmann, Charles Raven. *Hornet's Nest. The Story of Charlotte and Mecklenburg County*. Charlotte: McNally, 1961.

Brawley, James S. *The Rowan Story, 1753–1953*. Salisbury: Rowan Printing Co.., 1953.

Connor, R. D. W. (comp. and ed.). *A Manual of North Carolina*. Raleigh: E. Muzzel & Co., 1913.

Cope, Robert F., and Wellman, Manly Wade. *The County of Gaston*. Charlotte: Gaston County Historical Society, 1961.

Crouch, John. *Historical Sketches of Wilkes County*. Wilkesboro: John Crouch, 1902.

Cyclopedia of Eminent and Representative Men of the Carolinas of the Nineteenth Century, with introduction on North Carolina by Hon. Samuel A. Ashe. Vol. 2. 2 vols. Madison, Wis.: Brant & Fuller, 1892.

Davis, Edward Hill. *Historical Sketches of Franklin County*. Raleigh: Edwards & Broughton, 1948.

Dowd, Jerome. *Sketches of Prominent Living North Carolinians*. Raleigh: Edwards & Broughton, 1888.

Evans, General Clement A. (ed.). *Confederate Military History*. Vol. 4. 12 vols. Atlanta: Confederate Publishing Co., 1899.

Fletcher, Arthur L. *Ashe County, A History*. Jefferson, NC: Ashe County Research Association, 1963.

Foushee, Alexander R. *Reminiscences, A Sketch and Letters Descriptive of Life in Person County in Former Days*. Durham: The Seeman Printery, 1921.

229

Fowler, Malcolm. *They Passed This Way, A Personal Narrative of Harnett County History.* Harnett County Centennial, 1955.

Fries, Adelaide L., et al. *Forsyth, A County on the March.* Chapel Hill: The University of North Carolina Press, 1949.

Grant, Daniel Lindsey. *Alumni History of the University of North Carolina.* 2d ed. Durham: Christian & King Printing Co., 1924.

Griffin, Clarence. *History of Old Tryon and Rutherford Counties, North Carolina, 1730–1936.* Asheville: The Miller Printing Co., 1937.

A History of Catawba County. Compiled by Catawba County Historical Association, and edited by Charles J. Preslar, Jr. Salisbury: Rowan Printing Co., 1954.

Hollingsworth, J. G. *History of Surry County or Annals of Northwest North Carolina.* N.p., 1935.

Howell, Andrew J. *The Book of Wilmington.* N.p., n.d.

Johnson, Talmage C., and Holloman, Charles R. *The Story of Kinston and Lenoir Counties.* Raleigh: Edwards & Broughton, 1954.

King, Henry T. *Sketches of Pitt County.* Raleigh: Edwards & Broughton, 1911.

Lawrence, Robert C. *The State of Robeson.* New York: J. J. Little and Ives Co., 1939.

Lefler, Hugh, and Wager, Paul (eds.). *Orange County—1752–1952.* Chapel Hill: The Orange Printshop, 1953.

Leonard, Reverend Jacob Calvin. *Centennial History of Davidson County, North Carolina.* Raleigh: Edwards & Broughton, 1927.

Legislative Biographical Sketch Book. Session 1887, North Carolina. Raleigh: Edwards & Broughton, 1887.

Manarin, Louis H. (comp.). *Artillery.* Vol. 1. *North Carolina Troops 1861–1865, A Roster.* Raleigh: State Department of Archives and History, 1966.

———. *Cavalry.* Vol. II. *North Carolina Troops 1861–1865, A Roster.* Raleigh: State Department of Archives and History, 1968.

Montgomery, Lizzie Wilsen. *Sketches of Old Warrenton, North Carolina.* Raleigh: Edwards & Broughton, 1924.

Moore, John W. *Roster of North Carolina Troops in the War Between the States.* 4 vols. Raleigh: Ashe & Gatling, 1882.

Oates, John A. *The Story of Fayetteville and the Upper Cape Fear.* Charlotte: The Dowd Press, 1950.

Patton, Sadie Smathers. *Sketches of Polk County History.* Asheville: The Miller Printing Company, 1950.

Peele, W. J. (col. and comp.). *Lives of Distinguished North Carolinians.* Raleigh: North Carolina Publishing Society, 1898.

Polk, L. L. *Handbook of North Carolina.* Raleigh: n.p., 1879.

Powell, William S. *Annals of Progress, The Story of Lenoir County and Kinston, North Carolina.* Raleigh: State Department of Archives and History, 1963.

Pugh, Jesse Forbes. *Three Hundred Years Along the Pasquotank, A Biographical History of Camden County.* Durham: The Seeman Printery, 1957.

Quick, W. H. *Negro Stars in All Ages of the World.* 2d ed. Richmond: S. B. Adkins & Co., 1898.

Reed, C. Wingate. *Beaufort County, 2 Centuries of Its History*. Raleigh: Edwards & Broughton, 1962.

Rumple, Reverend Jethro. *A History of Rowan County, North Carolina*. Salisbury: J. J. Bruner, 1881.

Scott, W. W. *Annals of Caldwell County*. Lenoir, N.C.: News-Topic Print, 1930.

Sherill, William L. *Annals of Lincoln County, North Carolina*. Charlotte: The Observer Printing House, 1937.

Sondley, F. A. *A History of Buncombe County, North Carolina*. 2 vols.. Asheville: The Advocate Printing Co., 1930.

Taylor, L. E. *General Catalogue of Wake Forest College, North Carolina, 1834–5—1891– 2*. Raleigh: Edwards & Broughton, 1892.

Tomlinson, J. S. *Tar Heel Sketch-Book. A Brief Biographical Sketch of the Life and Public Acts of the Members of the General Assembly of North Carolina, Session of 1879*. Raleigh: Raleigh New Steam Book and Job Print, 1879.

Tompkins, D. A. *History of Mecklenburg County and the City of Charlotte from 1740– 1903*. 2 vols. Charlotte: Observer Printing House, 1903.

Turner, J. Kelly, and Bridgers, Jno. L., Jr. *History of Edgecombe County, North Carolina*. Raleigh: Edwards & Broughton, 1920.

Warren, Lindsay C. *Beaufort County's Contribution to a Notable Era of North Carolina History*. Washington, D.C.: Government Printing Office, 1930.

Weathers, Lee B. *The Living Past of Cleveland County, A History*. Shelby, N.C.: Star Publishing Co., 1956.

Weinborne, Benj. B. *The Colonial and State Political History of Hertford County, North Carolina*. Murfreesboro, N.C.: Edwards & Broughton, 1906.

Wellman, Manly Wade. *The County of Moore 1847–1947*. Southern Pines, N.C.: Moore County Historical Association, 1962.

———. *The County of Warren, North Carolina 1586–1917*. Chapel Hill: University of North Carolina Press, 1959.

Wheeler, John H. (comp.). *The Legislative Manual and Political Register of the State of North Carolina, for the Year 1874*. Raleigh: Josiah Turner, Jr., 1874.

———. *Reminiscences and Memoirs of North Carolina and Eminent North Carolinians*. Columbus, Ohio: Columbus Printing Works, 1884.

Whitaker, Walter. *Centennial History of Alamance County 1849–1949*. Burlington, N.C.: Burlington Chamber of Commerce, n.d.

Wright, Bishop R. R. *The Bishops of the A.M.E. Church*. [Nashville, Tenn.:] A.M.E. Sunday School Union, 1963.

Year Book. Pasquotank Historical Society. 2 vols. N.p., 1954–55.

OTHER MONOGRAPHS

Alexander, Roberta Sue. "North Carolina Faces the Freedmen: Race Relations During Presidential Reconstruction, 1865–1867." 2 vols. Unpublished Ph.D. dissertation, University of Chicago, 1974.

———. "Slavery Arguments in the South, 1820–1830." Unpublished M.A. thesis, University of North Carolina, 1966.

Bell, John Luther, Jr. "Protestant Churches and the Negro in North Carolina During Reconstruction." Unpublished M.A. thesis, University of North Carolina, 1961.

Billings, Dwight B., Jr. *Planters and the Making of a "New South": Class, Politics, and Development in North Carolina, 1865–1910*. Chapel Hill: University of North Carolina Press, 1979.

Bogue, Jesse Parker, Jr. "Violence and Oppression in North Carolina During Reconstruction 1865–1873." Unpublished Ph.D. dissertation, University of Maryland, 1973.

Boykin, James H. *North Carolina in 1861*. New York: Bookman Associates, 1961.

Evans, W. McKee. *Ballots and Fence Rails: Reconstruction on the Lower Cape Fear*. Chapel Hill: University of North Carolina Press, 1966.

Franklin, John Hope. *Free Negro in North Carolina*. New York: W. W. Norton, 1971.

———. *Reconstruction After the Civil War*. Chicago: University of Chicago Press, 1961.

Gutman, Herbert G. *The Black Family in Slavery and Freedom 1750–1925*. New York: Pantheon Books, 1976.

Hamilton, J. G. de Roulhac. *Reconstruction in North Carolina*. New York: Columbia University Press, 1914.

Hyman, Harold M. *Era of the Oath: Northern Loyalty Tests During the Civil War and Reconstruction*. Philadelphia: University of Pennsylvania Press, 1954.

Jenkins, William Sumner. *Pro-Slavery Thought in the Old South*. Chapel Hill: University of North Carolina Press, 1935.

Johnson, Guion Griffis. *Ante-Bellum North Carolina, A Social History*. Chapel Hill: The University of North Carolina Press, 1937.

Jones, Bobby Frank. "An Opportunity Lost: North Carolina Race Relations During Presidential Reconstruction." Unpublished M.A. thesis, University of North Carolina, 1961.

Lefler, Hugh Talmadge, and Newsome, Albert Ray. *North Carolina*. Chapel Hill: University of North Carolina Press, 1954.

Litwack, Leon. *Been in the Storm So Long: The Aftermath of Slavery*. New York: Random House, 1980.

Logan, Frenise A. *The Negro in North Carolina 1876–1894*. Chapel Hill: The University of North Carolina Press, 1964.

McKitrick, Eric L. (ed.). *Slavery Defended: The Views of the Old South*. Englewood Cliffs, N.J.: Prentice-Hall, 1963.

McPherson, James M. *The Struggle for Equality Abolitionists and the Negro in the Civil War and Reconstruction*. Princeton: Princeton University Press, 1964.

Mobley, Joe A. *James City: A Black Community in North Carolina 1863–1900*. Raleigh: North Carolina Department of Cultural Resources, Division of Archives and History, 1981.

Norton, Clarence Clifford. *The Democratic Party—Ante-Bellum North Carolina—1835–1861*. Chapel Hill: The University of North Carolina Press, 1930.

Olsen, Otto H. *Carpetbagger's Crusade: The Life of Albion Winegar Tourgee*. Baltimore: The Johns Hopkins University Press, 1965.

————. (ed.). *Reconstruction and Redemption in the South*. Baton Rouge: Louisiana State University Press, 1980.

Osthaus, Carl R. *Freedmen, Philanthropy and Fraud: A History of the Freedmen's Savings Bank*. Urbana: University of Illinois Press, 1976.

Perman, Michael. *Reunion Without Compromise, The South and Reconstruction: 1865–1868*. Cambridge: Cambridge University Press, 1973.

Powell, William S. *The North Carolina Gazetteer*. Chapel Hill: The University of North Carolina Press, 1968.

Raper, Horace Wilson. "William Woods Holden: A Political Biography." Unpublished Ph.D. dissertation, University of North Carolina, 1951.

St. Clair, Kenneth Edson. "The Administration of Justice in North Carolina During Reconstruction, 1865–1876." Unpublished Ph.D. dissertation, Ohio State University, 1939.

Sefton, James E. *The United States Army and Reconstruction 1865–1877*. Baton Rouge: Louisiana State University Press, 1967.

Tucker, Glenn. *Zeb Vance Champion of Personal Freedom*. Indianapolis: Bobbs-Merrill, 1965.

Wesley, Charles H. *Negro Labor in the United States*. New York: Russell & Russell, 1927.

Wilsen, Theodore Brantner. *The Black Codes of the South*. Montgomery: University of Alabama Press, 1965.

Yearns, Wilfred B. *The Confederate Congress*. Athens: University of Georgia Press, 1960.

Zuber, Richard L. *Jonathan Worth, A Biography of a Southern Unionist*. Chapel Hill: The University of North Carolina Press, 1965.

ARTICLES

Alexander, Roberta Sue. "Hostility and Hope: Black Education in North Carolina during Presidential Reconstruction, 1865–1867." *North Carolina Historical Review* 53, no. 2 (April 1976): 113–32.

Bassett, John Spencer. "Anti-Secessionist Leaders of North Carolina." *Johns Hopkins University Studies in Historical and Political Science*, series 16, no. 6. Baltimore: Johns Hopkins University Press, June 1898.

Boyd, William K. "North Carolina on the Eve of Secession." *Annual Report of the American Historical Association for the Year 1910*, pp. 165–77.

————. "William H. Holden." *An Annual Publication of Historical Papers published by the Historical Society of Trinity College, Durham, North Carolina*, series 3, 1899, pp. 39–128.

Burkhead, Reverend L. S. "History of the Difficulties of the Pastorate of the Front Street Methodist Church, Wilmington, North Carolina, for the Year 1865." *An Annual Publication of Historical Papers published by the Historical Society of Trinity College, Durham, North Carolina*, series 8, 1908–1909, pp. 35–118.

Davis, J. R. "Reconstruction in Cleveland County." *An Annual Publication of Historical Papers published by the Historical Society of Trinity College, Durham, North Carolina*, series 10, 1914, pp. 5–31.

"Death of a Prominent Colored Man." *North Carolina Journal of Law* 2, no. 1 (January 1905): 23–25.

Dorris, Jonathan Truman. "Pardoning North Carolinians." *North Carolina Historical Review* 23, no. 3 (July 1946): 360–401.

Eberle, Elaine C. "Marriage Registers of Freedmen." *Prologue*, Fall 1972: 150–54.

Farris, James J. "The Lowrie Gang An Episode in the History of Robeson County, N.C. 1864–1874." *An Annual Publication of Historical Papers published by the Historical Society of Trinity College, Durham, North Carolina*, series 15, 1925, pp. 57–93.

Hamilton, J. G. de Roulhac. "Party Politics—North Carolina 1835–1860." *The James Sprunt Studies in History and Political Science*, vol. 15, nos. 1 and 2. Chapel Hill: University of North Carolina Press, 1916.

Harrell, Isaac S. "Gates County to 1860." *An Annual Publication of Historical Papers published by the Historical Society of Trinity College, Durham, North Carolina*, series 12, 1916.

Lawrence, R. C. "The Lowrie Gang." *The State* 6, no. 48 (April 29, 1939): 10, 20, 22.

McCormick, John Gilchrist. "Personnel of the Convention of 1861." *James Sprunt Historical Monographs*, no. 1. Chapel Hill: University of North Carolina Press, 1900, pp. 3–97.

Nixon, Alfred. "The History of Lincoln County." *North Carolina Booklet* 9, no. 3 (January 1910): 111–78.

Padgett, James Absalom. "From Slavery to Prominence in North Carolina." *Journal of Negro History* 22 (October 1937): 433–87.

Ruark, Bryant Whitlock. "Some Phases of Reconstruction in Wilmington and the County of New Hanover." *An Annual Publication of Historical Papers published by the Historical Society of Trinity College, Durham, North Carolina*, series 11, 1915.

Scott, Rebecca. "The Battle Over the Child: Child Apprenticeship and the Freedmen's Bureau in North Carolina." *Prologue* 10, no. 2 (1978): 101–113.

Sitterson, Joseph Carlyle. "Lewis Thompson, A Carolinian and His Louisiana Plantation, 1848–1888: A Study in Absentee Ownership." *The James Sprunt Studies in History and Political Science*, 31. *Essays in Southern History*. Edited by Fletcher Melvin Green. Chapel Hill: University of North Carolina Press, 1949.

———. "The Secession Movement in North Carolina." *The James Sprunt Studies in History and Political Science*, 23, no. 2. Chapel Hill: University of North Carolina Press, 1939.

Wagstaff, Henry McGilbert. "States Rights and Political Parties—North Carolina 1776–1861." *Johns Hopkins University Studies in Historical and Political Science*, series 24, nos. 7–8. Baltimore: Johns Hopkins Press, July–August 1906.

Whitener, Daniel Joy. "Public Education—North Carolina During Reconstruction, 1865–1876." *The James Sprunt Studies in History and Political Science*, 31. *Essays in Southern History*. Edited by Fletcher Melvin Green. Chapel Hill: University of North Carolina Press, 1949.

Yearns, Wilfred B., Jr. "North Carolina in the Confederate Congress." *North Carolina Historical Review* 29, no. 3 (July 1952): 359–78.

Index